SOLUTION-FOCUSED SUBSTANCE ABUSE TREATMENT

SOLUTION-FOCUSED SUBSTANCE ABUSE TREATMENT

Teri Pichot

with Sara A. Smock

Routledge
Taylor & Francis Group
New York   London

Routledge
Taylor & Francis Group
270 Madison Avenue
New York, NY 10016

Routledge
Taylor & Francis Group
2 Park Square
Milton Park, Abingdon
Oxon OX14 4RN

Printed in the United States of America on acid-free paper
10 9 8 7 6 5 4 3 2 1

International Standard Book Number-13: 978-0-7890-3723-7 (Softcover) 978-0-7890-3722-0 (Hardcover)

Library of Congress Cataloging-in-Publication Data

Pichot, Teri.
  Solution-focused substance abuse treatment / Teri Pichot, with Sara A. Smock.
      p. cm.
  Includes bibliographical references and index.
  ISBN 978-0-7890-3722-0 (hardback : alk. paper) -- ISBN
  978-0-7890-3723-7 (pbk. : alk. paper)
    1. Substance abuse--Treatment. 2. Solution-focused therapy. 3. Solution-focused
brief therapy. I. Smock, Sara A. II. Title.

  RC564.P53 2009
  616.86'06--dc22   2008043460

Visit the Taylor & Francis Web site at
http://www.taylorandfrancis.com

and the Routledge Web site at
http://www.routledge.com

In loving memory of
Insoo Kim Berg
and
Steve de Shazer

Contents

List of Figures

Authors

Teri Pichot began her career as a psychotherapist close to 20 years ago. She has worked extensively with individuals, couples, and families distressed by many issues, including substance abuse and domestic violence. She received her master's degree in social work from the University of Denver, and she went on to obtain licensure as a clinical social worker in addition to achieving the highest level of both state and national certification as an addictions specialist. She is a Delta Society Pet Partner with her canine companions, Rockefeller and Jasper, and she enjoys partnering with them to provide animal-assisted interventions to her clients. She has designed and implemented innovative programs that utilize solution-focused therapy (with and without therapy dogs) with both adults and adolescents. She is currently the program manager of the Substance Abuse Counseling Program at the Jefferson County Department of Health and Environment in addition to maintaining a private practice in the Denver area. Teri has published numerous journal articles and books, and enjoys providing training on solution-focused therapy and its implementation with "challenging" populations. Teri's passion is assisting others (clients and professionals alike) to see that change is not only possible, but invigorating. Teri is well known for her energy, sense of humor, love of animals, and passion for her work. Her creative spirit, enthusiasm, and zest for change are contagious and are reflected in the therapists she supervises. She can be reached at www.therapydogsonline.com.

Sara A. Smock is an assistant professor in Addictive Disorders and Recovery Studies at Texas Tech University. She has completed outcome research on solution-focused brief therapy, examining its effectiveness with substance abusers. Dr. Smock has published and presented on the solution-focused brief therapy model. In addition, she is a member of the Solution-Focused Brief Therapy Association's founders group.

Foreword

A couple of years ago, my husband and I attended a solution-focused conference in southern Florida just days after the area had been hit by a series of severe hurricanes. Upon arrival, our first task was to rent a car and drive to the hotel where we were staying. Following that, we would drive to the venue where the conference was being held. We did not anticipate these tasks to be particularly complicated or daunting since we came prepared with the street addresses of both places, written driving directions, and a detailed map of the area.

We were therefore quite surprised to find ourselves completely lost and uncomfortably disoriented only minutes after leaving the airport. The hurricane winds had torn many of the road signs away, and there were mountains of sand and debris in places where we expected to see corners of buildings, highway exits, and stop lights. At first we just kept on driving in hopes that we would eventually find some landmark that would correspond to the map in the front seat. But we found none.

Finally we saw an open drug store. We pulled into what was left of the parking lot, went inside, and were greeted by a friendly and gracious man who recognized the look of distress on our faces and asked if we needed help. He turned out to be a professor at the school where our conference was being held. Grateful for his offer of help, we asked for directions. We were very surprised by what he told us.

It turned out that we had been going in exactly the opposite trajectory than what we believed, and if we had not stopped and gotten this essential advice, not only would we have not reached our desired destination, we would have ended up extremely far away from where we needed and wanted to go. And of course once we began traveling according to the route he described, landmarks that we had previously overlooked became meaningful and helpful. We safely arrived at our hotel feeling greatly relieved. We were confident that we would reach the conference as well.

The solution-focused approach to substance abuse treatment described in this book reminds me of our timely and extremely fortunate encounter with the Florida professor. A few words from him prevented us from potentially wasting hours of time struggling down obscure side streets that were in some cases nearly impassable in an attempt to reach roadways that did not correspond to the map we had in front of us.

The authors of this book go far beyond providing a useful map for treating substance abusers; they orient the reader to the real-life realities of their clients' lives, empowering them to recognize much needed therapeutic resources, exceptions, and poignantly meaningful personal landmarks that might otherwise remain hidden under the psychological "debris" of addictive behaviors.

Yvonne Dolan
Director of the Institute for Solution-Focused Brief Therapy
Munster, Indiana

Acknowledgments

Writing a book is an enormous undertaking, and we have many to thank for their help and support with this project. First, we thank Thorana Nelson for masterminding the concept behind this book and inviting us to be the authors. It was a privilege to work with her on this project, and we are indebted to her for all her help to blend our varied expertise. Second, we take a moment to express our deep gratitude to Insoo Kim Berg and Steve de Shazer. They both had a tremendous impact on our personal and professional lives. They challenged our thinking, valued our questions, and provided an environment rich with humor, compassion, and respect for individuality. Because of them, our ways of thinking will never be the same. We miss them and hope that they would be proud of how we represent the wonderful approach they created. Lastly, we thank the many clients we have worked with over our careers. It is through working with them that we have learned our greatest lessons.

I (TP) personally thank Yvonne Dolan for her continued support and words of wisdom. She has walked beside me during the writing of each of my books, and this one is no exception. She brainstormed the trouble spots, read each word of the manuscript, and provided invaluable suggestions all along the way. I truly value her mentorship and friendship. Second, I thank all of the therapists I have supervised over the years, in both agency and private practice settings. It is because of their many questions that I developed ways to better explain these simple yet difficult-to-master concepts. It was through explaining and demonstrating that I came to better understand them myself.

Finally, I thank Charlie Johnson, Karen Mooney, and Mark Hochstedler for the varied roles of support they continue to have in my life. Charlie is a dear friend and mentor who believed in me from the start and is always there to provide words of wisdom. Karen has taken a supportive role in my career and oftentimes stands behind my not-so-popular decisions to fight for client care when I otherwise feel completely alone and misunderstood.

She encourages me to keep going in a problem-focused culture and reminds me it is not for naught. And finally, Mark is my beloved husband and friend. He has been incredibly supportive of the missed time together for the sake of writing this book in my "free time." I cannot imagine a more supportive life partner. Thank you.

I (SS) thank the founder's group of the Solution-Focused Brief Therapy Association for welcoming me with open arms from the beginning. I have been so fortunate to learn from and work with so many wonderful individuals throughout the years. Thank you for all you have invested in my life. Second, I thank my assistants, Adam Froerer and Sara Blakeslee, for helping with this book project. My gratitude cannot be summarized in a few sentences. Thanks for all you do! Finally, I also thank my husband, Steve, for his continued support and encouragement. I look forward to the continued joys of our journey together.

Preface

After close to 20 years working in the field of addictions, I[1] continue to be discouraged that there are such a significant number of therapists working in the field who are relatively inexperienced. While there are some experienced old-timers, they tend to work from a recovery model (counseling based upon what worked for themselves for their own prior addiction), and not bring the research-based therapeutic approaches that are truly needed in this field. The ones who do work from a solid therapeutic model tend to work their way into a management position, leaving the true work (the work of engaging and making changes with the clients) again to the more recently hired, energized clinicians.

Now intellectually, I do understand this phenomenon since line staff in the addictions field do make fairly low wages, and the stress level is very high since the majority of clients come from external referral sources such as probation, child welfare, and so forth. These are not typically a happy bunch of people who are intrinsically motivated. They are oftentimes multiproblem clients with minimal financial and other tangible resources. They are frequently noncompliant with mental health or medical services (either due to lack of resources or lack of belief these services are needed). These clients frequently believe they are victims of life and various injustices (in some ways they truly are), and therefore shy away from looking within to determine what aspects of their lives they could actually change. They are oftentimes not forthcoming with necessary information, they are known for angry outbursts and feelings of entitlement, and frequently have co-occurring disorders that challenge the best of clinicians. Clinicians work under multiple layers of arduous albeit well-intentioned regulations from both federal and state governments. Regulations mandate all aspects of client care, making it a paperwork nightmare for a clinician who just wants to help people. Add to this the necessity of observing urine screens to ensure abstinence (not the most glamorous part of the job and not something most master's-level clinicians pictured when they envisioned their professional futures), and the field of substance abuse counseling becomes a lack-luster proposition.

Ironically, it is these very factors (the external referral sources, co-occurring disorders, difficulty to look to oneself to change, lack of resources, etc.) that are the characteristics that necessitate well-trained, experienced clinicians. As I look back on my career, I am amazed that some of my clients did as well as they did despite my lack of experience and knowledge about what truly results in change for clients. It is a vicious cycle, for the therapists' lack of experience and knowledge regarding how to address these difficult clinical issues in the majority of publicly funded treatment programs necessitates overly detailed regulations to protect the clients and ensure that the basics of good treatment are provided to these individuals. These overly detailed and burdensome regulations then increase the undesirability of the field to therapists who have gained the skills to become more lucratively employed elsewhere.

Now every profession has to provide some pathway for the training of new clinicians. My thoughts go to the medical field and the role that emergency room or surgical interns play in hospitals as these students learn the necessary skills to become skilled emergency room physicians or surgeons. However, in the medical field, these same students eventually graduate and continue to practice emergency medicine and surgery in the hospitals. This is not oftentimes the case in our field with substance abuse counselors. When I have spoken to recent graduates who are currently working in the field of substance abuse, it is commonplace for me to hear that they view this as a stepping ground to a more lucrative field of practice, such as private practice. This is especially true with the younger generation as they look to each job as an opportunity for them to gain additional skills to benefit them. Gone are the days of old of having a sense of "calling" or "purpose greater than myself" in life. In the community-based agency in which I work, it is very common for therapists to work hard to learn the field of substance abuse, only to leave the agency after four to six years (it is important to note that this is significantly longer than it was in other agencies in which I have worked over the years), to work for privately funded agencies or private practice, with fewer regulations and less troubled clients, and in addition, with clients who are more notably internally motivated for change. I frequently hear staff say, "I'm planning to stay a few years to learn substance abuse treatment since I can use that anywhere I go." There is no sense of giving back or developing the skills to be present and give back to the very clients who made the development of these skills even possible. There is a general sense that there will be someone else who will come along to care for the clients; the clients will somehow be fine. We have truly moved into a self-focused society at the very time that our clients' problems are becoming more complex and need experienced clinicians who are dedicated to care for them.

Now clearly, this book cannot solve the social quagmire of the world, nor change the social values of the upcoming generations. We will save that for a later date. However, it is precisely these challenges within the profession that make it the ideal setting for the use of solution-focused brief therapy. This field needs an approach that generates hope (in both the clients and the therapists). This field also needs an approach that intrinsically addresses many of the problems these clients have while simultaneously avoiding power struggles and energizing both the clients and therapist. Since the research clearly shows that "the client is actually the single, most potent contributor to the outcome in psychotherapy" (Miller, Duncan, & Hubble, 1997, p. 25), what would make more sense than to fully utilize an approach that wholeheartedly embraces who the clients are, how they think, and what they value and want? As Miller and de Shazer (1998) once wrote regarding the need to help clients change their lives, "It is a justification for therapy, and a test of it" (p. 366). During my many years in this field, I have put solution-focused brief therapy to the test out of sheer necessity and at times desperation, and it has passed with flying colors each and every time with the toughest client situations. I am a true believer.

However, I must confess that my initial thoughts when Sara and I were asked to write a book about using solution-focused brief therapy with substance abuse treatment was that it has already been done. I have already put my thoughts into print about how to integrate solution-focused brief therapy into work with substance abusing clients,[2] and quite frankly, writing a book takes a lot of effort. It should be saved for something new, innovative, and from the heart. However, upon further thought, I realized that this is an immensely challenging subject that is constantly evolving. I have continued to learn and am hopefully wiser today than I was when Yvonne Dolan and I wrote that book (Pichot & Dolan, 2003). I have oftentimes discovered new and exciting aspects of working with substance abusing clients while using solution-focused brief therapy that take the work to an even more purposeful level and thought, "Wow! I wish I had really understood that when Yvonne and I wrote our book. It would make an incredible difference in the reader's work with clients." I understand so much more now about how solution-focused brief therapy truly works and what it is specifically about each intervention that results in change for the clients. Now probably is the time to take this subject to a much deeper level—one that specifically targets the hows and whys of using this approach with this very special and yet challenging population. Now is the time to write a hands-on manual for the therapists in the trenches with these clients.

I am one of those old-fashioned people who do still believe that as a person I have a special calling—a gift if you will. My calling is to help therapists to be the best they can be and to use solution-focused brief therapy with challenging client populations such as substance abuse to make a lasting difference in others' lives. Our clients need therapists who not only want to make a difference, but have the skills and knowledge to make purposeful change. While a skilled therapist can make a therapy session look magical, it is a complex and purposeful process and requires a tremendous amount of work to understand and become skilled in the approach. Whether you are new to solution-focused brief therapy or to the field of substance abuse treatment or an old pro, it is our hope that this book helps you to understand this approach with this population just a little better, inspires you to do the work to hone your skills, and that in turn you will help your clients in ways previously unimaginable.

Teri Pichot
Littleton, Colorado

Endnotes

1. Any time the author uses first person throughout the text, she is referring to Pichot unless otherwise noted.
2. The way in which we are using the terms *substance abusing* or *substance abuse* throughout this book bears no correlation to a formal substance use diagnosis. We will be using these terms throughout this book as a way to identify a client who has some form of a substance abuse disorder, which very well may qualify for some form of substance dependence.

What to Expect From This Book

This book is intended as a hands-on, practical guide for therapists who want to learn how to successfully integrate solution-focused brief therapy into their work with clients who are struggling with substance abuse–related problems. This book is written for both clinicians who work within a substance abuse treatment agency and those working independently in a private practice setting. This book is written to assist therapists in gaining the necessary skills to work effectively with externally mandated[1] clients in addition to clients who are voluntarily seeking services. We have woven substance abuse practice standards and federal regulations throughout our examples to assist the reader in learning how to apply these to a variety of treatment settings. It is our hope that you will find these lessons valuable and applicable.

Chapter 1 provides an overview of substance abuse treatment. It reviews the evolution of the field, provides the context for this book, and explains the key elements that exist in substance abuse treatment today.

Chapter 2 provides a solid overview of the solution-focused approach and reviews its basic tenets and explains the core interventions. Special considerations are given to its application to substance abuse treatment.

Although solution-focused brief therapy is a very simple approach, it is extremely difficult to master. Chapter 3 explains the inner workings of the miracle question and gives practical suggestions for successful application with clients who are struggling with substance abuse issues.

Assessment and evaluation are key components of substance abuse treatment. Chapter 4 explains how to meet practice standards and complete credible substance abuse assessments and evaluations that are consistent with the basic tenets of solution-focused brief therapy.

Although the majority of treatment services are typically provided in a group setting, Chapter 5 outlines the needed guidelines and structure to provide these services in an individual setting, either in conjunction with or in lieu of group services. In addition, the importance of and how to provide case management services are addressed.

Chapter 6 provides a step-by-step skeleton of how to apply solution-focused brief therapy within a group setting. A group transcript is used to provide examples of each element of the group format.

Chapter 7 provides a more in-depth look at the group process to demonstrate how to go beyond the group skeleton to ensure that the group environment is conducive to sound clinical care. Specific discussions regarding how to develop group themes, how to be cognizant of and address group norms, and how to effectively use analogies are included.

Chapter 8 addresses how to effectively integrate this approach with more traditional substance abuse treatment elements, such as 12-step recovery programs, adolescents, and clients who have co-occurring disorders. In addition, this chapter addresses cultural considerations when using this approach.

Chapter 9 provides sample forms of key documents, such as treatment plans, issues lists, homework sheets, and so forth.

Included in the appendixes is a detailed annotated bibliography of resources that we have found to be helpful in the field of substance abuse treatment and solution-focused brief therapy.

Endnote

1. We use the term *externally mandated* throughout this book to refer to clients who are seeking services due to legal requirements (i.e., child welfare, probation).

1

Substance Abuse Treatment
An Overview

> We have come to believe that there are many alcoholisms—perhaps as many as there are problem drinkers.
>
> **Insoo Kim Berg and Scott Miller**

Before we explore how to effectively apply solution-focused brief therapy in substance abuse treatment, it is important to understand how the use of substances has evolved throughout history. Let us take a look back in time to understand the historic use patterns in the United States and the resultant need for treatment services.

Substance Abuse in the United States

The History of Substance Misuse in the United States

While tobacco and alcohol were the first known substances to be used in this country, the introduction of other drugs soon followed. The Jamestown settlers first brought cannabis (also known as marijuana) to Virginia in 1611, and it quickly became a major crop in North America (Brecher, 1972). The next nonindigenous substance to arrive in the United States was opium. The primary use of opium in these early years was medicinal. However, it did not take long for the abuse of opium to occur. Brecher states that women were using opium while their husbands were out at saloons drinking. Morphine soon followed and began to be used as a substitute for opium in medicinal settings. Next, cocaine entered the picture and became a main ingredient in Coca Cola. While states began to prohibit the illegitimate use of some substances in the late 19th century, most were widely used and not made illegal by the federal government until the early 20th century.

Use of substances such as heroin and cannabis continued throughout the 1960s, at which time hallucinogen use became more widespread. While the manufacturing of the hallucinogen lysergic acid diethylamide (LSD) occurred during the 1930s, it was not until the 1960s that LSD was widely used and impacted the American culture. In the 1980s, methylenedioxymethamphetamine (MDMA or ecstasy) and other "club drugs," such as ketamine, gamma hydroxybutyrate (GHB), Rohypnol (flunitrazepam), and methamphetamine, returned and became a hit in the rave scene.

During the 1990s, the Substance Abuse and Mental Health Administration (SAMSHA) reported an increase in methamphetamine deaths (2007). In addition, the 1990s showed an increase in heroin use among high school students. A 100% increase in heroin use occurred from 1990 to 1996 according to the National Institute on Drug Abuse (NIDA) monograph *Monitoring the Future* (Johnston, O'Malley, & Bachman, 1997). Throughout the early years of the millennium there has also been an increase in the potency of marijuana (National Drug Intelligence Center, 2006) and a rise in prescription drug abuse (NIDA, 2006a).

The Legal and Social Response
In response to the increased use of substances, laws were passed to curtail the resultant social problems. Substance misuse was initially viewed as a moral issue (something that one could simply stop doing), and therefore the legal system was the logical way to address these concerns. One of the first legal acts passed concerning alcohol was the Whiskey Excise Tax of 1791 (Barr, 1999). While this was an attempt by the government to help reduce federal debt and not an attempt to control the use or distribution of substances, it did not take long for the government to begin controlling the regulation of substances. In 1848, the Drug Importation Act required all medications to be inspected for the cleanness and quality of substances used for medical purposes (Higby, 2002). It was at this point that the government first began to regulate and officially approve substances in the United States, despite the fact that substances such as opium and heroin were being widely used among Americans.

The peak of U.S. regulation of alcohol occurred in 1920 with the passing of the 18th Amendment and the Volstead Act. These legal declarations began the prohibition period in the United States, which outlawed the manufacturing and selling of alcohol. It is important to note that the United States outlawed alcohol, but other substances such as cannabis and heroin were still legal. It was not until later that these substances became illegal. The prohibition of alcohol was lifted by the federal government in 1933 by passing of the 21st Amendment. The federal government allowed each state the right to control the distribution of alcohol. Separate acts followed that outlawed the use and distribution of other substances.

The Treatment Response

In addition to various social and legal responses, numerous religious groups and organizations supported prohibition and viewed the abuse of alcohol and drugs as a sin. This resulted in the only assistance these early, well-intentioned helpers knew to give: to tell people not to drink or use drugs. While this may have worked for some, it left others with a sense of shame and stigma for their perceived lack of moral ability to discontinue their use. There was no true understanding of addiction, and therefore individuals in the early 20th century did not have official treatment available to help them deal with issues regarding the abuse.

The first structured model of how to address substance abuse problems was developed in the 1930s when a group of alcoholics came together out of desperation to provide support and develop solutions. This group later became known as Alcoholics Anonymous (1976). This group began the movement away from the moral view of alcoholism, toward the disease or medical approach. This movement was necessary to change the view of those who abused substances from that of being sinful to that of one having a disease that is beyond one's control. While these early efforts could not be classified as treatment, this opened the door to understanding and formalized treatment for this population, for this approach to treatment views substance abuse as a chronic illness. Early formalized treatment (initially residential) incorporated the basic tenets of Alcoholics Anonymous and the 12 steps, and was conducted by counselors who were former addicts and alcoholics themselves. Treatment programs based on this early model are still in existence at the time of this writing.

As the mental health field developed and became professionalized, the field of addictions also began to change. Agencies became more aware of the necessity of having formally trained therapists conduct treatment in lieu of exclusively recovering alcoholics and addicts. Engel's (1977) development of the biopsychosocial model led to using this approach with the substance-dependent population during the 1980s, and the use of this model continues to this day (as of this writing). This approach takes into account the many factors that contribute to substance misuse (biological, psychological, and social) and postulates that each client is using due to a unique combination of these factors. This therefore necessitates a more individualized course of treatment to address these underlying factors. Over time, concepts such as focusing on clients' strengths and discovering ways to motivate clients have become part of many treatment models across the United States. However, the prevailing belief remains that addiction is a chronic disease.

The Prevalence of Substance Use and Abuse in the United States

Statistics show a steady use and abuse of substances throughout U.S. history. It is said that 2.8 million people over the age of 11 in the United States used an illicit drug for the first time within the past 12 months (SAMHSA, 2006a). SAMHSA's 2005 National Survey on Drug Use reported that 19.7 million Americans ages 12 or older were current illicit drug users. The survey goes on to report that marijuana was the most common illicit drug used by Americans. Reported alcohol use varied among age categories, with the highest category (21–25 year olds) at 67.4% of the U.S. population. Heavy episodic drinking has been on a rise among young adults over the past several years.

It is also important to note the differences in substance use by gender and race/ethnicity. The National Institute on Drug Abuse (2003) reports the prevalence of past-month drug use in the United States. The report shows the ethnic group with the least illicit drug use (2.8%) as Asian/Pacific Islanders, and American Indian/Alaska Natives as the highest (9.3%). While men show a greater use of substances than women, up to 5.4% of women report illicit use. All of these statistics show that there is a need for effective treatment for substance abusers in this country.

Current Trends in the Substance Abuse Field

Treatment Trends

Curriculum- or Manual-Based Treatment
There has been a recent trend toward the use of manual- or curriculum-based treatment. Manual- or curriculum-based treatment is any type of treatment that has a manual or preset curriculum to follow during treatment sessions. An example of this is Driving with Care (Timken, Wanberg, & Milkman, 2004). This is a three-level education and treatment program

that was developed to be used with people who have been convicted for driving while their ability was impaired by substances. This manual provides worksheets, exercises, and discussion formats based upon cognitive-behavioral and psychoeducational approaches. A second example is Strategies for Self-Improvement and Change (Wanberg & Milkman, 1998), which was specifically designed for use with substance abusing offenders. This is a 9- to 12-month curriculum designed to prevent criminal recidivism and substance abuse relapse within community-based and correctional settings. At the time of this writing, both of these curricula are widely used in the state of Colorado as well as throughout the United States.

While the content in both of these cognitively based curricula has obvious strengths, using such an approach neglects to address the specific needs of individual clients, and the prescribed format restricts the therapist's ability to address individual clients' needs within the sessions since such curricula are designed to be done primarily in the prescribed order. Despite their rigidity, cognitively based manualized treatment curricula are becoming increasingly popular due to the evidence-based treatment emphasis in the United States (since the easiest and surest way to test a model to see if it is evidence based is to have a treatment manual). Thus, one lends itself to the other. While we support the need for accountability and strong outcomes in substance abuse treatment, a one-size-fits-all treatment approach fails to address the fact that individual differences obviously exist within the substance abusing client populations. We would therefore argue that the goal of providing evidence-based treatment should not compel therapists to marginalize, neglect, or mistreat the substance abuse client population for whom individualized treatment is essential for success.

Culturally and Gender-Sensitive Treatments

Any time therapists are using a prescribed treatment approach, there is the unintended consequence that treatment is tailored for the majority and may not be effective with the minority groups. Traditional treatments have struggled with this issue, and effectiveness has been challenging with minority populations and nonreligious people (Galaif & Sussman, 1995; Tonigan, Miller, & Schermer, 2002). Thus, there has been a recent awareness of the need for culturally sensitive treatments to help serve underrepresented populations. Almost 38.2% of clients entering treatment in 2003 were from a minority group (with 23.6% identifying as African American; Treatment Trends, 2003).

According to NIDA, the main gender difference in treatment is that women are less likely to enter treatment; however, their success rates are similar to those of men (Women and Substance Abuse, 2006). The National Institute on Drug Abuse suggests that women-specific treatment is especially beneficial for pregnant women and can provide services for women needing childcare, job training, transportation, and housing assistance. Because women who are pregnant face additional obstacles (such as prenatal care, care of other young children, nutritional needs, etc.) in addition to their substance abuse, it is imperative that therapists are sensitive to these needs and that additional case management services are provided to ensure success. In addition, postpartum women can experience challenges of postpartum depression as well as a lack of childcare and lack of adequate parenting skills. Add to this that postpartum women are at increased risk of relapse due to lack of sleep, increased stress, and their belief that the baby will no longer be negatively impacted by their use since they are no longer pregnant. Since women are less likely than men to enter treatment, most likely due to the factors just mentioned, it is imperative to offer gender-sensitive treatment that can help in meeting the logistical needs of women.

Treatment providers are becoming increasingly aware of the high prevalence of trauma that women who abuse substances have experienced. Many are victims of sexual assault or are survivors of child abuse or neglect. In fact, there is a strong correlation between substance abuse and sexual abuse (Dolan, 1991). Several studies show that a significant proportion of substance abusing women have suffered from traumas such as sexual abuse, domestic violence, and child physical abuse (Brems & Namyniuk, 2002; Freeman, Collier, & Parillo, 2002; Ouimette, Kimerling, Shaw, & Moos, 2000; Simpson & Miller, 2002). Many women use substances to cope with this past trauma, while others experience trauma as a result of their poor choices and resultant vulnerabilities caused by their use. This trauma and its aftermath necessitate the employment of trauma-informed professionals in order to resolve the lingering issues and to prevent these women from relapsing back into the painful cycle. This move toward a greater awareness of individual factors is key to effective, long-term recovery.

Individualized Treatment

The field of addictions (like most other fields) is riddled with contradictions. There is simultaneously a push toward manualized or curriculum-based treatment and another push toward ensuring that all treatment is individualized. In fact, individualized treatment is considered by NIDA to be one of the scientifically based approaches in the substance abuse field (2000b). This positive trend takes into account the fact that each client is unique, and therefore requires an individualized approach to increase the odds of success. This approach requires an individualized treatment plan, understanding of the client, and resulting treatment interventions. In summary, this trend is a move away from the cookie-cutter approach of one size fits all, toward honoring and respecting the clients for who they are.

Strength-Based Treatment

One of the latest trends in the field of substance abuse treatment is what is best described as strength based. This approach remains problem focused in that the professionals' focus remains on solving the presenting problem; however, it values and seeks to include the clients' strengths as part of the solution. While using a strength-based approach is a new trend in psychotherapy in general, it has found its way into substance abuse treatment as well. One of the most common strength-based models is motivational interviewing (Miller & Rollnick, 2002), or motivational enhancement therapy. This approach aids clients in increasing motivation to produce change. This and other strength-based approaches focus on clients' strengths instead of their deficiencies.

Ironically, part of this focusing on clients' strengths has resulted in the inclusion of solution-focused language within the field while discarding the foundational principles and philosophy. It has become increasingly common for agencies to blur the distinction between solution-focused and strength-based/problem-focused approaches when upon further investigation they are in fact working from a more traditional, problem-solving, medical model-driven philosophy. As therapists become more curious about the solution-focused approach, it is important to clarify the differences between solution-focused and problem-solving approaches, such as the strength-based model, in order to avoid misunderstanding and maintain well-formed, consistent treatment.

Substance Abuse Treatment Federal Agencies

Several federal agencies exist that aid in the research and treatment of substance abuse. We want to give a quick overview of the three most prominent: NIDA, NIAAA, and SAMHSA. The National Institute on Drug Abuse (NIDA) was established in 1974 as the main federal agency in charge of research to improve the treatment and prevention of drug abuse and addiction. NIDA's mission is "to lead the Nation in bringing the power of science to bear on drug abuse and addiction" (NIDA, n.d.). Their site is a helpful place to gain information, research, and statistics about drug abuse.

The National Institute on Alcohol Abuse and Alcoholism (NIAAA) is one of 27 institutes and centers that make up the National Institutes of Health. In 1970 the Comprehensive Alcohol Abuse and Alcoholism Prevention, Treatment, and Rehabilitation Act passed, allowing the federal government to create an institute to administer treatment and prevention of alcoholism. This was the birth of NIAAA. Its mission is to reduce alcohol-related problems by supporting and conducting research to be disseminated to mental health providers, politicians, and the general public (NIAAA, 2006).

The Substance Abuse and Mental Health Services Administration (SAMHSA) is a division of the U.S. Department of Health and Human Services. The mission of SAMHSA is "building resilience and facilitating recovery for people with or at risk for mental or substance use disorders" (SAMHSA, n.d.a). NIDA, NIAAA, and SAMHSA are helpful resources for clinicians.

American Society of Addiction Medicine

A fourth organization that has been instrumental in recent changes in the field of substance abuse treatment is the American Society of Addiction Medicine (ASAM). This organization developed a patient placement criteria (PPC-2R) that provides necessary standardization to the available forms of treatment (Mee-Lee, 2001, 2005). This was necessary to ensure that clients receive the level of care that is truly needed to match the client's need. According to the ASAM PPC-2R there are four defined levels of treatment services depending on the severity of the problem, ranging from outpatient to inpatient services. Level I is outpatient treatment. Treatment at this level involves outpatient treatment in an individual, group, or family setting up to a maximum of nine hours per week. Level II has two sublevels: intensive outpatient and partial hospitalization. Intensive outpatient includes a minimum of nine hours of outpatient services per week, while partial hospitalization includes 20 or more hours of programming per week. Level III consists of the most commonly recognized forms of residential/inpatient services. Within this level, services can range from a halfway house to treatment that is designed to stabilize medical and mental health complications. With Level III, therapists are the primary professionals providing the treatment services; although Level III.7 includes services that are monitored by medical personnel. The final level is IV, which is the medically managed intensive inpatient treatment. This level is used in the most extreme cases, and is more medical or psychiatric in nature, with physicians providing and managing the majority of care.

Current Mainstream Treatments

Although there are a vast number of types of treatment currently being utilized within the substance abuse field, the majority have at their core one of four key guiding forces. They are motivational interviewing, 12-step approach (also known as the Minnesota model or the medical model), cognitive/behavioral therapy, and harm reduction. Let us take a closer look at each of these.

Motivational Interviewing

Motivational Interviewing is one of the more popular models currently used in substance abuse treatment. It serves an invaluable role in assisting therapists to step away from the more traditional thinking in the field of substance abuse treatment toward a more empowering and motivational stance with clients. In this model the therapist remains the expert, and the goal is to assist the clients in seeing their addictive behaviors as problematic and in need of change. The therapist seeks to enhance the motivation of substance abusing clients to seek and continue treatment[1] (Miller & Rollnick, 2002). In this model, the focus is on assisting individuals in moving through the following stages of change:[2] (1) precontemplation (no recognition of a problem in need of change), (2) contemplation (recognizing the possible need to change and considering change), (3) determination (making the decision or preparing for change), (4) action stage (making changes), and (5) maintenance (maintaining current changes to prevent relapse). In the precontemplation stage, the clients do not see any need to make changes. This results in the clients wanting to continue their current behaviors. In the contemplation stage, clients are ambivalent about change. They are aware of both positive and negative consequences of their current behaviors, and are beginning to contemplate the need for change. Determination is a stage of experimentation with and preparing for change. The substance abuser readily admits that change is necessary, but makes little effort to change. In this stage, the clients take the necessary steps to prepare for the changes that lie ahead. The action phase is when the clients begin actively making significant changes in their lives. This is the stage that clinicians long for in their clients. Once significant change occurs, clients move into the maintenance stage. This stage focuses clients on maintaining their current changes and continuing down the same or better path. Clients can go through the stages several times before the change is lasting (Zimmerman, Olsen, & Bosworth, 2000). The emphasis on motivation for change remains the critical variable in moving from one stage to another (DiClemente, Bellino, & Neavins, 1999).

12-Step Approach (Minnesota Model)
This model takes a traditional 12-step approach to treatment that uses the principles of Alcoholics Anonymous and Narcotics Anonymous. This form of treatment began in the 1950s, and the basic tenets remain consistent in modern applications. This is the primary form of treatment that is often portrayed in the media, and is most well known in the general public. The main aspects of the Minnesota model are the possibility for change, the disease concept, the principles of Alcoholics Anonymous and Narcotics Anonymous, and treatment goals (Cook, 1988). This model postulates that substance abuse is a disease that needs to be treated, similar to a medical condition such as diabetes. Abstinence from all substances (excluding tobacco and caffeine) serves as the goal of treatment.

One of the main tenets in this approach is that substance abusing individuals must overcome their denial about their illness. When clients come to treatment saying that they do not have a problem with substances, it is thought that they are displaying their struggle with denial. Getting clients to face and deal with their denial is a major component of this model.

Cognitive-Behavioral Therapy
The cognitive-behavioral model is probably the most widely used type of psychotherapy. Components of this approach are commonly seen in most treatment applications (including motivational interviewing and 12-step programs). There are three main parts of cognitive-behavioral therapy for substance abuse treatment: functional analysis, coping skills training, and relapse prevention (Rotgers, 1996). Functional analysis assists clients in identifying their past drug use and the consequences of their behavior. Coping skills training serves as the second key element. It involves helping

clients come up with appropriate coping strategies. Finally, cognitive-behavioral therapy helps clients to develop relapse prevention strategies. In general, cognitive-behavioral therapy focuses on behavioral coping strategies, cognitions, beliefs, and expectancies (SAMHSA, 1999). Many current approaches for substance abuse treatment have cognitive-behavioral therapy at their core. It is a simple approach to learn and lends itself well to research.

Harm Reduction

Harm reduction is another approach to substance abuse treatment that has emerged in the past few decades. Its aim is to shift the focus from preventing or stopping drug use to preventing potential harms related to drug use. While the goal of most clinicians who use harm reduction approaches is to end the substance use all together, this is a step-by-step approach to change and seeks to work with the client to make changes in whatever ways the client is willing. Examples of this approach are the needle exchange program for injection drug users or the education campaign to increase the use of condoms to reduce the spread of HIV. Educating people on how to more safely use drugs is the immediate goal (Duncan, Nicholson, Clifford, Hawkins, & Petosa, 1994).

Modes of Treatment

Regardless of what kind of treatment one employs, there are many different ways that treatment can be administered, ranging from individual to group treatment modalities. Probably the most common mode of treatment for substance abusers is group therapy (we will explore this modality in depth in Chapters 6 and 7). In recent decades, the integration of family therapy in substance abuse treatment has occurred. One of the major goals of family therapy for substance abusers is prevention (SAMHSA, 2005b). Since substance abuse tends to run in families, family therapy allows intergenerational patterns to be addressed in order to prevent and treat alcohol and drug abuse. In addition, family therapy serves to change the family system, thereby decreasing the risk of relapse once the identified client returns to the family system. While several models of family therapy exist, some basic goals are improving communication, altering the family's structure, dealing with intergenerational issues, and altering faulty cognitions and behaviors. A great number of substance abuse treatment facilities include at least one component of family therapy. Most approaches support the notion that the family plays a major role in addiction and recovery.

Co-occurring Disorders

A great deal of substance abusers struggle with co-occurring disorders. The terms *co-morbid conditions* or *dual diagnosis disorders* are also used to describe this population. There is a recent awareness of the prevalence of co-occurring disorders, necessitating many agencies to insist that their therapists are dually trained in both substance abuse and mental health treatment. Substance abuse professionals are now most often expected to be proficient in mental health treatment in order to effectively treat this population. While this may not be the case in all settings, our intent is to provide basic information regarding key mental disorders that may coexist in clients within the substance abuse treatment field.

The three main categories of co-occurring disorders as described in the Treatment Improvement Protocol (TIP) series are personality, psychotic, and mood disorders (SAMHSA, 2005b). Personality disorders are broken into three clusters. Cluster A includes paranoid, schizoid, and schizotypal personality disorders. This group displays odd or eccentric behavior. Cluster B consists of dramatic, emotional, or erratic behavior and includes antisocial, borderline, histrionic, and narcissistic personality disorders. Some tips on how to handle antisocial personality disorder from a more traditional approach include confronting dishonesty directly, giving consequences to a client's behavior, and using peers to confront unwanted behaviors. Since antisocial personality disorder in particular has a high correlation with substance abuse (Flynn, Craddock, Hubbard, Anderson, & Etheridge, 1997), it is important to know how to handle these clients. The final cluster consists of avoidant, dependent, and obsessive-compulsive personality disorders. Anxious and fearful behavior can be witnessed in these individuals.

The second group, psychotic disorders, includes occurrences of delusions and hallucinations. Delusions are an altered perception of reality that hinder someone's functioning, and hallucinations are any false sensory perceptions (e.g., hearing voices). Those with this extreme type of mental illness are often present in substance abuse treatment centers (Gustafson et al., 1999). It is therefore important for substance abuse counselors to: (1) screen and refer psychotic clients, (2) understand the signs of psychosis, and (3) help clients discover early signs of reoccurrence (SAMHSA,

2005b). Note that sometimes hallucinations and delusions are caused by substances, making this differential diagnosis crucial in order to determine the most appropriate action. One way to assess if the delusions or hallucinations are caused by abusing substances or are symptomatic of a mental illness is by taking a thorough history. Taking a detailed psychological and substance use history (family members can be helpful if the client is unable to provide this) will help in determining the origin of the hallucinations or delusions.

The next type of co-occurring disorders that are frequently present are mood disorders. These include inappropriate, exaggerated, or a limited range of emotions or feelings. Specifically, the most common mood disorders are depression, mania, and bipolar disorder (SAMHSA, 2005b). Anxiety disorders may also appear as a co-occurring disorder with substance abusers. Panic attacks, social phobias, and posttraumatic stress disorder are just a few examples. As with any co-occurring disorder, substance abuse counselors may need to refer some individuals for further mental health treatment if they are not adequately trained in this area.

Correlated Medical Risk Factors

Due to the fact that substance abuse drastically lowers inhibition, impairs judgment, and decreases impulse control, clients who abuse substances are at increased risk of making poor decisions when under the influence of substances. Clients in this category are at higher risk of engaging in unsafe sex practices or sharing unclean needles when using intravenous drugs. Therefore, this population is at greater risk of contracting HIV, AIDS, tuberculosis (TB), hepatitis C, and a wide variety of sexually transmitted diseases. Sixty percent of transmission of hepatitis C is from injection drug use (NIDA, 2000a). Thus, the most effective way hepatitis C can be prevented is by lessening the amount of unsanitary drug injection. According to the National Institute on Drug Abuse, TB remains intertwined with drug abuse (NIDA, 2006b). These statistics show the need for harm reduction strategies to prevent the spread of these and other diseases.

A great deal of the substance abuse literature discusses the link between drug use and HIV (NIDA, 2005). Whether substance abusing clients have a positive or negative HIV status, HIV/AIDS is an important topic of discussion. One of the goals of substance abuse treatment is HIV/AIDS, tuberculosis, and other communicable disease prevention. It is important to discuss with clients how to protect themselves from contracting

HIV/AIDS and how to avoid spreading the disease if they are infected. Educating clients about the transmission of HIV and other diseases and the steps they can take to reduce their risk of contracting this and other diseases and spreading them is central to substance abuse treatment.

Matters become more complicated when a client in a group setting is HIV positive. The most important thing for substance abuse treatment programs to do when working with clients infected with HIV/AIDS is to make sure that they have a close relationship with healthcare providers in the community (SAMHSA, 2005b). Since clients with HIV/AIDS have numerous medical issues, it is imperative for substance abuse therapists to stay in regular contact with HIV/AIDS medical personnel. It is also important to respect the client's right to privacy in regard to medical matters when working with a client in a group setting.

Summary

Substance abuse has been a part of U.S. history from the beginning. While those abusing substances used to be viewed as morally lacking, addiction is now more readily understood from a biopsychosocial perspective and as a condition that is treatable. We are living in a time in which treatment services are readily available and therapists are aware of the need for individualized, strength-based, and culturally sensitive treatment. Times have changed for the better in this regard. In the following chapter we will explore what solution-focused brief therapy is and begin our journey in understanding how this approach to substance abuse treatment can transform the field.

Endnotes

1. This is the key distinction between motivational interviewing and solution-focused brief therapy (SFBT). In SFBT, the clients remain the expert on their lives and the therapist is solely the expert in asking well-formed questions to help the clients explore and evaluate their lives. In SFBT, the therapist does not need to enhance the clients' motivation. The therapist simply listens to hear what the client is already motivated to achieve and focuses there. The therapist does not have an opinion as to the best solution or if the client needs to remain in treatment to reach the desired solution.

2. It is important to note that motivational interviewing builds upon the original work of Prochaska and DiClemente (1984), Prochaska, DiClemente, and Norcross (1994), and Prochaska and Norcross (1999). Miller and Rollnick

(2002) focus on utilizing Prochaska, DiClemente, and Norcross's stages-of-change model to increase motivation in clients who are struggling with substance misuse. Although the stages-of-change model was created by Prochaska, DiClemente, and Norcross, we refer the reader to motivational interviewing since the field of substance abuse uses this as a foundational text.

2

Solution-Focused Brief Therapy
The Basics

> Problems are problems and they can best be understood in relation to their
> solutions.
>
> **Steve de Shazer**

Before we delve into how to provide effective treatment services, it is wise
to take a moment to set the foundation for our work together. In the true
spirit of solution-focused brief therapy,[1] we do not want to assume that we
are thinking about the approach in the same way. In this chapter we will
clearly describe what solution-focused brief therapy is, the overarching
philosophy and principles, and the six associated interventions.

Introduction

A Brief Look at History

Solution-focused brief therapy was originally created by Insoo Kim Berg and
Steve de Shazer in Milwaukee, Wisconsin, in the 1970s. Both were formally
trained in systems theory as social workers and completed graduate studies
at the Mental Research Institute in Palo Alto, California. These early influences of systems theory, Erickson's work, and the Mental Research Institute
(MRI) model are evident in the model they later created. Being a pragmatic
person, Steve wanted to determine what exactly it was that was resulting in
change for the clients, so he and a team of colleagues began to sit behind a
one-way mirror as Insoo met with client after client. They made notes about
what worked, and then asked Insoo to do more of that. If something did not
work, they gave this feedback to Insoo and suggested that she stop doing it
and try something else. Eventually they discovered some basic principles and

interventions that consistently worked for the clients (it is important to note that these clients were low socioeconomic, intercity, minority, multiproblem clientele). They later called this list of principles and interventions solution-focused brief therapy. Their work has spread around the world and is now integrated into a widely diversified collection of settings that include child welfare, mental health centers, substance abuse treatment facilities, jails and correctional departments, battered women's shelters, business coaching, and educational settings, just to name a few. Their original work is written in numerous groundbreaking texts (de Shazer, 1985, 1988, 1991, 1994; Berg, 1994; Berg & Miller, 1992; Miller & Berg, 1995; Berg & Reuss, 1998), all of which we truly value and used as the foundation for this book.

Dispelling the Myths About Solution-Focused Brief Therapy

Similar to the telephone game of childhood in which one person whispers the message to another to test the accuracy of the message over time, the greater the distance of the message from the original sender, the more distorted the message becomes. In order to increase one's odds of under-standing the correct message, it is important to position oneself near the source of the message, and to create some kind of feedback loop to ensure the message was heard as intended. Unfortunately, not everyone has had the opportunity to work closely with Insoo and Steve to have that kind of feedback loop, and the message has been combined with other philosophies and approaches over the years. This combining with other approaches has had a positive effect in that it has added to the richness of other approaches, but it also can make the understanding of what solu-tion-focused brief therapy truly is a difficult proposition due to this blend-ing and multiple versions.

I oftentimes refer to these differences in the versions of solution-focused brief therapy as different dialects of the same language. They often serve some function or need in a particular region, or other times simply tell something about the unique culture of those who speak that dialect. However, the subtle difference in the dialects can make communication difficult among those needing to communicate if these differences are unexpected or not understood. Someone new who wants to learn the lan-guage may later find that he or she does not understand the pure language at all since it was a specific dialect that was studied. As a result of these different versions of solution-focused brief therapy, various myths and negative perceptions have been perpetuated about this approach. These myths can lead people to the mistaken conclusion that "brief therapies [this writer was including solution-focused brief therapy in this general label] are most effective with clients whose problems are of short duration and who have strong ties to family, work, and community" (Department of Health and Human Services [DHHS], 1999, p. 44). While this statement may very well be true for some of the problem-focused brief therapies, the statement is grossly inaccurate for solution-focused brief therapy, which shows good success with clients with limited, if any, family or community resources and with prolonged, chronic problems (de Shazer & Isebaert, 2003; Eakes, Walsh, Markowski, Cain, & Swanson, 1997; Lindforss & Magnusson, 1997; Pichot & Dolan, 2003).

These subtle inaccuracies about solution-focused brief therapy are commonplace throughout the literature. For example, in conducting research for this book I came across many statements about solution-focused brief therapy that made me realize how misunderstood this approach can be. One such statement from the Center for Substance Abuse Treatment stated when referring to this approach, "The word 'problem' is avoided" (DHHS, 1999, p. 100). While it is true that a solution-focused therapist believes that it is most helpful to talk about a place in which the problem is resolved, this does not mean that a seasoned solution-focused therapist would avoid talking about the problem in all circumstances. To do so would risk being insensitive and even miss the spirit of the approach. Similarly, over the years I have heard solution-focused therapists inaccurately described as "problem-phobic" or "feeling phobic" since solution-focused brief therapy takes a more client-centered approach and does not actively explore these areas until they are indicated as necessary or helpful by the client or the client system.

Another example of a common myth of solution-focused brief therapy was voiced by Linda Metcalf (1998) when she wrote, "Avoid any tendency to promote insight and instead focus on the client's ability to survive the problem situation" (p. 14). I cannot fathom doing any kind of treatment without the partial goal of promoting insight. The goal of promoting insight in our clients is common to the majority of psychotherapy approaches, solution-focused brief therapy included. Our work could not be possible without the client gaining necessary insight, for good therapy is good therapy regardless of the approach one utilizes. However, the insight that clients most frequently gain during a solution-focused session is about the solution and what they will be doing differently to create the desired solution, rather than insight about the problem and its etiology (however, our clients frequently leave treatment with a greater level of insight about that as well, although this is not our intent nor the focus of treatment). These examples of myths are just a few of the many that exist about this approach, for it would be beyond the scope of this book to provide an exhaustive list. So given all the myths and distorted information, you may be wondering what solution-focused brief therapy really is anyway. Let us jump in and explore this.

Problem-Solving versus Solution-Building Philosophy

Treatment philosophy can best be categorized into problem-solving philosophy and solution-building philosophy. Problem-solving philosophy involves the standard course of evaluation and preparation for treatment in which all of us were trained. This guiding philosophy is consistent regardless of which theoretical approach one chooses (aside from solution-focused brief therapy). It is as follows:

- Evaluate the problem.
- Diagnose the problem.
- Utilize known information about the diagnosed problem.
- Evaluate client resources/strengths. (This step is only included when one is using a strength-based approach.)
- Determine the best course of treatment through the use of a treatment plan.
- Implement the treatment.

The therapist serves as the expert, and a thorough understanding of the problem is necessary before beginning treatment. McHahon (1990) states that the problem-solving approach involves the client learning a new skill or method to resolve a problem. She defines problem solving as:

- Problem description and data collection
- Problem assessment
- Intervention planning
- Intervention
- Evaluation and follow-up

Because identifying the problem and its root lies at the core of problem solving, this can pose a challenge when working with substance abusing clients who do not view their use of substances as problematic, making more motivational approaches such as motivational interviewing (Miller & Rollnick, 2002) a treatment model of choice when problem solving with this population. Although models like motivational interviewing still fall under the category of problem-focused approaches, the techniques employed to increase client motivation assist clients in becoming more willing to understand and address their problems.

Some, at times, mistakenly confuse the strength-based approaches as falling under the solution-building philosophy. Although the strength-based approaches highly value the clients and what they bring to treatment, the overall guiding philosophy in strength-based approaches remains on first understanding the problem at hand and then determining how to best solve it. Steve de Shazer (personal communication, January 7, 2004) once said during a conversation about this subject, "Strength is an interpretation and a generalization that accidentally hides details that might be usefully highlighted." This value of classifying and interpreting client aspects for the purpose of solving a problem is an integral component of the problem-solving approaches.

In contrast, solution building takes a radically different approach when evaluating and working with clients. It can best be described as the following:

- Determine the desired goals.
- Assist the clients in creating a detailed description of their goals.
- Assist the clients in evaluating where they are in relation to their desired goals.
- Assist the clients in evaluating times in which they were successful in moving toward the desired goals.
- Work backward to discover keys to success.

As part of my (SS) dissertation work, I searched the solution-focused literature to find the main tenets of solution building. I found that the three main components from the literature are identifying the solution, awareness of exceptions, and hope in the future. The key to working from a solution-building philosophy is understanding what the client truly wants and what is in the client's heart. More specifically, solution building relies on having the clients identify how they would like their lives to be despite the current presence of their problems.

For example, I have yet to have a client tell me that he or she truly just wanted to drink or use drugs and that was all that was important to him or her. The substance use has always been something the client is doing, but not what was truly most important. I have on occasion had a client tell me in a flippant fashion that he just wanted to be high; however, when I gently pushed to better understand why, he then told me that he wanted to be high to help him forget his problems. The substance use was a method to a desired end, not the goal itself. Another example: A common thing I hear from clients is that getting their children returned to their custody and "being a good parent" are most important. By using these as a starting point, and working from a systems perspective (which we will discuss in more detail in a moment), the therapist starts to discover the desired solution. The therapist then works backward to determine what steps the client took to achieve this desired solution. It is this imagining that the problem is resolved and then working with the client from this place in which the problem is resolved to discover the solutions that are illuminated from this future place (Berg, 1994, p. 98) that makes this philosophy truly unique from all other approaches. Let us now take a look at the key principles of solution-focused brief therapy.

Solution-Focused Principles

The principles of solution-focused therapy are found throughout the literature and are summarized in various locations. Here are two lists that seem to best capture the basics tenets of this approach. Scott Miller and Insoo Kim Berg (1995, p. 31) summarize the principles of solution-focused therapy as follows:

1. No single approach works for everyone.
2. There are many possible solutions.
3. The solution and the problem are not necessarily related.
4. The simplest and least invasive approach is frequently the best medicine.
5. People can and do get better quickly.
6. Change is happening all the time.
7. Focus on strengths and resources rather than weaknesses and deficits.
8. Focus on the future rather than the past.

Pichot and Dolan (2003, p. 13) provide this list of principles that summarize what is in the literature:

1. If it's not broken, don't fix it.
2. If something is working, do more of it.
3. If it is not working, do something different.
4. Small steps can lead to large changes.
5. The solution is not necessarily directly related to the problem.
6. The language requirements for solution development are different from those needed to describe a problem.

7. No problem happens all the time. There are always exceptions that can be utilized.
8. The future is both created and negotiable.

While volumes could be written on these principles alone, we believe that they will be adequately described throughout the rest of our writing. We encourage you to notice them throughout the rest of the text. However, there is one principle that bears highlighting due to its centrality throughout our work: The future is both created and negotiable. Our clients frequently come to us with a sense of fatalism. Their lives are set on a destructive course, and they can see no way to alter their path. By assisting clients in understanding that they do indeed remain in control of their destiny, their lives can be profoundly altered. They frequently come to us so focused on the problems that they become oblivious to possible solutions. Solution-focused brief therapy opens their minds to the possibility of solutions.

Universal Truths

I have come to learn that there are some facts in this world for which, upon closer inspection, one can see the factual element in play in a variety of settings. Gravity, for example, holds true in the field of science as well as in the life of a common person; matter gets pulls toward the earth's center regardless of one's beliefs or context. Another one of these facts (I refer to them as universal truths) is that whatever one focuses on gets bigger. Rhonda Byrne (2006) refers to this as the "law of attraction" (p. 4). For example, imagine yourself driving in a snowstorm (or a rainstorm for those of you in warmer climates). If you were to focus on the snowflakes as they hit your windshield, you would rapidly become disoriented and run off the road. However, if instead, you focus on the white line on the road, you would be able to remain on the road and navigate through the inclement weather to your destination. By doing so, would you be in denial that it was snowing? Of course not. You would instead be wisely focusing on your path and, in turn, be able to withstand the distraction of the snowflakes. Another common example is in the field of sports. Experts in the field of sports psychology frequently coach their athletes to focus on their goal. At times they use visualization to help the athletes imagine themselves winning the race or performing their best. This can be especially helpful during times in which the athlete is making mistakes or is struggling through a difficulty. Solution-focused brief therapy uses this same universal truth by teaching clients how to remain focused on what they want despite the distractions of the current problems, knowing that in doing so, they will be better able to navigate through life's difficulties.

Systems Perspective

Before proceeding with each of the interventions, it would be prudent to spend some time discussing the systems perspective and how this plays a part in solution-focused brief therapy, for without this information, it is not credible to use this approach with externally motivated, substance abusing clients. The field of social work (remember, this was the profession in which both Steve de Shazer and Insoo Kim Berg were originally trained) has its roots in systems perspective (Bertalanffy, 1968). This approach views the client within the context of his or her system. For example, each of us has our own unique systems to which we belong. Our clients frequently are involved with the legal system, child welfare, as well as other systems. In addition, they are part of families and a larger community in which there are laws and expectations. Lastly, as therapists, we have to provide services within the confines of regulation and standards of care that impact and actually become part of the client's system as a function of working with us (see Figure 2.1).

Therefore, solution-focused therapists actually view the client as the individual in front of him or her within the context of the client's larger system, and therefore have the goal of helping the clients imagine what life will be like once the problem is resolved and everyone in his or her system also agrees that this problem is truly resolved. This broader perspective ensures that the client is thinking in terms of the larger context (something that is truly needed when working with externally motivated clients). This systems perspective also provides the necessary framework for the therapist's questions, so that the therapist has no need to form opinions or take a side.

Remaining Neutral

The word *denial* is used throughout the substance abuse treatment literature since clients are notorious for not being forthcoming about the extent of their use. And why should clients volunteer this potentially damaging information since many stand to lose so much through their continued use? When the treatment approach has a problem-solving philosophy, and

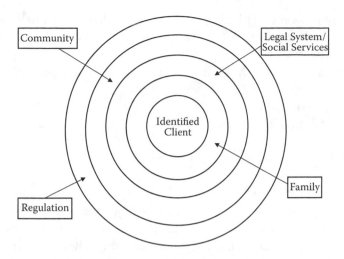

Figure 2.1 Sample Client System

therefore needs to fully understand the extent of the problem, this can pose a challenge, since the professional has no way to know if the facts pre sented by the client are entirely correct. In solution-focused brief therapy, this dilemma is avoided, since what remains the focus of evaluation is the system's desired goal and the degree to which this is obtained. This allows the therapist to remain completely neutral, with no need to evaluate the accuracy of the information the client presents since it is the role of those within the client's system to make the final judgment in this regard. By asking the clients questions regarding the perspectives of the other members in the system, the clients are required to make their own evaluation regarding the acceptableness of the answers. The following example demonstrates this concept:

Therapist (T): So how can I help you?
Client (C): I want to get my children back.
T: And how can I help you with that?
C: I need to prove to my caseworker that I don't have a problem with alcohol. She thinks I do, but I really don't. [The client just offered information that identifies another person in her system in addition to her child.]
T: So what difference would it make to your case for you to prove this to your caseworker?
C: Then they would know that I am a good mother. I am a good mother now, but they don't believe me.

T: So proving you don't have a problem with alcohol will help them see
    what kind of mother you already are? What else would help
    them see this?

C: That I am following through with appointments and getting a place to
    live. Maybe get some new friends.

T: And how will that help.

C: My friends aren't that great. They are always drinking, and it makes it
    hard.

T: So having new friends will make it easier?

By understanding who is in the client's system, the therapist is better
able to ask questions that will gather more objective information and easily determine the client's system's goal. There is no need for the therapist to
know for sure if the client has truly stopped her alcohol use or if the client
is a "good mother" since those determinations are the ultimate responsibility of the caseworker and the court system to ensure child safety. The
therapist's role is to ask purposeful questions that will assist the client in
determining what steps she will have taken to better the odds that the
court rules in her favor. By asking the client questions, from the caseworker's perspective, the client demonstrates that she is aware that stability and housing are also issues that must be resolved prior to her meeting
the system's goal of returning the child to a safe home. She has also disclosed information about changes that the client would like to see to make
it easier for her to reach the desired goal. The abuse of alcohol does not
need to be the focus of this discussion, but clearly will be absent once the
goal is complete. The therapist has no need to form an opinion (i.e., take
the client's or the caseworker's side), and is therefore free to remain on
the outside of the system. There is no need for a term such as *denial* in
this model. For such a term requires that the therapist make a determination as to "truth." In solution-focused brief therapy the client's system
determines what is true or acceptable in order to meet its goals, freeing
the therapist to remain neutral. So let us now take a look at the specific
interventions that make change possible in this model.

Interventions

Each approach or theory has its own set of interventions that are consistent
with the governing philosophy and make the approach unique. Solution-
focused brief therapy is no exception. While you may find that some of these

interventions are used in other theories, it is the combination of the intervention with the basic principles and governing philosophy that make the intervention effective and an integral part of solution-focused brief therapy. Let us begin with the intervention that Miller and de Shazer (1998) describe as the "centerpiece of this approach" (p. 366), the miracle question.

Miracle Question

The majority of the work in solution-focused brief therapy happens when a client imagines a place in which the problem is resolved. This plants the seeds of hope that change is possible, for now the client can see the solution, and this "taps into the clients' expectations for therapy: they come to therapy wanting a miracle" (de Shazer, 1988, p. 6). It is through the use of the miracle question that the clients are free to think beyond the problems that currently seem insurmountable, to allow them to identify resources that they may not remember or recognize when their minds are clouded by the problem. Bringing them to this future place in their imaginations allows them to suspend their disbelief that change is possible to explore a place of possibility. Peter DeJong and Insoo Kim Berg (1998) word the miracle question as follows:

> Now, I want to ask you a strange question. Suppose that while you are sleeping tonight and the entire house is quiet, a miracle happens. The miracle is that the problem which brought you here is solved. However, because you are sleeping, you don't know that the miracle has happened. So, when you wake up tomorrow morning, what will be different that will tell you a miracle has happened and the problem which brought you here is solved? (pp. 77–78)

Similar to so many aspects of solution-focused brief therapy, the miracle question initially appears quite simple, yet it is actually deceptively precise and purposeful. Many therapists have asked the miracle question only to have it fall flat and later wonder why they did not experience the magical answer that they saw in demonstrations and instructional videotapes. Once they have a clearer understanding of the purpose of the miracle question and how to best present it, they have much better success.

Setting up the Miracle Question
Initially, the question can sound rather odd and can be met with resistance if not presented purposefully and carefully. Many years ago I was training a therapist how to use this question with adolescents. After one of

the therapist's sessions, I met with the young therapist to hear how it went. The therapist told me that he was very proud that he had remembered to include each and every element; however, he then stated that after asking the question the client simply paused, stared at him, and said, "You are a dork!" The therapist lost all confidence and confided to me that he secretly believed maybe he did sound like a dork when working with this client, and had quickly retreated from the intervention. While most therapists' first experiences are not as traumatic or confidence shaking as this, it is very helpful to carefully set up the miracle question. By first asking the client permission to ask a potentially odd-sounding question and by stressing the potential benefit, the client is more likely to respond positively and weather the initial feelings of discomfort of exploring new territory.

In addition to ensuring that the miracle question is properly introduced, it is important that the therapist truly believes in the clients' ability to answer the question in a meaningful manner (de Shazer et al., 2007). It is this mindset that conveys faith in the clients' ability to change, and it is this faith that empowers the clients to live up to their potential and begin to hope. It is this hope that then leads the clients to action and eventual behavioral change. It is this gift of faith in the clients' ability to answer in a meaningful way and to sort pipe dreams from the attainable that enables the therapist to walk hand in hand with the clients through their miracle day as they determine the first and best steps that lead to a place in which the problem is resolved. Let us now take a closer look at the miracle question itself.

Key Components
There are five key components of the miracle question, and all are necessary to achieve the ideal results (Pichot & Dolan, 2003). The first is the idea that something occurs that is unexpected and unlikely to occur naturally. This is reflected in the wording, "A miracle happens." A miracle is most often perceived as a positive event that has enormous ramifications. It is this concept that ensures that the change will be worthwhile to the clients and not something that the clients perceive they could have easily obtained without assistance (remember, the clients are seeking help since they do not believe they can resolve their problems on their own). The original wording for the miracle came directly from a client with whom Insoo Kim Berg was working. Insoo asked her client what would need to happen during the session in order for their work together to be helpful, and the client responded that it would take a miracle. Insoo, always thinking on her feet, quickly responded, "Then suppose a miracle happened…"

For some people, the word *miracle* has a religious connotation; however, according to the *American Heritage College Dictionary* (1993) there are two definitions for the word *miracle*, and only one of these has any association with "supernatural" or "act of God." The second definition is nonreligious, and is simply something that "excites admiring awe" (p. 870). Because of these two accepted ways of defining the word *miracle*, I have found that clients who find religion to be helpful tend to view it in this context, while those who are not religious rarely associate the word *miracle* with religion or find it to be problematic. However, when working with a client who does not find the word *miracle* to be helpful, other words can be substituted as long as the original meaning is not lost. For example, I (SS) have heard Yvonne Dolan say "something shifts" instead of "a miracle happens." While it does not imply a change of as significant proportions as the word *miracle* does, it can be quite useful when needed.

The second element of the miracle question is that the miracle is defined. Traditionally, it is defined as "the problem that brought you here is resolved." While this wording is highly effective when the client has a clear idea what the problem is or when used by therapists who are highly skilled in using solution-focused brief therapy, I have found it to be problematic with the majority of clients who are mandated to receive substance abuse treatment, specifically when used by beginning and intermediate-level solution-focused therapists. The majority of these clients do not believe that they have a problem; the problem is others'. The only problem they see is that they are misunderstood and treated unfairly. When using the traditionally worded miracle in this context, the clients almost always think of an event (for example, their children are home) when the miracle question is asked. While a therapist who is highly skilled in solution-focused brief therapy can successfully work with a client in this context, the majority of beginning or intermediate-level therapists will soon find the miracle to be very superficial and unhelpful since the desired event may not be possible. Instead, I have found it most helpful to teach therapists to listen for a quality, skill, or trait that the client desires and then to use this wording in the miracle question. For example:

T: How can I help you?
C: You can't. I don't have a problem.
T: That sounds like a tough place to be. Help me understand why you thought it was a good idea to come see me today.
C: My probation officer said I had to come.
T: What is he hoping you will get out of coming?

C: He thinks I have a problem with methamphetamine.

T: What do you think?

C: I know I don't. I was just with a friend who was using.

T: So on a scale of 1 to 10, 10 being that your probation officer completely believes that you don't have a problem with drugs and 1 is the opposite, where do you think he is?

C: About a 2.

T: Where do you want him to be?

C: A 10.

T: So would it be a good use of our time to help determine what will be different when he is a 10?

C: Yeah!

T: OK. I have a very important question to ask you. It might initially sound a little strange, but it is very important. Are you willing to give it a try?

C: OK.

T: I want you to imagine that tonight when you go to bed, a miracle happens. And the miracle is that you now have the ability to convince your probation officer that you don't have a problem with substances. Now because you were sleeping, you have no idea that the miracle has happened. What are the first things that you notice ... even before you open your eyes ... that this miracle has happened?

C: I would be more relaxed...

In this example, it became clear that what was important to the client was to convince his probation officer that he does not have a problem with substances. In this situation, the therapist does not form an opinion about if the client has a problem or not. (The therapist remains completely neutral, trusting that in order for the client to convince the probation officer, any problem the client might have with substances would also have to be resolved.) In order to partner with the client to explore the client's miracle day, the therapist needs to define the miracle so that the client clearly understands what will be different. Although defining the client's miracle in this way is more limiting than the original wording of the miracle question, it provides the needed common ground to begin the work together.

I have found it most helpful to liken the client's larger miracle to a house. A house has multiple entry points: doors, windows, drain pipe, cracks, etc. Some ways are much easier to enter than others. Oftentimes our clients have tightly sealed their house, making it very difficult as a therapist to find a way into the house (such as the client just discussed). However, each client does offer some way of entry should the therapist patiently listen. While the front door would be a much more obvious way to enter (for example, how a therapist can enter with a self-referred client), entry through a drain pipe can be just as effective, for one still gains entry into the house. The goal is simply to enter the house, regardless of the path one has to take. When working with angry, externally referred clients, I find I frequently have to enter through a small crevice. However, once inside, I quickly hear who the client is and what is most important to him or her. I obtain the same results as if I was invited through the front door.

The third element of the miracle question is that the miracle is to occur tonight. This creates a sense of immediacy. As humans, we are very wise. We rarely extend energy unnecessarily or when there is no perceived benefit. Our clients' problems are oftentimes thought to be long standing, and therefore something that will take a great deal of time to resolve. Because of this, why should they begin to look for changes now? Because the miracle is described as something that occurs this very day, the clients receive hope that change may occur immediately, giving them reason to begin searching for hints of change right away.

The fourth element of the miracle is that the client is unaware that the miracle occurred. This element is crucial to stress, for without it the client has nothing to discover. This leads us to the fifth element: discovery. It is through discovering all of the tattletale clues that the miracle occurred that the client learns the multitude of things that he or she will be doing differently once the problem is resolved. These then become clues as to what the client could do differently to create change in the future. These elements are discovered through questions such as "What will be the first things you would notice?" or through relational questions such as "What would your wife notice?" It is also very effective to ask clients to step into the shoes of their children or even think from their pet's perspective. This is instrumental in assisting the client to discover details that prior to now have been overlooked.

The miracle question is the vehicle by which the client is able to suspend his or her disbelief and therefore explore life without the problem. It is this fundamental element that makes this question the foundation of all the work a solution-focused therapist does. In Chapter 3 we will explore additional aspects of the miracle question that will help beginning and intermediate-level therapists hone their skills to increase their effectiveness with this central question. Now let us take a look at scaling.

Scaling

Scaling is an invaluable tool that helps to make otherwise vague concepts measurable. The use of scales is commonplace in many professions, such as nursing. Nurses frequently use scales to have patients rate the amount of pain they are experiencing. This helps to gauge the amount of medication needed and progress being made. When used in this way, the higher the number, the more pain the patient is experiencing. Similarly, it is commonplace to take a patient's blood pressure, weight, and temperature as a routine part of a medical exam. All of these are forms of scales, which provide meaningful information to the professional. Similarly, mental health professionals have utilized the benefits of scaling through Likert and self-anchored scales. An early example of the use of a self-anchored scale is one that was developed by Wolpe (1969, 1973) to measure anxiety. It was called the Subjective Anxiety Scale. This is a 100-point instrument. The client is asked to think of the worst anxiety he or she has ever experienced, and this experience then becomes the reference point for 100. The client then is asked to imagine what absolute calm would be like, and this becomes the 0 on this scale. Scales such as this have high face validity, but have little ability to collect reliability data since these are individualized for each client (Bloom & Fischer, 1982, p. 169). According to Bloom and Fischer (1982), these types of self-anchored scales "can be used to evaluate internal thoughts and feelings, or the intensity of those thoughts or feelings, that other measures cannot tap" (p. 169). Solution-focused brief therapy takes full advantage of these beneficial aspects of self-anchored scales.

When Insoo began to use scaling, she found that more than 10 points was overly cumbersome. It was too much to expect a client to be able to differentiate between 56 and 57, for example. Throughout her work, she used a scale of 1 to 10. Steve de Shazer, on the other hand, was known for using 0 to 10. Consistent with the basic tenets of solution-focused brief therapy, what the solution-focused therapist scales are aspects that are desired. These may be progress toward the client's miracle or any smaller element, such as motivation, confidence, or any number of other desired aspects. This is one of the most unique factors of solution-focused scales.

In solution-focused scaling, the therapist clearly defines both ends of the scale based upon the factor being measured, leaving the client to determine the meaning of the numbers between the 1 and the 10. For example, when working with a client who is struggling with depression and anxiety about getting through the day, the therapist would be curious as to what will be present once the depression and anxiety are no longer an issue. Let us say for the sake of this example that it would be peace. The therapist might then anchor the scale by saying, "On a scale of 1 to 10, 10 being that you have a sense of peace and knowing that you can get through whatever comes your way and 1 being the opposite, where would you say you are today?" This form of scale then focuses the client on what is desired and assists the client in identifying progress that has already been made. Scales can best be categorized into diagnostic scales and therapeutic scales.

Diagnostic Scales

Diagnostic scales are those that are used by the therapist to better understand what the client is saying. These can be used to determine if something the client is mentioning is important and would be useful to explore further, or to better understand the specific element that the client desires. The following excerpt demonstrates this:

T: Let me just take a moment here to make sure I am hearing you correctly. You have been talking about your past issues with your husband, and I want to make sure our future conversation is going in the way you need. So, on a scale of 1 to 10, 10 being that you are completely sure what you need to do and 1 is you have no idea, where are you today?

C: A 10.

T: OK. Then on a completely different scale, 10 being that you know what you need to do and how to do it and 1 is that you know what you need to do but have no idea how to do it, where are you today?

C: I would say I'm a 10 on that as well.

T: OK. Very helpful. One more scale to make sure I understand. On this scale, 10 being that you know what you need to do, know how to do it, and are very comfortable doing it and 1 is that you know what you need to do, know how to do it, but are very uncomfortable actually doing it, where would you say you are?

C: On that one, I'm about a 2. I know what to do and how to do it, but I'm scared.

This series of scales was instrumental in clarifying for the therapist exactly which element needs to be the target of the work together. In this case, the client has the needed knowledge and confidence in her decision, but there is still something that is blocking her from taking action.

The therapist can now ask the miracle question using this information. It might be worded as follows:

> So, I want you to imagine that tonight when you are sleeping a miracle happens, and the miracle is that you are completely comfortable with your decision. You know it's the right one and you are now comfortable taking action. However, because you were asleep, you have no idea the miracle happens. What will be the first things that you notice when you wake up, even before you open your eyes, that let you know the miracle happened?

Diagnostic scaling is also an effective way to gather more information about the problem (to meet standards of care) without leaving the context of the solution. For example, when working with a client who makes statements that life is not worth living, it is imperative that the therapist clearly understands if the client is at risk for attempting suicide. In this instance, a safety scale as follows would be instrumental.

T: So, I hear that you are having a very difficult time right now. I'm impressed that you made it to this appointment. I'm wondering, on a scale from 1 to 10, 10 being that even though life is very difficult right now, you know that you will make it through and 1 is that there is no way you will make it through and you will kill yourself, where are you right now?

C: Well, I have thought about killing myself, but I know I wouldn't do that.

T: That's good. What number do you think best represents where you are right now?

C: I would say about a 3.

T: Great! What lets you know you are a 3 right now and not a 2?

C: Well, I have tried to kill myself in the past, and I'm not there.

T: What is different about now that lets you know you are not at risk for killing yourself?

C: Well, I have my daughter now. I could never do that to her. I have other ways to get through.

T: That's wonderful. What are some of those ways?

By using scaling, the therapist is able to gather useful information, such as the client has had one past suicide attempt and that things are different for her now that she has a daughter. She is aware of the potential pain and harm losing her mother would have on her daughter, and the client currently has skills and tools to cope that she previously did not have. All of this is obtained by carefully wording the scale to be very specific to what the therapist needed to know (the 1 was defined in such a way that in Colorado we would have had to implement a psychiatric hold and the 10 was defined as to acknowledge the client's difficulties and pain yet still adding the safety element that we are working toward). The therapist is now ready to ask the miracle question to address the issues at hand. It might be worded as follows:

T: I would like to ask you an odd question if that is OK with you. I think it will really help you as you are going through this difficult time. Is that OK?

C: Sure. I guess.

T: OK. I want you to imagine that tonight when you are sleeping, a miracle happens, and the miracle is that even though you are going through this very difficult time, you have what you need to get through it in the best way possible. But because you were sleeping, you have no idea that the miracle happened. What will be some of the first things that you notice when you wake up that will let you know the miracle happened?

In this example, the miracle question is worded in a way that validates what the client says is her reality. She is going through a difficult time. To pretend she is not could be perceived by the client as naive and insensitive. By wording the question in this manner, the therapist is able to target the area of focus (to get through the difficult time in the best way possible), which respects the client's external reality. Now let us take a look at therapeutic scales.

Therapeutic Scales

Scaling is not only useful as a diagnostic tool but is valuable clinically as well. When a therapist asks a client to scale any element of his or her goal, the client is making a connection between the present and the desired result. This can be done on a broader level by asking clients to scale where they are in relationship to their miracle, or on a more specific level by asking them to scale where they are in relation to a specific element, such as confidence. By continually linking the present and the future, the therapist is displaying assurance that the miracle can be reached, and therefore increasing the client's hope that this will become a reality. By using scales in this manner, they become a sort of bridge or ladder between where the client is now and where he or she wants to be. By routinely scaling where the client is in relationship to the goal, both the therapist and client gain a better awareness about the progress being made.

Now in my early days as a solution-focused therapist, I used to keep copious notes about where clients scaled themselves, thinking that these were crucial in case the clients could not remember their ratings from the previous sessions. During one such session I was sitting behind the one-way mirror with a trusted colleague. I listened intently as the therapist in front of the mirror asked the client where she was in relationship to her miracle. She rated herself as a 7. The therapist asked, "Now where were you last time we met?" I quickly referenced by notes, always prepared. The client then said, "A 6." From my notes, I knew the client was mistaken. She had answered a 7 during the previous session, meaning that in comparison to her number given today, she had not moved up the scale. I gave the findings to my colleague questioning if we should call the therapist and inform him of the mistake. It was then that he patiently explained a fundamental lesson about solution-focused scaling. It is not the exact numbers that matter, but what the client is meaning by offering them. In this example, the client was communicating that she did notice improvements. As life circumstances change and clients shift their focus from the problems to the solutions, it is common for them to adjust their numbers to better match their reality, even though this may not be a conscious process. It is prudent for therapists to focus their energies into better understanding what the client is communicating through these offerings. I still keep detailed notes, but now my notes are about what the client is truly meaning, understanding that this changes each session as the client progresses toward the miracle.

Beginning solution-focused clinicians often ask, "But what if they get worse?" First, I would caution such a therapist about the word choice of *worse*. Such a word implies judgment and an expected timeline. Client change is not necessarily linear despite our efforts to quantify it through the use of linear scales. It is possible that a client's number will drop (this is actually a very normal occurrence when learning any new behavior), but it is avoiding the normal temptation to interpret this and remaining curious that make the difference. For example:

T: So on a scale of 1 to 10, 10 being you have completed your goals and 1 being the worse it has ever been, where are you today?

C: A 3.

T: And where were you last week? [Deliberately asking rather than referring to last session's notes]

C: A 4.

T: OK. So, your number has dropped slightly. I realize this might initially seem like a silly question, but I have learned never to guess. Is that a good thing or a bad thing that you are a 3 today? [I have had many clients tell me it is a good thing since they needed to slow down and solidify some element of the previous number. It is always important to ask and not assume.]

C: I'm rather disappointed in myself. I didn't do well the past few days.

T: OK. So this was not a planned change. [Pause] So it makes me wonder, since you didn't plan to decrease your number, how did you keep from going even lower and being a 2?

Scaling is a vital way to not only measure change toward the client's miracle, but also provides the needed structure to move up the scale toward the desired result. It can be tempting for beginning therapists to switch to a problem-solving mode at this point of the treatment (for example, asking what the client can do to be higher on the scale in future sessions.) However, it is imperative that the therapist remains cognizant that it is by assisting the client to work from a place in which the problem is resolved that differentiates solution-focused brief therapy from other approaches. Therefore, part of the structure of solution-focused brief therapy is to then ask the client at the end of a session where he or she would like to be on the scale at the time of the next session (Pichot & Dolan, 2003, p. 40). This allows the clients to set their interim goals and determine what the next part of the journey should be. The therapist then asks for details about what the clients would notice that lets them know the progress has been made, who would notice, and so forth. This stepping forward and looking back is a central theme in solution-focused brief therapy. Now let us explore difference questions.

Difference Questions

As Steve de Shazer (1988) so eloquently writes, "For brief therapy to be satisfactory, the present needs to be salient to the future. Otherwise there is no sense in the client's doing something different or in seeing something differently" (p. 190). Difference questions are the tool that assists the client in determining if proposed or current behavioral changes are beneficial in the overall goal of reaching the client's miracle. Difference questions are purposefully scattered throughout every solution-focused interaction.

They are the salt that brings out the natural flavor that otherwise might go unappreciated. Anytime a client mentions something that will be occurring in the miracle day, it is imperative that the therapist gains a clear understanding regarding if this detail would be different. "Once something different is noticed, then the excitement builds again as the observers look for similar events and patterns" (de Shazer, 1988, pp. 2–3). This noticing and exploring serve to deepen the conversation and add meaning, for actions that are discovered to make tremendous differences become apparent and illuminate the steps between the present and the desired future. The difference questions add what I (SS) like to call the "so what" factor. The so what factor simply means: *So what* if your miracle occurs? Is this something worth pursing? If the clients do not find value in having their miracle or some smaller aspect occur, why bother? The effects of the miracle must be important to and for the client in order to provide the necessary motivation to make the at-times difficult changes ahead. Here is an example of how this is done:

T: So, we have been spending a great deal of time talking about how your life will be once your miracle happens, and I can't help but wonder [pausing to ensure the inflection of voice clearly conveys curiosity and not any minimization of the previous conversation], so what? How would your life be better because of these changes?

C: [The client hesitates, initially surprised by the question.] It would be completely better and make all the difference! [The client's voice is suddenly more energized, and she becomes noticeably more animated as she begins to explain. Suddenly, the client appears to fight for the changes she previously was only describing.]

Asking what difference the miracle will make has a way of deepening the overall effect of the miracle, giving it purpose. By determining the value of the goal, the goal will thereby become more desirable and worth pursuing.

Relationship Questions

As discussed earlier, all clients exist within a system. No one lives a life that is not touched by or that does not touch others. It is this central tenet that makes this approach so powerful. Clients oftentimes come to us due to someone else's complaint or concern. This is especially true in the field of substance abuse counseling. This approach offers ways in which the therapist can begin at this other-focused point and still skill-fully work toward client change. There is no need to redirect the client or insist that the clients focus on their own issues or flaws. We can sim-ply work with who the client is and what he or she offers. Relationship questions provide a powerful way to bring these individuals from the client's system into the therapy session. By asking clients what difference their friends and family would notice, the clients are able to see others' perceptions and evaluate the importance that change in their life will have on those they love. Through this form of questioning, clients gain a better vision of how their changes will impact others. For example, "The client's 'feeling better' will lead to some different behavior on her part, and this different behavior will prompt other people to respond to her differently. These different responses can come to serve as reinforce-ments for the client's different behaviors, thus also reinforcing the inner changes" (Miller & de Shazer, 1998, p. 366). Let us look at how this might look for an adolescent client:

T: So how can I help you today?

C: I don't know. I don't think I need to be here.

T: That must be a tough place to be. How can I help?

C: Well, my mom said I had to come.

T: What was she hoping would be different as a result of you coming here?

C: I don't know.

T: OK. That's fair. I ask some tough questions sometimes. Let me try this one instead. I'm wondering, on a scale of 1 to 10, 10 being that your mom is completely OK with how you two are getting along and 1 is she couldn't be more upset and worried, where would you say she is?

C: About a 2.

T: How about you? Where would you put things on that same scale?

C: About a 3.

T: Wow! You guys are pretty close! Does it surprise you that you both are seeing things similarly?

C: Yeah, I guess so.

T: So, I'm wondering, would it make a difference for you if you both were higher up on that scale?

C: Yeah!

In this example, the therapist is able to create a common goal between the client and his mother. This was achieved by asking the client questions from his mother's point of view. Although the client and his mother most likely have very different complaints, the client is now able to take his mother's point of view into account as he works his way up the scale in this and future sessions. This brings us to an important outcome of relationship questions: their ability to create empathy. This insight and empathy naturally increases motivation and desire for change, while simultaneously ensuring that the outcome takes into account all elements that must be addressed in order for the problem to be truly resolved. As this example illustrates, relationship questions are frequently incorporated into all of the other forms of interventions. In the above example, we used scaling and difference questions in combination with relationship questions to discover a common goal.

Exception Questions

It is a very common occurrence to discover during client conversations that the problem is not always occurring. (Remember, this is one of the basic principles of solution-focused brief therapy.) It is impossible for the problem to be happening all the time. Unfortunately, clients commonly hone in on the times in which the problem is occurring and overlook the times in which it is not. As Miller and de Shazer (1998) state, "Solutions to clients' problems are already present in clients' lives. Solutions are present as exceptions to clients' problems, and as personal and social resources that clients may draw upon in solving their problems" (p. 371). The key is assisting the clients in changing their focus so those times in which the problem is not occurring (exceptions) become more noticeable.

The difficult thing about exceptions is training one's ear to hear them. As therapists, we were taught to evaluate problems. It is rare for a therapist to have official training in listening for solutions; it is frequently an incompatible skill. I have seen many well-intentioned therapists who are new to the field of solution-focused brief therapy become excited about exceptions. Soon, they are holding tight to times in which the client was able to thwart the problem, doing their best to help the clients see how they could do this again if they would only try. They then become discouraged as their valiant efforts are meet with the "yeah, buts"; all the reasons using that past exception will not work in this instance. Exceptions are only useful if the client identifies them as such. The therapist's role is to highlight these exceptions so the client takes notice. It is in these times of noticing that the client then naturally evaluates if the uncovered exception would be of use in today's context. A wise therapist uses the client's "yeah, buts" as a useful indication that he or she has become overly invested in an exception being more helpful than the client has determined it to be.

Clients naturally bring us their problems. After all, that is what they want changed. They do not intend to ignore their successes; they simply are focused on what went wrong. As a solution-focused therapist, our task is to be keen listeners for exceptions. The following dialogue illustrates this point.

T: How can I help?

C: I relapsed this week. It was just horrible.

T: I'm so sorry to hear that. I'm really glad you made it here for your appointment. How did you stop using so you could be here?

C: I just knew I had to come.

T: Is that different for you to be able to stop when you know there is something that you need to do?

C: Oh, yeah! I use to just keep using and think, "Well, I've already blown it. Might as well keep using."

T: But you didn't this time.

C: No.

T: How did you stop?

Exception questions help clients to identify what has worked and how they were able to do this. In this example, instead of focusing on the relapse, the therapist focuses on the discontinuation of use. The client did not intentionally omit information about how she discontinued her use, but was instead focused on the relapse. The therapist understood that there was more to be learned in understanding how the client discontinued her use. Through gentle questions, the therapist uncovered that this ability to stop using and attend scheduled appointments is indeed an exception, one that the client readily acknowledges once highlighted. Once the client determines that the behavior is different, it is time to fully explore how the client did this. It is through this exploration that the client will gain the insight and ability to do this in a more purposeful manner in the future should she find it helpful. Now let us explore the sixth intervention, compliments.

Compliments

Compliments are the solution-focused therapist's way of verbally high-lighting areas of client conversation that would otherwise be overlooked. They can be as simple as Insoo Kim Berg's characteristic "Wow!" or Steve de Shazer's quiet handshake for a job well done, or they can be more com-plex. Oftentimes, simple is best. Now, it is important to stress that com-pliments are not at all similar to the behavioral intervention of positive reinforcement. When using compliments, the therapist's goal is to simply express positive surprise as a beginning place for further exploration. It serves as a genuine way to stop the conversation to ensure that both thera-pist and client can better understand what was just said and how this fits with the larger miracle. While the therapist initially is the one who deter-mines if a conversation point deserves further exploration, it is the client who then makes the final determination if the issue in question was truly deserving of the compliment.

There are several elements that are required. First, the compliment must be truly genuine. Therefore, each therapist must determine a way of complimenting that is comfortable and naturally fits his or her personal-ity. For example, Insoo's "Wow!" fits me very well, while I would appear awkward and insincere if I were to use Steve's handshake. Another form of compliment that I use frequently is to simply ask, "Is that new?" It serves to briefly interrupt the session and highlight things that are new or differ-ent. Following up with questions such as "Is that a big deal?" further serves to highlight and give noticed changes the attention that is warranted.

Second, compliments should be genuinely interspersed throughout all interactions. It is a common error to believe that compliments should be saved for a specific time during a session (they are commonly used as part of an end-of-session message, but the intervention itself is used through-out all solution-focused sessions). Compliments can be a word of pleasant surprise (e.g., Wow!), an inflection of voice, or a change in eye contact or body language. All are used in a purposeful way to gently redirect the cli-ent's attention onto what is currently occurring that is consistent with the client's miracle.

Third, a solution-focused therapist only compliments things that are consistent with what the client (or the client's system) has already iden-tified as important. Therefore, the compliment comes directly from the client, not the therapist, for it is not what the therapist thinks is impor-tant but what is important to the client. This serves as a reminder that the therapist is to remain neutral, and does not have an independent opinion about what is useful. Therefore, many solution-focused compliments take the form of gently questioning if something is useful, and if so, how did the client accomplish this. Yvonne Dolan writes about a form of compliment that Insoo Kim Berg frequently used. She called it a two-step compliment. It goes as follows (Pichot & Dolan, 2003, p. 26):

1. Express positive surprise in reaction to one of the client's accomplishments.
2. Ask the client how she or he did it.

These forms of compliments provide some of the most unobtrusive and effective ways of highlighting client exceptions when done in a genuine way. With practice they can become second nature as the therapist learns to spontaneously respond out of pleasant surprise and curiosity. They are a wonderful way to highlight and explore the many exceptions that clients bring to us each day.

Summary

Each form of psychotherapy has its own way of viewing and working with clients that make it unique. Throughout this chapter we have described the assumptions, principles, and interventions that together are unique to solution-focused brief therapy. It is a very simple approach, yet one that takes a lifetime to master. In Chapter 3 we will take the basics one step further to assist you in understanding how the miracle question transforms the hearts and lives of our clients.

Endnotes

1. The terms *solution-focused brief therapy* and *solution-focused therapy* are frequently used interchangeably within the literature and field of therapy. We have chosen to use the term *solution-focused brief therapy* throughout this book since it is the actual title of the approach and is descriptively most accurate. However, I have discovered that at times it can be wise to refer to the approach as simply solution-focused therapy when working in highly political settings in which the term *brief* can have negative connotations.

3

Beyond the Solution-Focused Basics

He [Steve de Shazer] did not merely assume the best about people; he did something much more difficult and infinitely more respectful: He deliberately refrained from arbitrarily interpreting behavior based upon assumptions or making assumptions based upon interpretations.

Yvonne Dolan

Solution-focused brief therapy has been described by many as a very simple approach; however, in reality it is extremely difficult to truly master. It is common for therapists and students upon leaving a workshop about solution-focused brief therapy to say, "It just makes sense." However, once these same professionals try to implement the approach with their clients, they find that what seemed commonsensible is truly very difficult to practice. Berg and Reuss (1998) summarized this phenomenon best when they wrote, "It takes a great deal of discipline and clear-headedness to stay simple" (p. 153). In this chapter we will take you beyond the basics of solution-focused brief therapy to explore the hows and whys that make solution-focused brief therapy truly effective.

Introduction

Watching an experienced solution-focused therapist work with a client using the miracle question has a magical element. The questions are precisely timed and adeptly worded. Somehow, all of the client issues that were initially overwhelming and in need of intervention are suddenly resolved. The therapy has a solidness to it, although it can be difficult to explain how something so seemingly simple could possibly achieve such profoundly lasting results. When I began using this approach, I was met with skepticism by other professionals. There was an expectation in the field that change occurs only through understanding problems. Since solution-focused brief therapy challenges this rationale, others found it difficult to believe that I was truly resolving the problems that standards of care required that we address regardless of my explanations. This was especially true with complex, multiproblem substance abuse cases. Many of these clients had been caught by the referral source in multiple lies, and it was challenging to explain how an approach that takes the client at face value could possibly address all of the problems at hand—even the ones the clients denied. When I taught new therapists how to use solution-focused brief therapy with clients who had very complex clinical cases, I quickly saw that the therapists were missing key elements and were not able to achieve the desired results. Although they were technically using all of the interventions, there was something missing. The resultant therapy was superficial. They were unable to connect with who the client truly is, and the underlying problems remained untouched.

Initially I found this perplexing since in my experience, solution-focused brief therapy just worked. It was then that I first discovered that there was something that skilled clinicians do when they use this approach that is commonly not described in the literature or directly taught. It was not a deliberate omission, but something that had been set aside as previous writers labored to put all of the richness and other important details of solution-focused brief therapy into print. My guess was that skilled clinicians do not consciously think about what is guiding their word choices or the direction of their questions, just as gifted musicians do not instinctively analyze how the melodies they intuitively hear in their heads flow from one note to another. Due to their experience, they most likely are using their clinical intuition to ensure the therapy results are solid. Unfortunately, therapists new to this approach and working with such challenging client populations need these elements clearly delineated, so they can not only learn to implement the approach well, but also articulate to others how this approach results in profound and lasting change. This challenged me to dissect solution-focused brief therapy and determine how it truly works and how I could best teach others. Here is what I discovered.

Not-Knowing Stance

Anderson and Goolishian (1992) first coined the concept of not-knowing. They state:

The not-knowing position entails a general attitude or stance in which the therapist's actions communicate an abundant, genuine curiosity. That is, the therapist's actions and attitudes express a need to know more about what has been said, rather than convey preconceived opinions and expectations about the client, the problem, or what must be changed. The therapist, therefore, positions himself or herself in such a way as always to be in a state of "being informed" by the client. (p. 29)

This not-knowing stance goes beyond remaining neutral. It requires a genuine setting aside of what we know, what we believe, and what naturally comes to mind when working with clients. It is through this setting aside, coupled with a genuine faith in the clients' ability to effect change, that we can truly hear and understand the clients and what they want, along with the most effective path to obtain this. This ability to set aside is one of the most difficult things we have ever learned. With time, it becomes a natural way of viewing clients. So much so that I have found myself taken by surprise at times by other professionals' reactions to the way in which I work with clients.

For example, I was recently giving a one-day presentation about solution-focused brief therapy to a group of professionals who work with high-risk pregnant and postpartum women. At the end of the day, I opened the conversation up to invite case examples, so participants could gain a better understanding of how I would use this approach with clients such as theirs. During such presentations, I frequently invite the participant who has questions about a specific case to spontaneously role-play the client with me, stressing that each client is unique, and it is oftentimes difficult to answer hypothetically. After fielding some more routine questions, I turned to a therapist who had calmly raised her hand. She said, "I have a client, and I want to know how you would handle this." She then went on to tell me that her client eats the couch. Immediately, the room erupted into laughter. I did my best to ignore the laughter, seeking to find an appropriate way to interrupt the audience and demonstrate that I understood that this woman was not being disrespectful or making light of this approach at all. In fact, it was because she was so intrigued by this approach that she dared to wonder how she could use solution-focused brief therapy with her challenging client. The following dialogue between the curious therapist and me ensued.

Teri: Now hold on. I want to better understand [hoping to gently quiet the laughter]. So your main concern is that your client is eating the couch.

Therapist: Yes. She has been doing it since she was young. I wouldn't have even found out except she answered yes to the question on the questionnaire that asks about eating things that aren't food. [More laughter from the audience, but now the audience quieted more easily since many were wondering what I was going to do with this.]

Teri: I see.

Therapist: When I go over to her house, there are big chunks out of the couch. [Showing me with her hands the size of the missing pieces]

Teri: OK. Now I know this may sound like a strange question, but it is very important, so please bear with me here: So how is this a problem? [More laughter from the audience. One exacerbated professional yelled, "Because it's pica!" clearly believing that I had not heard of this diagnostic category.]

Therapist: Because it doesn't have any nutritional value.

Teri: No, no, no. I understand all that. I'm sorry. What I meant was, how is this a problem from the client's point of view?

Therapist: What? From the client's point of view?

Teri: Yes. I understand all the potential hazards of such behavior, but what I don't yet understand is how is this a problem from the client's point of view.

Therapist: I guess it isn't.

Teri: OK. So then what is she hoping to be different by working with you and by telling you this?

Therapist: Well, I guess that her mother gets off her back about it. [Clearly perplexed that I wasn't more interested in directly addressing the client's odd behavior]

Teri: And how do those two things fit together?

Therapist: Because her mother is worried about her because she is eating the couch. She actually ate an entire bed already. [More laughter from the audience, as I did my best to remain focused and convey the power of using this approach in such circumstances]

Teri: OK. I think I understand. The client's mother is very worried about her, and the client would like things to be different between her and her mother, correct?

Therapist: Yes.

Teri: So that would be how I would word the miracle question for this client—that she has the ability to create the kind of relationship she wants with her mother.

Audience member: So you would just ignore that potential intestinal blockage and poor nutrition is occurring? [Said with a definite sarcastic tone]

Teri: [Turning back to the therapist] I didn't hear you mention that the client was having any medical problems as a result right now, correct?

Therapist: Correct.

Teri: And does the client believe that eating the couch is a good idea?

Therapist: No. I think she is embarrassed about it. She just can't help it.

Teri: OK then. I believe in this case I would be more effective in addressing the client's problem by actively working toward something that is important to the client: improving her relationship with her mother. I am not unaware of the potential dangers of her behavior. However, I would rather that the client was actively working with me as a professional and working toward her goals. I believe that if I tell her what she has to do, she will no longer tell me what is truly going on. I believe that the couch issue will be resolved in the client's miracle. I would be eager to learn how she did it.

Therapist: That's right! [Said with excitement as she realized the power of this approach] I am the first professional she has ever told about this. I can see how working with her where she is has a greater chance of working.

While I was interacting with the audience that day, I was again reminded of how different this approach is. While the audience member was actively thinking in diagnostic terms to label the client's problem, by adopting a not-knowing stance, I instead was driven to understand the situation from the client's point of view. While the diagnosis of pica was technically correct, it was not useful to me. This information would not help this client change her behavior nor give me any insight into how the client was thinking or what she wanted. Clients oftentimes engage in activities that are not in their best interest. By setting aside the preconceived opinions and notions about the client's actions, the solution-focused therapist can better understand who the client is and what is motivating the client to take action. By becoming curious about the situation and the desired solution from the client's point of view, the presenting problems are addressed, for the therapist and client are working from a place in which the problems are resolved. While I was initially dismayed that the professional in the audience seemingly did not believe I was credible since I did not readily demonstrate that I was aware of the name of the client's problem, I quickly realized it was because of my own sense of pride. Pride is not helpful to my clients. Once I regained my focus on the client and what she wanted, the treatment course again became solid, for it was a path that fit with her. It is through this not-knowing that we are able to truly hear and thereby help our clients.

Listening

Listening is such a basic skill in counseling. However, it remains one of the most difficult counseling elements to both teach and perfect. Regardless of the experience level of the therapist with whom I provide supervision, I have noticed that the need to truly hear the client remains the most common theme of our work together. It is only fitting that we begin this chapter with a few words about the importance of truly hearing what is at our clients' hearts. As Miller and Berg (1995) so emphatically state, "Each person experiencing an alcohol problem is *different*" (p. 16). This inherent uniqueness requires the professional to develop a finely tuned ability to listen, for both what is important to each client and what the most fitting solution is for the problem at hand, for "most often, these problems do not have a single correct solution" (De Jong & Berg, 1998, p. 10).

Initially therapists oftentimes have a great deal of difficulty setting aside their clinical assumptions and interpretations as they are working with clients. With time and supportive supervision, they are gradually able to learn to listen to their clients with a more factual ear. They learn to listen to what the client is truly saying, asking clarifying questions as needed to truly understand, and refraining from taking this information and making more of it than what the client is actually saying. This is a skill that takes a tremendous amount of effort to obtain. As with learning any new skill, it is common to overcompensate during the learning process. At times I have seen therapists who are learning this new skill mistakenly become so focused on hearing the client that they set aside their clinical judgment. It is then that I remind them that their focus should be twofold when listening from a solution-focused perspective. They should simultaneously listen for first, what is in the client's heart, and second, what are the clinical elements in play.

Listening for What Is in the Client's Heart

Every time the client and therapist interact, the therapist should be able to clearly identify what is most important to the client at that moment. At times the clients will clearly say what is in their heart, while at other times the therapist needs to ask carefully worded questions to uncover this. The following dialogue is an example of this.

Therapist (T): How can I help you today?
Client (C): I just need to get this done [referring to treatment].
T: OK. Let's do that. I don't know you that well yet, so is it OK for me to ask you a couple of questions to get to know you?
C: I guess.
T: OK. Well, you mention that you need to get this done. I have learned that each client's reason for this is very different. How will your life be better once we get this done?
C: I will get my kids back and get back to my life.
T: Oh. Sounds like your kids are very important to you.
C: Yes. They are everything to me.

The therapist has learned that this client's children and regaining custody of them are at her heart. Any future interactions with the client will be much more meaningful and change will be more lasting if this is remembered and taken into account. At times therapists have asked me why this step is necessary. Aren't children always at the heart of every parent? While this is frequently the case, there are oftentimes different things at the client's heart at any given moment. Although most parents are deeply in love with their children and will do anything for them, that does not mean that at times there will not be something else that is weighing heavy on their hearts. It may be embarrassment over a failure, sadness over a loss, or joy over an accomplishment. At any given moment, what is in our hearts as humans fluctuates. Knowing this and taking the time to discover what is currently important to the client are key to ensuring that each and every interaction is meaningful and well matched for the client.

Listening for the Clinical Elements

While the therapist is listening for what is at the client's heart, the therapist must also be cognizant of the clinical elements in play. Let us continue with our client dialogue to get an example of this.

T: So you mention that your children are everything to you. How can I help you get them back?

C: Well, I have to get this evaluation done and whatever you make me do.

T: What are you hoping that the evaluation will show?

C: That I don't have a problem with methamphetamine. I used it once over 10 years ago, but my caseworker just can't let that go.

T: What do you think that your caseworker will need to see to know for sure that methamphetamine is no longer a problem and that your children will be safe? [The therapist is introducing the shared goal of keeping the children safe. Safety is a clinical element since the children have been removed from the home, and is something that is reasonable to assume that the client also wants for her children, although she probably would not agree with the caseworker about what is making them unsafe.]

C: That I am able to keep a job and pay the rent.

T: OK. Are those important to you as well?

C: Yeah. I can get a job. I just haven't done it yet.

T: Good. What else?

In this example there are several clinical elements that were discovered. First, there is the caseworker's concern about methamphetamine use. While the client states that she has not used the drug in 10 years, the caseworker's concern must be acknowledged since she is an influential member of the client's system. Her continued concern is a red flag, and although we do not know if the client is currently using or not, the caseworker must be seeing something that is resulting in her concern. Second, the children have been removed from the home, indicating that there are safety concerns for the children. As a therapist, I should now look for any way that I can naturally compliment the client's connection, love, and desire for her children's well-being. It is reasonable for me to assume that the children's safety is paramount to both the caseworker and the client. It is a way that I can link them toward a common goal. During future conversations, the therapist would be wise to highlight areas of safety and times in which the client is being preventive by putting the children's welfare first. Without the therapist clearly identifying the clinical elements in play, these important areas might go unnoticed in future conversations, resulting in a more superficial intervention. Lastly, areas of self-sufficiency and motivation are clinical areas. The therapist would be wise to listen for times in which the client is able to motivate herself to do the things she already knows how to do (these are exceptions). This could provide the clues to how she can do this on a more regular basis should she decide this would be helpful. These basics of listening for both what is at the client's heart and the clinical elements in play are the foundation for all interactions with clients when working from a solution-focused approach. With those solid, let us now take a closer look at the miracle question and how it results in change.

How the Miracle Question Creates Change

The miracle question is at the heart of solution-focused brief therapy. It is through this intervention that the client's attention is transitioned from the presenting problem to a problem that is solved (Berg, 1994, p. 98). Our clients oftentimes come to us after enduring a great deal of despair and heartache. Either the clients themselves have identified a problem, or as frequently is the case for substance abusing clients, someone else (commonly another professional) has identified a problem and then ensured that the clients fully understand the problem areas that must be resolved prior to the professionals leaving the clients' lives. In either case, the clients come to us discouraged, frustrated, and focused on the problem. The miracle question is the ideal way to assist the client in discovering how life will be once the problem is resolved.

Knowing When to Ask the Miracle Question

During a workshop that I attended during the early part of my career as a solution-focused therapist, I remember an audience member asking Steve de Shazer exactly when one should ask the miracle question. I sat quietly waiting to see just how Steve would answer this question. Steve thought for a moment and then in his wonderfully playful, yet purposeful way stated, "After twelve-and-a-half minutes." He then let the audience in on his playfulness by explaining that there is no exact minute that is right in all occasions, that his giving a precise time was in jest. However, he went on to explain that if you do not know what is important to the client after a short period of time, and therefore have not asked the miracle question already, maybe one needs to ask the miracle question to figure out what is important to the client. What I took away from this conversation was just how central the miracle question is in solution-focused brief therapy.

In working with clients, I have found it most helpful to ask the miracle question as soon as I have a very clear picture of what is in the client's heart and what he or she is hoping to gain by coming to see me. This is frequently very soon within the first session. The key, again, is truly hearing the client. If I have not really heard what is important to the client and for what he or she is yearning, it is not yet time to ask. It is best that I keep listening and ask better questions that will help me hear this important element. It is oftentimes helpful to ask clients how our time together would be useful. Another way to phrase this question is, "How would you know that our time together today was worth it?" These forms of questions provide a tool to get a clearer picture of what is important to the client and set the foundation for the miracle question. (It is important to note here that in my private practice working with self-referred clients, I have found Steve's advice of asking the miracle question even when I am not sure of what is most important to be very helpful. When I am unsure what is most important, the miracle question is a wonderful way to help me to better hear what I have missed. However, I have found that with externally referred and frequently angry clients, I have better success by continuing to listen.)

In addition, I have found that is it imperative that both the client and I truly understand what the miracle would be before I ask the miracle question. In my earlier work with Yvonne Dolan (Pichot & Dolan, 2003), we wrote about the importance of having a clearly defined miracle (p. 78). We go on to state that when working with externally motivated clients, it can be helpful to go beyond the standard definition of the miracle (the problem that brought you here is resolved) to identify a quality, skill, or trait that the client views as beneficial and a good use of our work together. By listening for a quality, skill, or trait, I am better able to remain focused on elements that I can truly influence and to avoid defining the miracle question with life events (i.e., my children are returned), which may or may not come true. In doing so, I am much better able to use carefully chosen words to help the client and me walk together through the at times confusing language of the miracle question. It also helps clients who are angry that they have to be in therapy remember that I did hear what was most important to them and, in turn, helps them remained focused on what they stated would be helpful for us to address together.

Slowing the Client Down

Since our clients have become accustomed to describing the problem, they have most likely overlooked clues to the solution. Due to the universal truth we discussed in Chapter 2 (that what the client focuses on gets bigger), the client's problems have become all-consuming. Only serving to complicate matters is the fact that it is human nature to rush and to not thoroughly appreciate the details. These factors bring to light the importance of changing our clients' focus and then slowing them down so they can more clearly notice details in order to create an environment for change.

When I work with therapists who are new to this approach, it is common for the therapist to allow the client to quickly review the client's miracle day. While a highly skilled therapist can hear the important elements and guide the client into purposeful directions to discover change as the client quickly reviews his or her miracle day, I have found this to be the exception. More commonly, I have found the therapist to reach the end of the client's miracle day only to then look to me with an inquisitive expression and with confusion as to the point of the intervention. I have found it most helpful to encourage therapists to instead take a much more active role in discussing the miracle day, seeking to slow the day down to discover each and every detail in a purposeful fashion.

It is common for clients to depreciate elements of the miracle day that are the direct result of behaviors that the client did. Once these elements are brought to the client's attention, clients frequently credit "dumb luck" or external factors for these changes, oftentimes overlooking the small things done by the client that resulted in these significant changes. Because of this tendency to overlook the very things the client did that created the necessary changes, the goal of the miracle day is to help the client to methodically discover these specific elements and to identify possible things that he or she could actually do tomorrow (if not sooner) to begin the change process. These are things that currently exist in our clients' lives, but things that they have overlooked by focusing on the problem. Insoo Kim Berg (1994) writes, "Answering these miracle questions will provide him with clues on what first steps he needs to take to find solutions and will show him how his life *will* change, thus giving him hope that his life *can* change" (p. 100). By working slowly and purposefully, the therapist can then ask additional questions about each discovered detail so that the client can then evaluate each aspect to determine its potential worth. Miller and Berg (1995) state, "The more clearly you are able to specify exactly how you want things to be different after your problem is solved, the more likely it is that you will be able to unlock the door to that solution" (p. 35). Taking a slow pace as the therapist and client walk through the client's miracle day is key to discovering and exploring these details. Once found, there is no need for the therapist to instruct the clients to then recreate the elements discovered in the miracle day in their everyday lives. If the client finds them to be instrumental, the client will naturally do them without external prompting.

Keeping the Client in Bed

Although this may initially sound odd, I have found it useful to instruct therapists who are new to this approach to have the client remain in bed for a moment or two in his or her imagination after they ask the miracle question. As humans our brains first begin to regain consciousness and orient ourselves to the day before we even open our eyes each morning. It is a fact that many may overlook, if not encouraged to slow down and fully appreciate, these moments before the hustle and bustle of the day begin. For example, when I awoke this morning, I lay in bed appreciating the warmth of the covers as my eyes remained tightly shut. I heard my husband's breathing as he slept, and I heard the quiet stirrings of my two canine buddies in the darkness. I found my mind wandering, briefly scanning my memory to determine what day it was and what was on today's agenda. Was it a weekday or the weekend? Do I have appointments, or do I have a more relaxing day ahead? Do I have time to lie here and enjoy the morning, or do I need to force my eyes open and begin my day? It is in these moments that one determines when and why to get out of bed. These moments oftentimes set the tone for the day. This may seem rather rudimentary; however, this basic noticing, thinking, and making purposeful decisions are oftentimes the very skills our clients have been lacking. Without assisting our clients to explore these first moments of the miracle day, the clients frequently move to behavior, and the miracle day can take on a more external and superficial feel. Here is an example of how this might look:

T: Now I'm going to ask you a strange question. I want you to imagine that tonight when you go to bed, a miracle happens. The miracle is that the problems you mentioned to me earlier are resolved. Unfortunately, you were sleeping and have no idea that this miracle happened. So, I'm wondering what will be the very first signs— even before you open your eyes—that this miracle has occurred.

C: Well, that I have a job to go to.

T: Now hold on. That would be a wonderful miracle. Before we get too far along, I'm wondering what you would notice maybe even before you get out of bed, when you are still laying there with your eyes shut.

C: Oh, I guess I would notice that I'm more at peace.

T: Wow! Is that different for you to be more at peace?

C: Yes. I always feel so stressed out and worried.

T: But on this day, you feel more at peace.

C: Yes. It is wonderful. I am able to lie there and breathe.

T: And what difference does it make for you to be able to just lie there and breathe on this morning?

C: Well, I feel more able to start my day.

T: What else do you notice as you lie there?

C: I am able to think about my day.

T: What kinds of things are you thinking about your day as you lie there?

C: Things I have to do. How I should get them done.

T: Is that different?

C: Yes. Very.

T: How so?

C: I feel more organized and ready to get up.

T: And how does that change what you do next?

C: I get up.

T: And how do you know it's time to get up now as opposed to later?

C: Because I have things to do.

T: Is this different for you to get up at this time?

C: Yeah, I guess so.

T: How is it different?

C: I usually hit the snooze button a few times.

T: But you don't on this morning.

C: No.

T: How do you do that?

C: Because I'm more prepared to face my day.

By encouraging the client to explore the miracle day prior to her getting out of bed, she was able to identify feelings (a sense of peace) and cognitions (organizing and planning her day) in addition to behaviors (breathing and getting out of bed). This allows the client to experience her day in a more holistic way. In addition, it provides additional clues as to what she did to create this change. She discovered that by thinking about her day, she felt more prepared, and in turn had the motivation to get up and begin her day. Had we allowed this client to go straight into behavior, we would have started her day with her going to her job, and missed the very elements that help her first prepare for her day and get her feet on the floor.

It is also important to mention that in using this technique the therapist must listen carefully for when the client has fully explored possible cognitions and feelings and is ready to get out of bed. I have witnessed therapists who are new to this approach well-intentionally insist that clients remain in bed well after this task had been completed only to have the unintended result of the clients feeling like they were held hostage and not allowed to move on. It is a delicate balance, one that requires careful listening and respect for the client's answers.

Interrupting

As therapists, we hate to be impolite. We do not want to interrupt or be perceived as rude. However, I have found that it is very important to realize that when I am working with clients, I am expected to take the lead, and a more assertive stance is not seen as rude (if done with tact), but as purposeful and necessary to ensure that the work at hand is done well. A misconception of solution-focused brief therapy is that the therapist takes a nondirective stance. Cantwell and Holmes (1994) refer to how solution-focused therapists work as leading from one step behind. This way of leading requires that the therapist be comfortable with interrupting in order to keep the conversation moving in a solution-focused direction. When working with self-referred clients on an individual basis, I have found that a slower, relaxed pace can be very effective. There is minimal need to redirect the client, and little damage can occur from allowing the client to drift from the subject matter from time to time as long as, as the therapist, I do not become distracted and lose sight of the therapeutic course.

However, working with clients who have been referred by the legal or child welfare system and who are not at all in agreement about the issues at hand (especially within a group setting, which we will discuss at length in Chapter 6) can present quite another matter. I frequently liken the experience to a snowball that starts to form at the top of a hill. At the top of the hill just a few snowflakes begin to stick together and are relatively harmless, yet as the collection of snowflakes begins to accumulate and heads down the hill, the snowball quickly gains mass and speed. At first the small complaints and problem talk look innocuous, but left unheeded, they can become unwieldy and confound the best of therapists. The tiny snowball can soon become capable of engulfing anything in its path. I have found that having a tight verbal structure, and compassionately interrupting as soon as the conversation goes astray to better understand and redirect the conversation toward solution talk, can be instrumental in both therapist and client remaining focused on the matter at hand.

For example, it is common for clients to stray from the question when they have been asked the miracle question. They can at times innocently drift into another conversation, or add elements that do not make sense in the context of the miracle question. If the therapist simply follows the client along, both become distracted and the intent of the miracle question becomes lost. The therapist then may become confused as to how to return to the miracle question, if the therapist even realizes why they are no longer talking about the miracle day. The client has then unwittingly led both of them off of the therapeutic course. It is imperative that the solution-focused therapist realize that while the clients are the experts on their own lives, the therapist is the expert of the therapeutic process, and should therefore speak up and skillfully redirect the client when the therapeutic course is jeopardized.

A second common example of when the therapist is wise to notice and intervene is when the client's answer is completely unrelated to the question that the therapist just asked. While this may seem rather rudimentary, it is surprisingly common for the therapist to remain unaware of when this occurs. Here's an example of how interrupting can be used to remedy this.

T: How can I help you today?

C: My caseworker thinks I have a problem with drugs. I don't! She doesn't believe anything I say. She is just out to get me. [The client's answer does not answer the therapist's question, but is just information about the problem. Uninterrupted, it is likely to continue for a while.]

T: Wow [interrupting, but said in a clearly genuine fashion], you have a lot going on! That sounds tough. How can I help you with that? [The therapist expresses empathy and compassion, but then gently re-asks the question, which has been slightly reworded for extra padding.]

C: You can get her off my back!

T: I hope we can work toward that together. What else is important to you? [With skillful wording and genuine curiosity, this can be the turning point from the client being externally motivated to what is in the client's heart.]

C: I want to get my children back. I'm just lost without them.

T: I can tell they are very important to you.

C: Yes.

T: How are you surviving with them being gone?

C: I'm not. I can't sleep. My wife won't forgive me. It's not my fault!

T: This must be so difficult for you. Would it be a good use of our time together to help you find a way to get through each day just a little better?

C: Yeah. I think so. It's just so hard right now.

In this example the therapist has to interrupt and refocus the client on their work together. There is no good that will come from a verbal tirade about the injustices he has suffered. This refocusing onto a productive discussion "is not a way of denying the deprivations and injustices in clients' lives, but of getting beyond them" (Miller & de Shazer, 1998, p. 373). It is important to remember that clients come to us because they want their lives to be different. What could be more compassionate than to move them gently in that direction when they have gotten off course? Now that we have reached the client's heart, we are ready to ask the miracle questions. Let us continue with the dialogue:

T: OK. I have a very difficult question to ask you. Some have thought it strange, but I have found it to be very helpful. Would you be willing to give it a try?

C: Yeah, I guess so.

T: All right. I want you to imagine that tonight when you go home and go to bed, a miracle happens. The miracle is that you are somehow able to get through each day despite how difficult it is. You can do it. Unfortunately, you were asleep and you don't know that the miracle happened. So, what I want to know is what will be some of the things that you notice first thing when you wake up tomorrow morning. Even before you open your eyes?

C: That my wife was there.

T: Is that different?

C: No, she is always there, but on this morning, it feels different.

T: How so?

C: Like she and I are in this together. You know it used to be like that when we first met. [The client is now leaving the miracle day. Although it is to describe an exception, it is leaving the miracle day. The therapist needs to make a purposeful decision if it is better to stay with the miracle day or follow the exception.]

T: And yet on this miracle day, you have that back.

C: Yeah.

T: So on this miracle day, what is different as you lie there in bed that lets you know you are both in this together?

C: There is just a sense.

T: And how are you different because of it?

C: I have more confidence.

In this example, the therapist had to make a purposeful decision if it was best to follow the exception or to remain in the miracle day. As a general rule, I have found it easier to return later to follow up on a discovered exception than to return to the miracle day once the client has lost his or her focus on the future. Because of this, I most frequently will choose to continue in the miracle day and make a mental note of the various exceptions or other possibly useful clinical paths for later conversations. In this example, I am not sure if the exception would hold useful clues to today, but I do know that if the client can envision a positive change in the future, that is more likely to be helpful in providing an increased sense of hope as he goes through this difficult time.

Yes Sets

A valuable tool that can be used during any point during a solution-focused conversation is a yes set (Erickson et al., 1976; Erickson & Rossi, 1979; de Shazer, 1982). This is a short series of questions that is asked in close succession, questions that are expected to elicit an affirmative answer from the client. Before I move forward with a client, I oftentimes find it useful to ensure that I heard the client correctly. I can confirm this by repeating what I believe I heard and then asking the client to confirm that I indeed have the information correct. This can take a more subtle form by simply pausing at various points in the conversation and watching the client intently for signs that the client is indeed following the conversation in agreement. I find this useful in helping me to slow down and remember all of the tiny elements before I move forward with the client. The extra time and repeating allow me to adequately process the information, hear the important elements, and ensure that I remain with my client throughout the intervention. In doing this, the client feels more comfortable that we are proceeding in a direction that is based upon what the client already stated to be true. The client is then more willing to take the next step. As Steve de Shazer (1985) writes, a yes set "helps to get the client into a frame of mind to accept something new" (p. 91). Here is an example of how this can be helpful with our previous dialogue:

T: So let me just make sure I am hearing you correctly, since what you are saying is so important.

C: OK.

T: So on this miracle morning, you and your wife feel more like a team, like you are in this together.

C: Yeah!

T: And because of this, you have more confidence, right?

C: Exactly!

T: And you haven't had this in a while, so this is a really big deal…

C: Yes, it is!

T: So I can't help but wonder, how does this change who you are or what you do next?

C: It makes a huge difference!

T: How so?

When using a yes set such as this, the therapist builds a connection and can frequently feel the client's excitement and energy level rise as each question is confirmed. When I use yes sets, they bring to mind those tiny rubberband-powered child toys; I remember having a plastic lady bug and a toy car. In order to get them to race forward on their own, one had to rev them up by quickly rolling the toy's wheels across the table a couple of times before setting it down—such a simple action, but it made the tiny toy seemingly come alive. By using these simple yes sets throughout the miracle question, the therapist not only is provided with valuable feedback that he or she is on the correct path, but also reassures the client that they are moving together hand in hand toward a purposeful goal. Lastly, they provide the needed energy and excitement to continue our journey together.

Maintaining Balance

When observing an experienced solution-focused therapist work with a client, the content of the client answers has a solidness. While the client speaks about changes in behavior, the conversation contains other important elements of relationships, emotions, cognitions, and so forth, that are necessary for lasting, meaningful change. The answers sound genuine and not rote. Each answer demonstrates the discovery of new, uncharted territory. In trying to discover what these experienced therapists were doing to create these answers, I found that instinctively the therapists were varying the types of questions to elicit answers from the clients in three general categories:

- Being
- Thought/cognition
- Behavior

These three elements are noted in Figure 3.1. Let us look at each in more detail.

Being Questions
The questions in the being category include how the client feels and who the client is. I have found that it is not necessary to ask the client directly how he or she feels when asking the miracle question. Clients readily volunteer this when they believe it is relevant. According to de Shazer et al. (2007), "Emotion arises as the client needs or wants it to arise and the SFBT therapist acknowledges it but typically does not try to elicit a more detailed description of what the feeling is nor what the client attributes it to" (p.

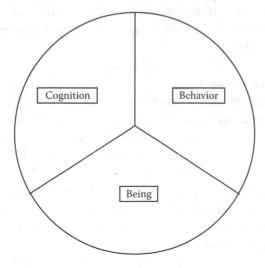

Figure 3.1 Elements of Balance

154). I find questions about how something changes who the client is to be much more powerful questions, for they imply that the client is changed from the inside out on the miracle day and encourage the client to not only look to behavior, but within as well. Asking a being question in this broader context allows the client to answer in whatever way is most accurate.

Clients frequently answer the miracle question initially with being answers. Answers such as "I would feel more peaceful" or "I would be more at ease" are examples of this. These forms of answers give valuable clues about the client's desired emotional state or way of being within the world. Alone, they do not provide any direction or guidance as to how the client obtained this inner state, for feelings are oftentimes the result of the client's way of thinking or an external event. Therefore, they need thought/cognition or behavioral questions to determine the path to this desired way of being. However, they are an important piece of the puzzle.

At times, it can be helpful for the therapist to directly ask a client a being question, for being questions help to deepen a conversation that has become rather superficial in nature. I liken these forms of questions to adding color into a black-and-white drawing. The color is not necessary to understand the content of the drawing, but splashes of color oftentimes add a richness and beauty that would otherwise be lacking. Conversely, a picture that only contains splashes of color frequently lacks definition and can be in need of interpretation. Likewise, it is important that the therapist carefully monitor the balance of the conversation and ask behavior or thought/cognition questions when the conversation becomes overly vague and needs more clarity.

Thought/Cognition Questions

Thought/cognition questions are those that direct the client's attention to what the client is thinking at any given time. Since our feelings are oftentimes the direct result of how we think or make sense of situations, these questions provide valuable clues as to what the client will be doing differently on the miracle day. Clients do have the ability to change their thought patterns should they find this to be useful. Clients frequently mention that they notice they are thinking differently first thing on the miracle day. By asking clients to explore how they are thinking differently and then inviting them to explore what difference this different way of thinking makes, therapists help the client to gain valuable clues as to how they can then create these desired changes.

Another form of thought/cognition question is to ask the client how they make sense of a situation. This allows them to explore how they are interpreting situations in their surroundings on the miracle day that is resulting in life being how they want it to be. Asking clients thought/cognition questions is useful when the conversation becomes overly superficial, for it allows the client to understand what thoughts are resulting in the client's behavior. They are also very useful when the conversation has become overly vague and externally focused. However, overuse of thought/cognition questions can result in a philosophical and impractical feel to the conversation, signaling that a different form of question is needed to regain balance and make the discussion more tangible.

Behavior Questions
Behavior questions are those that explore what the client will be doing. These are extremely important, for it is most frequently the client's behaviors that are identified by the client or someone in the client's system as being problematic. It is through understanding what behaviors will be different that the client and therapist gain a glimpse of the details of what will be different once the miracle occurs. However, a line of questioning that focuses only on client behaviors has a very superficial feel and can sound rote in nature. Our clients most often already know what they should be doing differently, and this has made little difference in their choices. While carefully exploring what the client will be doing differently on the miracle day is critical to behavioral change, it must be used in careful balance with being and thought/cognition questions in order to result in lasting and meaningful change. Let us look at how these three forms of questions work together by revisiting our previous example:

T: OK. I have a very difficult question to ask you. Some have thought it strange, but I have found it to be very helpful. Would you be willing to give it a try?

C: Yeah, I guess so.

T: All right. I want you to imagine that tonight when you go home and go to bed, a miracle happens. The miracle is that you are somehow able to get through each day despite how difficult it is. You can do it. Unfortunately, you were asleep and you don't know that the miracle happened. So, what I want to know is what will be some of the things that you notice first thing when you wake up tomorrow morning. Even before you open your eyes?

C: That my wife was there.

T: Is that different?

C: No, she is always there, but on this morning, it feels different. [Being answer]

T: How so?

C: Like she and I are in this together. You know it used to be like that when we first met. [Thought/cognition answer]

T: And yet on this miracle day, you have that back.

C: Yeah.

T: So on this miracle day, what is different as you lie there in bed that lets you know you are both in this together?

C: There is just a sense. [Being answer]

T: And how are you different because of it?

C: I have more confidence. [Being answer]

T: So let me just make sure I am hearing you correctly, since what you are saying is so important.

C: OK.

T: So on this miracle morning, you and your wife feel more like a team, like you are in this together.

C: Yeah!

T: And because of this, you have more confidence, right?

C: Exactly!

T: And you haven't had this in a while, so this is a really big deal?

C: Yes, it is!

T: So I can't help but wonder. How does this change who you are or what you do next? [Therapist is offering the option of getting out of bed by offering a being or a behavior question.]

C: It makes a huge difference!

T: How so?

C: Well, I get out of bed and start my day. [Behavior answer]

T: And then?

C: I guess I would take a shower and start getting ready for the day. [Behavior answer]

T: Is that different?

C: Yeah. I usually just get up whenever and don't clean up.

T: But today is different.

C: Yes. I know I need to get ready. [Thought/cognition answer]

T: What lets you know?

C: I need to get a job.

T: And yet today you are doing something about it. Why today?

C: Because I know that my wife loves and accepts me. [Thought/cognition answer]

T: And so this changes your morning. [Inviting a move back to behavior]

I have found it most useful to begin the miracle question as I did in this example, by asking general questions that allow the client to answer from any of the three perspectives (being, cognition, or behavior). By doing this, the client is able to naturally work from the mode that fits the client best. Many of our clients are more cognitive, while others are more affect based, and others still are more concrete and behavioral. By allowing the client to choose, solution-focused brief therapy remains culturally and gender sensitive, allowing clients to process information in a variety of ways. The therapist then only gently guides the client to ensure there is adequate balance to create lasting change. For example, when working with a client who is overly feeling based, I would purposefully ask direct questions about behavior or cognition. I would avoid asking any being questions, for the client will readily give me information in this area. In order to create the necessary balance to result in change, the client needs to envision what she will be doing and thinking differently in order to change her emotions.

Exploring Each Additional Element

As the therapist and client walk through the miracle day, each and every difference contains possible clues for the client. When training therapists in using the miracle question, I encourage them to take each element that the client offers and to carefully explore it, only moving forward once they are certain there is nothing else to learn. In doing this I have found there are three forms of questions that are helpful to fully understand the possibilities that each element may contain:

- Is it different?
- What difference does it make?
- How did you do that?

Let us look at each of these in more detail.

Is It Different?

It is important that when clients begin to tell us about their miracle day we clearly understand which parts of their day are truly different. It is common for clients to tell us about aspects of their miracle day that are not different at all. We should not assume we can identify what is different. In the above example, the first thing our client mentioned on his miracle day was that his wife was there. However, once the therapist asked the client if that was different, the client stated that it was not. This redirected the therapist to continue looking, for there was something different; having his wife there felt different. Understanding what exactly was different—a sense of partnering with his wife and being on the same team—was key to this client's miracle. There is a significant difference between the difference questions we discussed in Chapter 2 and asking if something is different. Inquiring if something is different simply guides the therapist in understanding if something offered by the client is useful to explore in more detail.

What Difference Does It Make?
Once the therapist has identified something that is different on the miracle day, it is time to use the difference questions we discussed in Chapter 2. By asking this form of question next, the therapist is able to deepen the element discovered and find the meaning the element holds. Clients are not likely to work hard to change something that will not make a significant difference. Clients are very wise and will rarely waste their time on something that will not result in meaningful change. By taking the time to understand what difference a noticed change will make, the client is more likely to become invested to make the needed behavioral changes.

How Did You Do That?
Once we have discovered a change that is different on the miracle day and is one that will make a meaningful difference for the client, it is important that we then help the client to explore how exactly the client brought about the change on the miracle day. This helps to create a clear path or series of steps for the client to follow in the future should the client decide to recreate this desired change. In addition, it serves a valuable function of assisting the client to understand that the desired change was not a random event that was the product of dumb luck, but the direct result of something the client did or thought that can now be reproduced. The following example shows how these three steps work together.

T: What else do you notice on this miracle day?
C: That I eat breakfast.
T: Is that different?

C: Yeah. I usually don't take the time to eat breakfast. I'm never up on time.

T: But today you are.

C: Yes.

T: What difference does it make for you on this morning to have the time to eat breakfast?

C: It makes a big difference. I'm able to relax, and have a few minutes to gather my thoughts while I eat. I'm also not as cranky when I have breakfast.

T: Wow! So this does sound really different. I'm curious about how you pulled it off on this morning to have this time to eat breakfast?

C: Well, I got up right away when my alarm went off.

T: I remember you mentioned that. Sounds like that was a very important step.

C: It was. I really need to do that.

T: What else made the difference on this morning that allowed you to have the time to eat breakfast?

C: I had clothes clean and ready to go.

T: Wow. I bet that took some planning.

C: Yes, but it does make a difference.

By using this same three-step process with each element that clients offer, therapists are able to help clients gain a clear understanding of what steps are needed in order to make changes in their everyday lives to start the change process. At the end of such a session I have found it to be common for clients to identify various changes that they discovered while answering the miracle question that they now want to implement. As a result of seeing how such small changes have the potential to make such significant differences in their lives, it is only fitting that these changes become a reality.

Summary

While watching a skilled solution-focused therapist can make solution-focused brief therapy appear amazingly simple and even magical, it takes time and practice to perfect this approach. In this chapter we have begun the complex process of analyzing some of the many elements that make this approach effective, but we have only scratched the surface. In the next chapter we will explore how solution-focused concepts can be used when completing substance abuse evaluations and assessment.

4

Assessment and Evaluation

Knowing when to push, when to let go, what to listen to, and what to ignore—all these skills are based on the profound respect for human dignity and working to restore a sense of who they are and what they want to be.

Insoo Kim Berg

Assessment and evaluation have a valuable role in clinical care, and substance abuse treatment is no exception. Assessment in substance abuse treatment frequently involves an extensive process that requires analysis of the many factors causing, maintaining, and contributing to the client's problem, its severity, and its consequences. Several different types of assessment exist, such as diagnostic criteria, standardized testing instruments, and clinical judgment. In this chapter we will talk in-depth about the nature of assessment in the field of substance abuse and how solution-focused clinicians use assessment in their clinical work.

Problem-Focused Approaches to Substance Abuse Assessment

In every field of study, there are accepted standards of practice. They not only provide guidance for clinicians in the field, but also are the benchmarks to which professionals are held should the unexpected happen and a client be harmed. Should something go wrong, and a clinician have failed to attend to these standards of care, the clinician will be seen as providing substandard care and be liable for damages. A wise clinician takes these standards to heart regardless of the theoretical model employed since these make up the framework of the yardstick by which the therapist will be judged. In addition to the potential legal implications, there is some merit to the thinking that one should be able to determine if treatment is effective by looking at some common elements, such as the client's overall level of functioning in various life areas. Some examples of these may be

71

the client's employment, relationships, and so forth. Following this logic, it only serves to reason that there would be some common areas of assessment that could then, by conclusion, be measured pre- and posttreatment in order to determine effectiveness. Each theoretical approach will give different meaning and weights to each area of assessment, but all agree that good and effective treatment should result in good client functioning in each area at the conclusion of care. According to the Department of Health and Human Services (DHHS, 1999, p. 46), there are 10 core assessment areas in the field of substance abuse:

- Current use patterns
- History of substance use
- Consequences of substance abuse (especially external pressures that are bringing the client into treatment at this time, such as family or legal pressures)
- Coexisting psychiatric disorders
- Information about major medical problems and health status
- Information about education and employment
- Support mechanisms
- Client strengths and situational advantages
- Previous treatment
- Family history or substance abuse disorders and psychological disorders

In addition to the elements that make up the standards of care for client assessment, specific client populations have been identified as being at elevated risk when using substances, and therefore being in need of additional assessment and treatment standards. In the United States at the time of this writing these groups include (45 CFR 96.120–.137):

- Pregnant women
- Women who are addicted and who have dependent children
- Injecting drug addicts
- Those who have tuberculosis
- Those infected with human immunodeficiency virus (HIV)

Again, regardless of one's theoretical model, these identified groups simply follow logic. For example, it is logical that a woman using substances while pregnant will be at increased risked due to the potential harm to the unborn child. Any well-trained treatment professional would naturally be more concerned about the health of the mother and unborn child when learning that the mother was actively using or had been using substances during key developmental stages of the pregnancy. As therapists, we frequently wear multiple hats, and at times we need to take off our therapist hat and replace it with our client safety hat. In the case of a pregnant woman actively using substances, the professional must first determine if the client and her unborn child are safe or in need of additional services prior to beginning psychotherapy. This may necessitate coordination with her prenatal care provider (or providing assistance to access prenatal care), referral to a level of care that decreases her exposure to active drug use, and so forth. However, once the client is determined to be safe, the clinician can switch back to the therapist hat and resume clinical services. Then, the degree to which the history and assessment information will be paramount in the treatment process will be determined by the therapeutic model being used. Regardless of how extensively the assessment data were used during the treatment episode, all clinicians would then again use the same discharge criteria (which were identified during the assessment process) in determining success. In the case of our pregnant substance-using woman, the outcome measures would be the health of the baby at birth, the ability of the woman to effectively parent the child, and the environmental factors the woman puts in place to ensure the ongoing health of herself and her child (i.e., housing, daycare, nutrition). Let us look at how solution-focused brief therapy uses assessment information.

The Solution-Focused Approach to Substance Abuse Assessment

Meeting Standards of Care

Upon first glance one might mistakenly think that a solution-focused therapist does not value assessment. For if a therapist believes that the client's solution may not be connected to the client's problem, then why spend a significant amount of time exploring the problem? In the majority of the current literature about solution-focused brief therapy, you will not find a significant amount of time devoted to evaluation and assessment. Up until now books about solution-focused brief therapy have prioritized technical clarifications and further development of the approach primarily through detailed descriptions of its practical clinical and social applications in the everyday world and very little about assessment. Indeed, some might even wonder if assessment and evaluation have a place in solution-focused brief therapy at all. This can create a professional dilemma, for standards of care requires a thorough assessment of clients. How can both be true? This was a question that I pondered for quite some time during my early years as a solution-focused therapist.

When I asked my solution-focused mentors about assessment, their initial response was always that understanding the problem was irrelevant to the solution. While I understood this to be true from the tenets of solution-focused brief therapy, I struggled to comprehend how this approach could be viewed as credible without including this standardized element. So I kept asking. I was convinced the approach worked, so I was determined to understand this apparent conflict. On many occasions, I was told by my mentors that I should just complete whatever assessment forms were required by regulation and view this as separate from solution-focused brief therapy.

While I did this for a while, I still did not understand how this approach could be viewed as credible when this required assessment information was viewed more as a bother and a nuisance. However, I did find this separation between clinical work and gathering required information to work well in my private practice, since the clients I worked with in that setting came to me with a clear understanding of a problem and of what they wanted to be different. In those cases, I did begin initial sessions with the miracle question (after a brief period of pleasantries and asking what they hoped to be different by coming to see me) and complete the therapeutic conversation prior to gathering assessment data. At the end of the session, I transitioned into a list of topic areas that as a professional I was accountable to gather. The subject areas included medical status, mental health status, current medications, history of harm to self or others, substance use, and an "other" category for anything else the client thought I should know. In addition, I asked direct questions in order to determine a diagnosis for billing purposes. Other areas, such as relationships, presenting problem, legal issues, employment, and so on, were naturally collected during the treatment component of the session without any need for me to focus the direction of my conversation onto those problem areas. However, I did discover that I naturally modified my questions in response to the information I learned about the client's problem. For example, when I learned that a client was having difficulties in her marriage, I might ask, "So what would your husband notice that is different about you on this miracle day?" This question naturally acknowledged the problem the client mentioned, but focused our work together on the solution to the problem. Despite my success in a private practice setting, this approach was not successful in an agency setting with clients whose only reason for seeking services was oftentimes at someone else's requirement (i.e., child welfare, probation). It was not until I took the time to discuss the matter with Insoo Kim Berg and listened to how she interacted with others about clients that I began to understand.

On many occasions when I was with Insoo and other mentors and we were discussing client cases, I discovered that they would make reference to various problems of which they were aware, but then their questions and ponderings would come from a solution stance. For example, when talking about a client who was involved in the child welfare system who had a diagnosis of major depressive disorder, the following type of statements was common:

> She looks so sad. I wonder what the caseworker would be noticing about the client during the next home visit or what we will be seeing next time we see her that would let us know that things are looking better. I wonder what the caseworker will see that lets her know that she doesn't have to worry about the client harming herself anymore. I think I will ask her a scale next time about how she is managing her mood. Probably should also think about a medication evaluation if the client thinks that would be helpful.

I soon discovered that in cases such as these, the solution-focused therapist was well aware of the potential clinical issues (in this case depression and possible risk of self-harm and need for psychotropic medications) and was in turn directly exploring possible solutions regarding them. By scaling the solution (ability to manage mood) the therapist would also indirectly gather specific information about the problem. It was implied through this discussion that this problem (the depression) needed to be resolved prior to the client reaching her miracle. It was then that I discovered that solution-focused therapists are still using their clinical training and awareness of the potential dangers of client issues. However, instead of gathering more information about the problem, they are actively gathering information about the potential solution. This is how solution-focused brief therapy meets the standards of care—by being aware of the problems and ensuring that the problems are resolved prior to treatment's end.

I then surmised that if the therapist working with the above-mentioned client was required to complete a problem or issues list (a required form in most substance abuse treatment agencies), a solution-focused therapist's list would closely resemble the problem-focused therapist's list. Both therapists would list symptoms of depression as one of the client's concerns. The only difference would be the designated disposition of each issue. This would be directly influenced by the therapist's model being employed. In either case, both the solution-focused and problem-focused therapists would agree that the same issues need to be resolved prior to treatment being successful. In addition, the solution-focused therapist believes that the more the therapist can become aware of the areas in which potential solutions are needed (a problem-focused therapist would call these "problems") through natural conversation, the better, for they will be less of a distraction to the treatment. In contrast, a problem-focused therapist believes that these issues or problems need to be clearly stated so that they can be actively resolved during treatment. In either case, the therapist will be cognizant of the issues at hand and actively work to resolve the issues, thereby meeting standards of care.

Whether you are working in private practice or for an agency, there are several ways to gather information for assessment. When you are working in a private practice setting or in an agency that has fewer regulations, you can effectively gather the majority of information through the specific solution-focused interventions during the treatment session itself. Let us take a look at how that can be done.

Assessment Through Solution-Focused Interventions

One of the most effective ways to gather assessment information is through the use of the miracle question. Developed as a means to assist clients to envision a desired future despite their current belief that a positive future is unobtainable, the miracle question helps the therapist and clients to assess how things will be different once the miracle has occurred. Since in its purest form, the miracle is defined as "the problem which brought you here is solved" (DeJong & Berg, 2008, p. 84), the solution-focused therapist is directly gathering information that is specifically related to the absence of the problem. While most would not think of the miracle question as an assessment tool, it is. Most assessment tools, especially in the field of substance abuse, look for deficits and pathology in the client and tend to focus on the past. Since one can rarely know for sure the origin of a problem, a logical conclusion would be to assess what one does know (i.e., how he or she wants his or her life to be different in the future). The miracle question thereby offers a unique future perspective on assessment.

A second helpful intervention for assessment is scaling, for regardless of the therapeutic intent of the scale, scales always provide the therapist with the secondary benefit of tidbits of information about the problem that can be gleaned while the client describes his or her relationship to the solution. The following example illustrates this point:

Therapist (T): So you say that things have been difficult. Just so I understand better, on a scale of 1 to 10, where 10 means that despite how difficult things have been you are doing very well, getting everything done that you need to, etc., and 1 means that you can't even get out of bed, where would you say you are?

Client (C): Well, I am out of bed. I would say about a 6.

T: Wow! A 6! What lets you know you are that high?

C: Well, I was able to get to my appointments all week, I have kept my house fairly clean, and I've taken care of myself OK. I just haven't been able to do all the other things I wanted to get done.

T: That's very impressive. Even though you are having a difficult time, you are able to get done everything you had to do. Is that right?

C: Yes. I get those done, but not anything else.

In this example, the therapist learned that despite the client's difficulty, she is not experiencing depression at a level that is negatively impacting her responsibilities. Through scaling, the therapist is able to find this important evaluative fact while listening to how the client would like her life to be different in the future. Scaling is an intervention that gathers important information without engaging in problem talk.

A third solution-focused intervention that provides evaluative information is relational questions. By understanding what difference various changes make or will make to others in the clients' lives, clients frequently disclose information about the problem. The following dialogue demonstrates this:

T: So how can I help you today?

C: My caseworker thinks I have a problem with alcohol.

T: And what do you think?

C: I don't think that I do, but I can't get my kids back until she changes her mind.

T: And what will she be seeing that will let her know that you don't have a problem with alcohol?

C: She will see that I'm going to work, I'm on time for my appointments, there is food in the house ... you know. All that kind of stuff.

T: Would this be different?

C: Yes and no. It would be different for me to be on time and go to work.

T: And what would be different that resulted in you being able to do those things?

C: I'd get enough rest and be able to get up on time.

T: And how would you have done that?

C: I probably wouldn't have partied the night before.

T: What would you have done instead?

C: Maybe just hang out with the kids. Maybe play a game with them or something.

In this conversation, the therapist learned that the caseworker sees some evidence of a problem with alcohol. Some of the problems she most likely noticed are "partying," difficulty getting to appointments on time, and difficulty holding down employment. There is no need to know exactly what criteria are met for an alcohol-related diagnosis (unless required for payment or regulation purposes). It is clear for purposes of evaluation that alcohol issues are negatively impacting this client's life and need to be resolved prior to treatment being completed. Now let us take a look at how evaluation can be done in a more highly regulated agency setting.

Formalized Assessment

When I was first trained in completing substance abuse evaluations, I was taught to look for evidence that the client had a problem. It was not long before it became apparent to me how difficult an undertaking that truly was, for clients were quick to deny that a problem existed, resulting in a very unpleasant power struggle to obtain needed information. I always left the interview questioning if the client was being forthcoming and generally concluding that he or she probably was not. The clients most likely left feeling like they were being judged (which they were). It then almost seemed logical why in my college training I was instructed to assume that the client was minimizing (for that was part of the disease of addiction). Unfortunately, that advice did not provide me with any clues as to how to obtain the accurate information, for if I assumed the client was minimizing, my only recourse was to guess as to what the correct information was. This would still leave me with inaccurate information. So, with no further ideas of how to effectively evaluate the client, I came up with my own plan. It was simple. I would look for evidence that the client did not have a problem. It only seemed logical that the client would not try to hide this information, and in fact would be highly motivated to join with me in the search, thereby eliminating the power struggle. If there was not the needed evidence that the client did not have a problem, it would not be something that I was charging against the client, but would simply be a matter of fact. Therefore, it would not be an accusation against the client, but an invitation to work together in treatment to create the needed evidence. Not only did this solve my immediate problem, but it was much more consistent with solution-focused brief therapy as well.

Definition of the "Client"

In order to effectively work with a client who is mandated for services by someone else, I found it most helpful to change my definition of the "client" from the person sitting in front of me to the client's system (see Figure 4.1).

Each client has his or her own unique system based on his or her circumstances (Bertalanffy, 1968). In addition to the client's obvious members of the system (family, probation, child welfare, community), I added "regulation" as the final ring in all client systems, for as soon as clients begin working with me as a professional, these substance- or agency-related regulations become part of the elements under which I must operate, and therefore which we must consider. This allowed me to remain genuinely neutral when working with the client, and only educate the

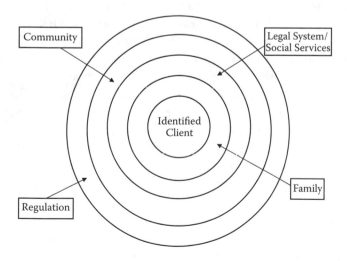

Figure 4.1   Sample Client System

client about the various regulations as they became relevant to the client's decisions. This systemic view of the client allowed me to return to the solution-focused belief that there is only a problem if the client (in this case anyone in the client's system) views it as such.

The Role of Neutrality in Evaluation and Assessment
One of the most freeing elements of my newfound way to approach evaluation was that I was to remain completely neutral. I was no longer asked to believe or disbelieve the client or the facts he or she presented. This concept derived from a conversation I once had with Insoo Kim Berg, during which she told me that I was to leave no footprints when working with clients. I viewed my footprints to be my opinions and judgments. This freed me from the lie detector role (something in which I was not accomplished despite the previous expectations). At times professionals have questioned me about this, wondering how the client could perceive me as caring and compassionate if I did not believe them. It is then that I remind them that concepts such as believing are like a two-sided coin. If one chooses to believe a client, then by omission one also chooses to disbelieve the client. It is impossible to accept one without the other.

When trying to explain how a professional can remain completely neutral and yet remain compassionate and genuinely involved, I liken the analogy of a travel agent. When one seeks the services of a travel agent to plan a trip, it does not even occur to the travel agent to believe or disbelieve the customers as they tell about the places they have traveled before or where they want to go. It is irrelevant to the business at hand. While the travel agent most likely will listen to these stories, she then skillfully turns the conversation to where the customer would like to travel next. The customer never thinks that the travel agent is not compassionate or caring because the travel agent has no opinion about if a proposed destination is right or wrong. The customer understands that the travel agent can be very caring and compassionate without having a stake in the chosen destination (in fact, a travel agent who tries to influence the destination would most likely be viewed as intrusive or meddling). However, an experienced travel agent will make known various facts of which the customer should be aware in making the decision (i.e., weather patterns, culture, politics) to assist the customer in making a good decision. Likewise, the solution-focused therapist asks good questions to assist the clients in fully evaluating each choice from the context of all members of their systems to ensure the clients are ultimately satisfied with the decisions.

Evidence There Is No Problem

When completing an evaluation from this stance, one uses the same evaluation forms and biopsychosocial tools (a common instrument in the substance abuse field is the Addiction Severity Index [ASI]). These forms allow for a systematic way of gathering self-reported information from the basic domains of medical, employment/support, substance use, legal, family/social, and psychiatric. In addition, other methods of data collection that provide objective evidence, such as urine screens and standardized testing instruments, are extremely useful to remain evidence based and avoid any need for subjectivity. When reviewing all of the data, the therapist needs to identify any possible red flags (items that prevent the therapist from ruling out substance abuse as a possible scenario). Evidence that the client does not have a problem can only be found in the absence of red flags. The following is a nonexhaustive list of possible red flags:

- Any inconsistency within the client's report or between types of reports: If there are any inconsistencies within the data, it is difficult to determine the cause without forming an opinion. These inconsistencies could be between what the client stated occurred and what is documented in a police report; it could be inconsistencies between the amount or frequency of drug use the client reports during the interview and that shown by the testing instruments, and so forth. Information that is accurate is more likely to be reported consistently in multiple forms. While it is possible that accurate information could be reported inconsistently, it does bear further exploration and is considered a red flag.
- Lack of consistent objective evidence of no substance use: This can be a difficult area, since most people do not have any evidence (i.e., urine screens) that they have been substance-free. If this is the only possible red flag, this would not prevent a client from having the necessary evidence that he or she does not have a problem. However, many clients who come to substance abuse treatment agencies have already been requested to provide urine screens by their referral source to determine if they are using substances. In these circumstances compliance with this request and providing consistent negative urine screen results would be needed to offer evidence that they do not have a problem with substances. For example, say a client was referred to an agency by child welfare due to possible concerns for substance use. The caseworker had requested that this client provide a urine screen within 24 hours at a testing location. If the client did not comply with the caseworker's request, this would be a red flag and prevent us from having evidence that the client does not have a problem with substances (while there are many possible explanations for why the client might not have provided the urine screen, one

explanation could be substance use, thereby preventing us from ruling that out). Conversely, any positive urine screen result will automatically prevent the client from having the necessary evidence that he or she does not have a problem with substances.

- Any objective party who has any concerns about possible substance use: This relies on the basic concept that an objective party has no reason to make false allegations against the client. If there are concerns about possible substance use by a credible source, this prevents us from asserting that the client does not have a problem. This is one of the ways that using a systemic approach helps to bring possible issues to light without the therapist having to determine the validity of the concerns.
- Legal charges or documented involvement with illegal substances: This one is rather straightforward. Anytime that the clients have obtained charges or documentation that links them to substances, this warrants services to address the issues at hand. Legal involvement would be part of the client's system and prevents the client (as we are defining the term more broadly) from saying there is no problem.
- Use of substances during pregnancy or other situations that are hazardous to the client or someone else: This concern comes from the regulation ring of the client's system (see Figure 4.1). As previously noted, federal law identifies a pregnant woman using substances as problematic. Similarly, most states identify a person driving under the influence of a substance as problematic due to the potential danger to self or others. These are examples of when the therapist is obligated to educate the client about the regulations and how the larger system views various behaviors. A therapist who does not identify these as problematic and recommend treatment to ensure these behaviors are resolved would violate standards of care.
- Continued problematic use of substances following treatment or lack of any treatment following a period of problematic use: When I train therapists how to conduct evaluations, I frequently talk about the importance of remaining credible should the matter need to be presented to a judge. While some clinicians never find themselves in front of a judge, this is a rather common occurrence in the field of substance abuse when working in agency settings, since so many of our clients come to us from the legal or child welfare systems. I would rather make my decisions assuming that I will have to defend my work in a court of law rather than be taken by surprise and find my credibility at risk. Because of this, I strongly recommend that therapists take a more conservative stance when looking for red flags. I have found it better to recommend services to rule out a possible problem than to grapple with the emotional turmoil of later learning that a child had suffered injury on behalf of a parent's substance abuse because I mistakenly believed a client when

he or she told me substance abuse was no longer a problem. When the child welfare and the legal systems are involved, there is just too much at risk for me to guess. You will have to come to your own conclusions in this regard.

This red flag is one of those gray areas that should something go wrong and the client later be determined to have a problem with substances, the therapist who did not recommend services even though the client disclosed that he or she did not complete any formalized treatment following a period of problematic use will be highly criticized and found substandard. This is a difficult area for a solution-focused therapist, for we do believe that it is possible for clients to recover from substance abuse issues without formalized treatment. This area of spontaneous remission of substance abuse problems has been researched (Granfield & Cloud, 1999; Cloud & Granfield, 2001). Unfortunately, it is not widely accepted, and reliance on this is not a defense that would bode well in a court of law.

- Any indicators on the standardized testing measures that indicate problematic use or inconclusive results: Lastly, the use of standardized testing measures such as the SASSI, ASUS, ASAP-II, and BDI-II (see later in this chapter for more information about these measures), as well as use of formal diagnosis, can be very helpful in providing objective evidence. If the client scores within normal limits on these instruments, this can provide some of the best evidence when combined with other forms of data (such as consistent data, lack of concern within the system, etc.) that the client does not have a problem with substances. However, should the client's results be inconclusive (due to an elevated defensiveness score) or indicate problematic use, this prevents the client from gaining the evidence needed to demonstrate that substances are not a problem. We have found the SASSI to be especially helpful in this regard. While it is rather simple for a client to conceal diagnostic information during an interview should that be desired, it is important for us to mention that any diagnosis for which the client qualifies would automatically be a red flag.

Once all the information has been gathered, and the therapist has determined that there are no red flags raised by the client data, the solution-focused therapist then looks to see if the one required element to prove that the client does not have a problem is present: that no one in the client's system views the client's behavior as problematic. Now you might be wondering how any client could meet all of the requirements to prove that he or she does not have a problem with substances. Depending upon the setting in which you work, you will have varying percentages of clients who come to treatment with the necessary evidence. I have found that a significant percentage of clients in my private practice come with the necessary evidence, while a very small percentage of clients who come through the county-based treatment center present with the needed evidence. This seems to correlate with the reason they are initially seeking services. In my private practice, most are self-motivated, and therefore they are more preventive in nature when they seek evaluation for substance abuse. It would stand to reason that a greater number of these clients could easily demonstrate that substance use is not a problem. In contrast, at the county agency the majority are externally mandated after significant legal problems and consequences have required their involvement in substance-related services. It is logical to conclude that a greater number of these clients would have difficulty providing the necessary evidence that they do not have a problem with substances. Now let us take a more in-depth look at some of the more common standardized testing instruments that are used in substance abuse evaluation.

Substance Abuse Assessment Instruments

There are a vast number of well-designed, standardized testing instruments available for use. Our discussion is in no way meant to be exhaustive, only to highlight some of the ones most often used or the instruments we have found to be most helpful. An important caveat when using any standardized testing instrument in a solution-focused fashion is to remember that we are not using the testing instrument to discover problems or to diagnose the client. Instead, we are using the instrument as a way to validate information that the client already disclosed during the interview. Because of this, we only consider valid anything that matches what the client already disclosed. Anything that is not consistent is a genuine puzzlement, which is offered to the client to help us better understand the initial discrepancy. If the client has no explanation, then the information is dropped as something that has no relevance and is a possible red flag. This lack of judgment and lack of belief that the testing is "correct" is most likely the key difference between how a solution-focused therapist will use testing data and how a problem-focused therapist will use data.

Another way that a solution-focused therapist may use the testing instruments to assist in client change is to encourage clients to determine the meaning of their scores and explore how the clients want to change for the positive. For example, if a client received a score on one of the instruments illustrating difficulty with substances, the therapist would first ask if this score was an accurate measure. Then, the therapist would ask the client where he or she would like to see himself or herself in the future on the instrument. This would lead to a discussion regarding what will be different for the client when that place is obtained and how the client will have achieved this. Let us now take a look at a few of these instruments.

SASSI-3 (Adult) and SASSI-2A (Adolescent)

The Substance Abuse Subtle Screening Inventory (SASSI) classifies individuals as to whether they score similarly to those who have a substance dependence disorder (Miller, 1985). This instrument pays specific attention to the client's attitudes, values, and beliefs and is able to indicate if a client is at high risk to develop problematic substance-related behaviors in the future based upon the person's way of thinking or current values. This instrument consists of 52 true-false items and takes 10 to 15 minutes to complete. The following are five subscales of the SASSI: Obvious Attributes, Subtle Attributes, Defensiveness, Family, and Correctional. In addition, there are two scales that provide direct information about the clients' way of using substances: Face Valid Alcohol and Face Valid Other Drug. The SASSI-3 (the latest adult version at the time of this writing) has been shown to have a reliability of .93 when determining if drug users possess a substance dependence disorder (Miller, 1997b).

ASI

The Addiction Severity Index (ASI) is a structured interview given by a clinician to assess for alcohol and drug use and other problems. Questions are grouped into six problem areas: medical status, employment/support status, drug/alcohol use, legal status, family/social history, and psychiatric status. The therapist then uses a 10-point severity rating scale to objectively indicate areas in which treatment services are needed. A separate client scale is also used to gather information about the client's perception of need. In addition, the ASI can be used as a pre- and postinstrument in order to demonstrate outcomes. Although the manual states that the interview takes between 20 and 30 minutes, we have found it to take closer to 45 minutes when working with complex client cases to thoroughly explore each area in a way that allows the therapist to also be prepared to write solution-focused treatment plans at the end of the evaluation. The interrater reliability of the instrument is .89, and the test-retest reliability is .92 (McLellan, Luborsky, Woody, & O'Brien, 1980; McLellan et al., 1985).

ASUS

The Adult Substance Use Survey (ASUS), developed by Ken Wanberg (1992), is a self-report measure. The five subscales that are included are:

1. Lifetime involvement in drugs across 10 categories
2. Disruptive consequences and problems related to drug use
3. Antisocial attitudes and behaviors
4. Mental health or emotional distress
5. Defensive test-taking attitude

The internal reliability for the scale ranges between .80 and .95 (Wanberg, 1997). I have found the most helpful scales from a solution-focused perspective to be the Involvement Scale (to see if the data are consistent with the interview), the Disruption Scale (the relationship between the Involvement and Disruption Scales can be used as potential evidence to substantiate a client's statement that he or she is ready to make changes), and the Mental Health or Mood Scale (to see if the data are consistent with the interview).

ASAP-II

The Adolescent Self-Assessment Profile (ASAP) was also developed by Wanberg (1992) and consists of 225 items. The domains within this measure include: in-depth assessment of drug involvement (which substances, extent, exposure, etc.), the consequences and benefits of drug use, family factors, psychological factors, school disruption, legal factors, peer influence, and many others. The reliability of the instrument ranges from .73 to .94 (Wanberg, 1999). I have found this instrument to be a very helpful tool in assisting clients to discuss these areas of concern with their parents. As I go through each scale and explain what it means, I then look to the client to ask if the information fits. I then invite the client to explain to his or her parents more about each element and how it fits for him or her. This oftentimes provides the forum needed to ensure that the parents have the information they need to make informed decisions about their child and the services that are needed. The scale format assists the parents in understanding where their child lies in relationship to children who are simply experimenting with substances.

AUI

The Alcohol Use Inventory (AUI) is a 228-item assessment from Pearson Assessments. This inventory examines the different ways in which individuals use alcohol, the individual's degree of concern about the use of alcohol and its consequences, and the benefits and negative consequences associated with alcohol use. The primary scales within this inventory are the following: benefits, styles, consequences, and concerns and acknowledgments. The reliability of the AUI is reported by subscale internal consistency and ranges from .54 to .89.

BDI-II

Although the Beck Depression Inventory II (BDI-II) is not a substance-related testing instrument, it plays a valuable role in substance abuse evaluation. Depression has been shown to be positively correlated with alcohol use (Brennan & Moos, 1996; Brennan, Moos, & Mertens, 1994) and other drugs of abuse (Havassy & Wasserman, 1992). Mental health disorders frequently go hand in hand with substance-related disorders, and the use of this simple tool to screen for depressive symptoms can be invaluable. The BDI is utilized primarily as a self-report tool that takes between 5 and 15 minutes to administer. The scoring for the BDI involves tallying the raw score and determining where it falls on a scale of severity that ranges from 0 to 63. The greater the score, the more severe the depression. The reliability for the BDI ranges from .73 to .92, with a mean of .86 (Beck, Steer, & Garbin, 1988).

ASAM PPC-2R

While the American Society of Addiction Medicine Patient Placement Criteria, Second Edition, Revised (ASAM PPC-2R) is not really a standardized assessment tool, it is commonly used throughout the field of addiction as a way to standardize treatment recommendations and should be mentioned (Mee-Lee, 2001). This instrument provides a standardized way of organizing the data collected throughout the evaluation process so that the therapist can determine which of eight possible levels of care (from early intervention through the most intensive level, medically managed intensive inpatient treatment) would best meet the needs of the client. The appropriate level of care is determined by categorizing client data into six dimensions: acute intoxication or withdrawal, biomedical conditions and complications, emotional/behavioral conditions and complications, treatment acceptance/resistance, relapse/continued use potential, and recovery environment. These criteria can then be used to justify which level of care is needed, the amount of care within each level, and when treatment services are complete. Solution-focused brief therapy can be effectively used within each level of care.

Case Example

Over the years, I have discovered that life has an uncanny way of providing poignant examples for the subject matter about which I am writing at any given time. Unfortunately, I again found that to be true this week as I wrote this chapter on assessment and evaluation. Early this week, I was saddened to learn that a client for whom we had recently completed a substance abuse evaluation committed suicide. Even after close to 20 years, that news always makes me take pause; there is no easy way to accept when we are unable to help a client despite our best efforts. Part of the requirements from our regulatory agencies is that I complete a thorough incident report upon the death of any client to ensure that the client received the best possible care. In the past, such incident reports were a source of angst as I struggled to explain how we had truly provided exemplary care despite solution-focused brief therapy's expectation that the client be the expert and the model's lack of emphasis on history. Saying that the client did not bring up depression or suicide ideation during the conversation was hardly sufficient defense, nor was explaining that we simply focused on the client's goals or miracle. When unfortunate things happen, a clear indication that client risk factors have been explored is not only good client care, but also necessary on a personal level to relieve my own fears of falling short for my clients in their darkest times. This time (maybe as a result of my current focus on writing this chapter and doing my best to clarify how both can be true), I was able to truly remain focused on my feelings of loss for the client as I reviewed our work without any need for a defensive posture. Here is what I found:

> BDI-II: The client's total score was 8, which placed her in the minimal range (normal level). I then looked at question number 9, which specifically asks the client about any thoughts of suicide over the past two weeks. My client had circled 0, indicating "I don't have any thoughts of killing myself." I then noticed that the client had written something beside question number 7. I found this odd since clients usually simply chose among the available answers, and rarely offer additional commentaries. So although I would not normally look at this question when screening

for suicide ideation, I read her answer. The question was exploring the client's self-concept. She had circled the answer 1, indicating "I have lost confidence in myself." But there in tiny print she had written "getting better." I smiled at how, if we only listen, clients help us find the solutions within the problem questions.

ASUS: The client's Mood Scale was in the sixth decile rank. While it is elevated, I have found that most of the clients at our agency tend to score in this general area. I then turned to the second page to explore the client's actual answers (the only true way to understand a client's thinking). I immediately looked at question 16 in the Disruption Scale since it is the first question on this instrument that asks about past suicide attempts. To my relief, she had answered "never." I then turned to the questions that make up the Mood Scale. These questions are to be answered by the client from a lifetime point of view. I have oftentimes thought that I probably would score in the sixth decile range as well should I ever take the instrument on a whim, since it only takes an answer of "yes sometimes" on a variety of questions regarding "feeling down and depressed," "nervous and tense," "moods up and down," "worry about things," and "discouraged about the future" to render such a score. How many of us could honesty answer "never" throughout our entire lifetime on those questions? Finally, I reviewed question number 47, due to its specific focus on "not wanting to live or like taking your life." Consistent with all of the previous client data, the client had circled the lowest possible answer: "hardly at all."

SASSI-3: There is only one scale on the SASSI-3 that could potentially indicate possible depression, and that is the DEF (defensive) Scale. This scale is actually a bipolar scale, meaning that both a high and a low value can be meaningful. The SASSI-3 provides a normal range for each scale, and it is most telling when a scale falls outside (in either direction) this range. On the female version (this instrument is normed for each gender), the score would have to be a 2 or lower to indicate possible depression. My client's score was 10.

ASI: In matters such as this, I find the data collected by the ASI to be most helpful, for a skilled clinician not only asks the prescribed questions, but also asks a multitude of follow-up questions until the client is completely understood. If I were to find anything we missed, it would most likely be on this instrument. I quickly turned to the "Psychological Status" section and reviewed the client's answers for both the past 30 days and her lifetime. True to my hypothesis, there was indication of past depression. While she denied any feelings of depression or anxiety in the past 30 days, she did indicate she had had past difficulties in these areas. I smiled with relief as I saw my therapist's notes indicating this was many years ago, and despite no current concerns, the therapist had recommended a mental health evaluation due to some odd answers and inconsistencies regarding past abuse in her childhood and resultant mood issues in her adulthood. The therapist had done well; she did not believe nor disbelieve, but had flagged inconsistencies as indicators of a need to rule out possible issues.

I submitted my report to our regulatory agencies, thinking that would be the end. We clearly had done everything we could and had the necessary evidence to substantiate it. What I did not expect was a voicemail message to greet me the following morning. It was Karen from our state regulatory agency. She expressed her condolences for the loss of our client, but then went on to say how clear it was from the report that we had done everything we possibility could, that it was quite thorough, and that she wanted to use our report as an example for other agencies for how incident reports should be done. While I was relieved that others agreed that we had done our best, the chart review and Karen's message brought to light that had we not used the very instruments that Sara and I just discussed, the outcome would have been quite different. Although the regulatory body accepts solution-focused brief therapy as a possible therapeutic approach, when the time comes to evaluate if clients receive adequate care, we all need to express this in a way that everyone, regardless of theoretical approach, can clearly understand. Good client care is good client care.

Summary

While upon initial glance, providing a thorough assessment or evaluation does not appear to be consistent with the basic tenets of solution-focused brief therapy, it is important to understand the value of providing this. Such evaluations not only provide the necessary information to substantiate our decisions should our actions be called into question, but they also provide the necessary credibility and self-confidence in our work. Clients who find themselves in the midst of horrific life consequences due to their use of substances (such as legal charges or the loss of parental rights) are not always comfortable disclosing the extent of their problems. This can place a professional in a difficult position since accurate treatment recommendations are critical in order to ensure child and community safety. By taking the stance of searching for evidence that a problem does not exist, the professional can avoid adopting a pessimistic view of the client, while ensuring that needed services are recommended until such evidence becomes apparent. In the following chapter, we will take an in-depth look at case management and individual services, and how these can be done from a solution-focused stance that ensures credibility and good client care.

5

Case Management and Individual Work With Clients

Goals are established to help determine how the client and therapist alike will know when the problem is solved. Without this step, therapy could reasonably go on forever.

Steve de Shazer

Introduction

As newly trained therapists leave the universities and begin their careers, most dream of working in private practice or at least working with clients on an individual basis. It is commonplace to have applicants ask with a hopeful tone upon interviewing for a job in the field of substance abuse treatment, "Do you do individual work too, or is it just group?" When they learn that it is most common to conduct the majority of work in a group setting, some are noticeably disappointed. Despite this industry norm, some work is done on an individual basis out of necessity. Some clients need individual treatment services, all clients need case management and treatment planning, and still other clients have minimal legal involvement and seek services from individual practitioners who only offer individual sessions. Because of this, solution-focused therapists need to be well versed in applying these basic tenets to case management and individual services as well. In this chapter we will explore when and how case management and other individual services are used in the field of substance abuse treatment, and how these same services can be effectively provided utilizing solution-focused brief therapy.

Individual Sessions

Individual services include any service that is conducted by a therapist with one client. This includes providing therapy sessions, case management,[1] crisis counseling, and the like. Individual services are provided for different reasons when working within an agency setting as opposed to working within a private practice. Let us look at each of these settings in more detail.

Agency Practice

While the client's initial evaluation is customarily conducted on an individual basis within most agencies, the majority of services provided after this appointment are usually completed within the presence of other clients. Some agencies even conduct group intakes in an effort to be more cost-efficient and ensure quicker access to treatment services. During these group intakes, several clients complete their intake paperwork within the same room and receive instructions for completion as a group. Clients are then pulled aside for a brief, private interview for treatment planning; however, the bulk of the appointment is conducted in a group setting. Following evaluation and intake, individual services are primarily offered within agency settings for all clients for three reasons:

1. When clients are inappropriate for group services
2. To create treatment plans and review treatment progress
3. To provide case management services

When Clients Are Inappropriate for Group Services

There are several circumstances in which clients might be or become inappropriate for group services. The first is when clients' personal issues are notably emotionally charged, resulting in them being angry or distraught, unable to focus on the group content or other clients, or unable to respond to the therapist's directives. In order to function appropriately within a group setting, clients must be capable of listening attentively when others are speaking and apply this conversation to their own goals. When clients are experiencing intense emotions, it can be difficult for them to manage these without the therapist's immediate attention. Since the therapist must constantly tend to the needs of all of the clients within the group, a client such as this would be distracting to the group process. An example of this would be a client who is unsuccessfully managing chronic stressors occurring within his or her life and feels overwhelmed and unable to focus or address them without constant direct intervention. In situations such as these, the therapist should schedule individual treatment sessions in lieu of the group sessions to address the chronic crisis, only returning the client to the group setting once the client is stabilized and able to benefit from the group format.

The second situation in which clients would be inappropriate for a group setting is when a client experiences an acute crisis. For example, we have seen this when a client comes to group directly from court in which the outcome was not favorable to the client. The client was too angry to benefit from the group process and instead needed to leave to come to terms with the judge's decision. Other examples are when a client's family member is in the hospital and the client is preoccupied with his or her welfare, or a client who is experiencing some sort of medical condition such as flu, resulting in the client being distracted by his or her physical symptoms. In cases such as these, the therapist may decide that the client should attend to the issues at hand in lieu of attending group. Other times, it may be necessary for the therapist to schedule a single individual session to assist the client in gaining the necessary skills to address the crisis.

The third circumstance in which a client would be inappropriate for a group setting is when a client is presenting a distraction to the group as a whole and has the potential to negatively impact the group's norms despite efforts taken by the therapist to mitigate damages. For example, on occasion, clients come to group with the proverbial chip on their shoulder. Everything is someone else's fault, and there is absolutely nothing they either want or believe they need from treatment. While this stance on some level is fairly normal for our clientele, most clients readily identify something that they would like to gain since they "have to attend group anyway" due to a lack of evidence that substances are not problematic. Most clients aptly set aside their attitude and embrace the process following the first group session. However, on occasion, we run across clients who stand firm to their initial belief that there is nothing to be gained. In such a situation, it is important to work with these clients individually rather than in a group setting so that their "this is stupid" attitude does not hamper the treatment process for others. It is at these times that maintaining a solution-focused stance during the individual session can make a profound difference.

To Create Treatment Plans and Review Treatment Progress
Treatment planning is the backbone of clinical care. Without a solid treat-ment plan, both therapist and client risk wandering aimlessly. Solution-focused brief therapy is a form of brief therapy. Because of this, people frequently assume that clients only remain in therapy for a few sessions. While this is true for some (usually those who have minimal legal involve-ment), it is definitely not the case for all. Because of this, I am oftentimes asked how I define *brief,* and my answer is always, "Not one more ses-sion than is clinically necessary." This necessitates that the therapist then has a yardstick by which to determine when clinical issues are addressed. Treatment plans serve this role. By reviewing the treatment plans regu-larly, both client and therapist are able to quickly identify changes and make necessary modifications to maximize the clients' time in treatment. We recommend that treatment plans be reviewed at a minimum of every four to six weeks. While regulations vary from state to state, the required timeframe by which a treatment plan must be reviewed can be as long as every 90 days or even longer. Waiting this long to review a client's progress may risk keeping the client longer than is necessary.

Meeting with clients individually to review treatment plans provides the therapist with valuable information as to the specifics regarding the way in which the clients completed aspects of their treatments plans. Solution-focused treatment plans are unique in that they frequently are comprised of interventions that allow the clients to explore and design their own solutions (see Chapter 9 for sample treatment plans). Therefore, a detailed review with the client is necessary in order to fully understand the clients' progress. During these sessions, clients' treatment plans may be signed off as completed, additional plans created, or existing plans modified, depending on the clients' needs and referral sources' concerns.

To Provide Case Management Services
Case management covers a wide array of activities that the therapist com-pletes on behalf of the clients (treatment planning and progress review being just one category of these). Many of these activities include corre-sponding with the referral sources and other professionals[2] within the cli-ents' systems as well as locating needed resources within the community and making referrals on the clients' behalf. All of these services necessitate documentation as a way to provide evidence for the clients, which also falls under this category. However, the treatment services in this category that are of most relevance for the purpose of this conversation are those that involve a direct conversation with the client. These may be scheduled

or spontaneous, depending on the nature of the conversation or the ease with which the client can be contacted to schedule an appointment. It is commonplace for the majority of these meetings to be spontaneous for those clients who may not have a telephone, those who are homeless, or others who simply do not regularly return phone messages, making it challenging to schedule an appointment. Because they are conducted by the therapist from a solution-focused stance, the therapist can purpose-fully address clinical issues during any interaction.

There are two kinds of agendas for meetings such as these. The first is to conduct a more formal individual therapy session. This may be in response to a clinical concern raised by someone within the client's sys-tem, or it may be to address an acute crisis or issue of concern that was observed within the agency. For example, I have used sessions such as these to address poor hygiene, inappropriate dress, and a marked change in the client's mood, just to name a few. Sessions such as these are very effective forums in which to address specific behaviors or concerns that the client might not otherwise initiate during a regularly scheduled group session, making them nice additions to the group schedule. The privacy of an individual session allows the therapist to provide or gather facts about how the client is being perceived by those in his or her system so that this information can then be taken into account by the client during future group sessions. The issue may be resolved during the individual session, or the client may decide to begin addressing it during his or her usual group sessions (this can easily be done in a group setting since there is no need for the client to verbalize the problem or issue when working toward resolution within a solution-focused group session).

While the content for case management sessions such as these is fre-quently introduced by the therapist or someone within the clients' system, rather than the clients themselves, a solution-focused therapist will simply present the issue at hand as something the clients should know. The focus then quickly returns to how the clients want their lives to be and what steps the clients will have made to achieve this. The issue at hand is skill-fully woven into the clients' miracles as something that is resolved. The therapist then works with the clients backward to determine the solution that the clients utilized to resolve the problem.

The second agenda for individual sessions is to address facts of the case, such as positive urine screens, missed appointments, positive changes noticed, and so forth. These are oftentimes done in a spontaneous way, since these conversations rarely need a significant amount of time. In addi-tion, this more casual stance of asking the clients if they have a moment prior to group to chat reinforces the message that these are just facts in their cases of which they need to be cognizant. These conversations serve as a form of feedback to the clients about the kind of evidence they are currently gathering. The information is never done in an accusatory tone, and is relayed in the spirit of ensuring the clients can make informed decisions and include this information in their work in future sessions. Here is an example:

Therapist (T): Hi, Cindy. How are you?
Client (C): I'm doing OK.
T: Do you have a few minutes we can talk before group?
C: I guess. [They then move to a private location.]
T: I wanted to let you know that your urine screen came back positive for cocaine. [Said in a neutral tone to allow the client to interpret what is being said without fear of judgment from the therapist]
C: No way!
T: Yeah. I just received it today. [Again, said while maintaining a neutral stance despite the client's reaction. It is key during a conversation such as this for the therapist to truly have no opinion about if the client used the drug or not. The test result is simply a fact that the client must address.]
C: I'm going to be in so much trouble!
T: How can I help? [Asked with genuine empathy and concern]
C: I'm never going to get my daughter back now!
T: It sounds like that is still very important to you.
C: Yes [as she starts to cry].
T: May I ask a few questions? [Asked to create a yes set and get the client's buy-in]
C: Yes.
T: I want you to imagine that it's a couple months down the road and you haven't had any more positive urine screens.
C: OK.
T: What did you do differently to pull that off?
C: I don't know.
T: But it is important to you, right? [Verbally backing up with a yes set to help the client past an "I don't know"]
C: Yes.
T: OK. Then let's think. What did you do differently to get all negative urine screens?
C: Well, I guess I will have stayed away from Joseph.

T: OK. What lets you know that was a good idea.

C: He's still using, and I get tempted when I'm over there.

T: OK. What else? [The therapist here purposefully chooses the verbal path that leads toward what the client will be doing differently and avoids the path that will most likely force the client to confess to drug use. There is no need for a confession, just behavioral change.]

Private Practice

The majority of services provided in a private practice setting are frequently individual (while it is important to note that group can be a common treatment modality in a private practice setting as well). Many individual practitioners also provide couples and family services, but not all provide group services. Private practitioners who are skilled in group facilitation tell me that at times they are unable to offer groups, for they do not always have enough clients at one time to benefit from utilizing this treatment modality. However, this is not problematic since clients who are in need of substance abuse treatment services readily respond to individual services as effectively. Clients who present for services from private practitioners tend to have more financial resources (either health insurance or the ability to pay for services themselves), allowing them to afford the more expensive individual treatment modality. As a group these clients tend to have fewer systemic problems and external mandates for treatment. While the solution-focused therapist in a private practice setting still works from a systemic model and involves everyone within the client's system, the treatment tends to be less complex and most often only involves the clients and their immediate family members (oftentimes just through the use of relationship questions).

It is often mistakenly thought that clients who seek services from a private practitioner will not present with substance misuse as the problem. However, I have found that once a therapist is well established in the field as having expertise in addictions, word spreads and clients are frequently referred for the sole purpose of addressing substance abuse problems. One of my favorite clients first contacted me by saying, "I'm an AA [Alcoholics Anonymous] refugee who has been in intensive therapy for two and a half years. I have a dual diagnosis of substance abuse [her actual diagnosis was alcohol dependence] and PTSD. The 12 steps make me worse, not better." She was seeking services from me because her current therapist believed she was in denial because she always drank more after attending AA and therefore no longer went. I saw this client a total of four times before she completed her goals and no longer needed my help. Another client called and simply said, "I've developed a bit of a problem with chardonnay." Irrespective of what first brings the client through the door, the work from a solution-focused perspective remains the same, for the work is done from a place in which the problem is resolved, regardless of what that problem is.

Level of Acceptable Risk

Working with clients inherently involves risk: risk that we miss a crucial clinical element, risk that our clients are not disclosing everything necessary for us to make good clinical decisions, risk that our clients will harm themselves or others, risk that we are simply human and make a bad call, and so forth. Clients who are in need of substance abuse treatment services are at elevated risk of accident, overdose, suicide, homicide, and many other tragic ends. Working with this population by definition increases the therapist's risk. Therapists can decrease their risk through the use of standardized testing instruments, formal evaluation, clear and thorough documentation, external evidence such as urine screens and breathalyzers, and so forth.

As therapists, each of us has to determine the level of risk that we are willing to accept. We can then control our risk level through one of two ways: either choose clients who appear to be at decreased risk (those with minimal co-occurring mental health issues, etc.) with minimal external involvement or utilize formal evaluation, documentation, and monitoring procedures to ensure necessary evidence that good care was given should it come into question. For example, when I work within an agency setting as a program and clinical supervisor, I am acutely aware that I am working in one of the highest risk settings. The agency admits any client who requests services, our clients have little or no tangible resources, they are involved with multiple legal systems, most have co-occurring disorders, many exhibit erratic or unpredictable behavior or affect, active intoxication is common, and many have a history of violence. Add to this, I am liable for the actions of the therapists I supervise. While I do my best to ensure I remain aware of the therapists' actions through weekly individual and group supervision, the use of a one-way mirror, and the review of client charts, working under these conditions only serves to elevate my risk exposure since they may miss something due to their lack of experience or other human element. To mitigate this risk, I put into place formal evaluation procedures, standardized testing, and monitoring procedures such as urine screens and breathalyzers, and ensure that everything is thoroughly documented. These all provide a paper trail that I (or the court, if necessary) can follow to provide evidence that standards of care were met.

When I work within my private practice, I am still held to the same standards of care. My risk level immediately decreases since I am only responsible for my own actions. However, because I do not have access to monitoring procedures such as a breathalyzer or urine screens, my risk level again increases since I would have no way to determine if a client was really telling me the truth if I smelled alcohol during a session. I would have to rely on my own judgment of the client's ability to drive home safely, and so forth. In addition, I prefer not to complete lengthy, formal evaluations or provide written evaluation reports and summaries in my private practice (all of which are necessary with higher-risk clients). Because of this, I have made the decision to carefully screen potential clients before agreeing to meet with them, referring those who are more complex to agency settings. I purposefully do not see clients in my private practice who are legally mandated into treatment or who are seeking services for substance use but do not personally view their substance use as problematic. I am also leery of clients who have gone through several therapists (specifically if the potential client blames the past therapists for the reasons for termination) or present as needing therapy for years. The risk level is simply more than I am willing to accept in this setting. I only see clients who are seeking services because they or someone in their family would like something to be different. This kind of client requires only moderate documentation and evaluation notes and the occasional standardized testing instrument or formal letter. This level of evaluation and documentation is sufficient to provide the necessary proof that I am meeting standards of care should it come into question. When working with clients in need of substance abuse treatment services, it is prudent for therapists to carefully evaluate the level of risk that is acceptable and to make purposeful decisions to ensure that the necessary steps are in place to manage the risk that is present.

Abstinence versus Controlled Use
When working with a client in a private practice setting, the therapist is able to use solution-focused brief therapy in a more easily recognizable form (similar to that described in the solution-focused literature). Since the clients tend to have fewer external systems involved (i.e., probation,

child welfare), they are able to make more decisions without taking into account so many external elements. For example, while in an agency setting, the client is more likely to be involved with external systems such as probation or child welfare. These agencies most often determine if abstinence is required in order to be compliant with treatment. However, when working with lower-risk clients (those who do not have legal involvement and are seeking services of their own volition) in a private practice setting, the clients are the ones who determine the role that substances will have in their miracles. Some clients determine that they can drink in a controlled fashion, while others are clear that they cannot drink again. Regardless of the clients' decision, it remains the therapist's role to continually ask the clients questions to ensure that they are taking into account the perspectives of everyone within their system (including the community) when they define *success*. This ensures decisions that are lasting and realistic.

I am frequently asked if this means that I will silently support a client to brazenly violate the law by using an illegal substance. The answer is always very simple. Clients who are not involved with the legal system most often are making purposeful decisions (aside from using an illegal substance) to abide by the laws. While they may have become addicted to an illegal substance, many hold conventional pro-social values and do their best to maintain their conventional life despite their drug use. Therefore, clients who I see in my private practice who are breaking the law by using an illegal substance commonly experience cognitive dissonance and seek to change. The clients who do not hold pro-social values most frequently are already involved with the legal system at the time they seek services. This external involvement then becomes a part of the clients' system that mandates them to discontinue the use of the illegal substance.

Individual Skeleton

When working with clients individually during a treatment session, substance abuse issues are addressed through the same process as other presenting problems. As Steve de Shazer (1994) wrote, "We dealt with these cases [those involving substance abuse] 'as usual' and the success rate for the 'abuse' cases turned out to be no different from that for other cases" (p. 242). Clients oftentimes require fewer sessions when they are meeting with a private practitioner (partially because their cases are far less complex), and these sessions are spread out over a larger span of time, allowing for the client to practice what was discovered during the session. When working with clients in a private practice setting, session frequency is oftentimes determined by the client. It is common for me to meet with clients in my private practice for only four to six sessions, yet these sessions are spread over three or four months. This duration allows me to assist the client in developing and practicing relapse prevention skills and the needed confidence to maintain these skills long term. Because the number of sessions is most often very low, it is also effectively used with minimal modifications in Employee Assistance Program settings as well. The following is the individual skeleton (see Figure 5.1) that is used when working with clients during an individual treatment session (Pichot & Dolan, 2003, pp. 30–42):

Because few if any modifications are needed to the traditional application of solution-focused brief therapy when working with clients who are

Individual Skeleton
1. Find out what needs to happen (client's goal) in order for treatment to be useful for the client.
2. Verify that the therapist's understanding of the goal is accurate by asking difference questions or scaling questions. If the goal is unclear, repeat step one.
3. Ask the miracle question and get as many details of the miracle as possible.
4. Listen for exceptions and follow up on them by getting as many details as possible. If no exceptions are identified, move on to step five.
5. Ask a scaling question to determine clients' current levels of progress towards their goals.
6. Referring to the previous scaling question, find out what the client has done to have reached and maintained current level of progress.
7. Find out where on the previously-mentioned scale (step five) the clients think others (probation officer, caseworker, children, spouse or partner, pets, employer, etc.) in their lives would rate them.
8. Find out what the client thinks the significant people identified in step seven would say that the client is doing which caused them to rate the client at the level described in step seven.
9. Ask the clients what difference they think significant others would say the behaviors identified in step eight are making.
10. Ask the clients where on the scale (in step five) they hope to be by the next session. Continue to ask questions about how the clients will know they are at this specific place on the scale, what will be different then, etc.
11. Use scaling questions for the clients to rate their confidence in their ability to sustain the changes (or to scale the referral source's confidence that the clients can sustain the changes). Although we list scaling confidence questions at this stage, we also use this question as needed at any stage throughout the therapy process.
12. Based on responses to questions one through eleven, invite the client to assign self homework

Figure 5.1   Individual Skeleton

struggling with substance-related problems, and because the majority of cases in the solution-focused literature are with clients in individual sessions, we invite you to review the references listed in the appendices for additional examples as needed.

How to Determine When Services Are Finished

Regardless of the setting in which the client is being treated, it is imperative that the therapist has a clear set of guidelines by which to determine when the client is no longer in need of services. Simon Budman and Alan Gurman (1988) wrote about a common misperception held by many professionals that "more is better" when it comes to number of sessions and length of treatment (p. 8). I continue to hear this sentiment echoed in the field today. While there is research to suggest that clients who receive a minimum of 90 days in treatment have better outcomes (National Institute of Drug Abuse, 2000b), it does not suggest that clients do better with treatment that significantly exceeds the 90 days or that more is better. In fact, there is research that suggests that the most significant proportion of change occurs within the first six to eight sessions of a treatment episode for clients receiving individual psychotherapy, and that clients frequently receive diminishing returns with additional sessions (Budman & Gurman, 1988; Cummings & Cummings, 2000). It is thereby logical to conclude that it could be advantageous to see clients in private practice for six to eight sessions over a minimum of 90 days (ironically, this is the precise pattern that clients tend to complete when they are in charge of scheduling their own sessions in my private practice).

However, I have found when working with more complex client systems within an agency setting that other professionals (including probation, child welfare, and the court system) frequently require a significant period of time before they have the necessary confidence in the client that the changes are permanent. There is oftentimes more at risk should the client fail (i.e., child or public safety). Because of this, clients within an agency setting tend to require longer lengths of stay. Despite this, it is important to note that clients within the agency setting frequently make significant changes within the first month or two of services as well, yet it is crucial that the clients understand the necessity of regaining others' trust as part of the treatment process. Therefore, gradually decreasing the clients' services (both group sessions and urine screen frequency) can be a helpful tool to maintain connection with the clients in treatment while giving them increased time between sessions to practice their skills and demonstrate their changes. This decrease in service frequency should be done on a schedule that is comfortable to all members of the client's system to ensure that the process builds confidence rather than erodes it. Let us now look at six factors that need to be considered in order to determine if a client has successfully completed substance abuse treatment services according to standards of care, regardless if the client is being treated in an agency or a private practice setting.

Treatment Plans Completed

As previously stated, treatment plans are the backbone of good therapy, for "setting specific goals clearly influences outcome" (de Shazer, 1988, p. 93). Goals are the agreed upon outcomes, and when written into treatment plans, they outline the contract for change made between therapist and client, and therefore should be the first consideration when determining if services are complete. This may be informally written into progress notes in a private practice setting, or formally written as required in an agency setting. Regardless of the level of formality, both client and therapist should have no doubt as to the specific goals and indicators of when the goals have been completed. Once both client and therapist agree that the goals have been completed and that there are no additional goals that would be helpful, it is time to explore the next element.

No Reported Concerns Within the Client's System

When clients enter treatment, they frequently come bearing a list of problems or grievances that they would like to be resolved. This list becomes the issues list from which both therapist and client work to ensure that the clients' lives are better when treatment has concluded. When working in private practice, this list is oftentimes not written down; however, therapist and client verbally sort the list together to determine which items will be addressed during treatment. These elements then become part of the treatment plan. When working with clients in an agency setting, other members of the clients' systems frequently have issues to add to the list of what must be addressed prior to treatment being concluded. In addition, regulations and standards of care (as mentioned in Chapter 4) also necessitate additional elements that must be added to the list. Therefore, this list is usually written down into a formal issues or problems list when working in an agency, with a clear delineation of which agency will address which issue in order to demonstrate that the appropriate disposition has been noted (see Chapter 9 for a sample issues list). Regardless of the formality used for the function, each issue must be addressed or assigned to an appropriate party prior to discharge.

Evidence of Lack of a Problem

The degree of evidence needed to substantiate that the problem has been resolved varies significantly according to the setting. For example, when I work in private practice, I do not have access to any method to prove that the client is substance-free. Therefore, I only accept cases in which verbal proof is sufficient, referring all others to agency settings. However, verbal evidence is hardly neither sufficient nor appropriate when working in an agency setting with clients who are involved with the legal system, who have put others in harm's way, or who have lost the trust of others. In such settings, it is necessary to obtain the form of evidence that is widely accepted in your geographic location. In Colorado, at the time of this writing, that would be random urine screens (that are physically observed and also screen for alcohol). While other methods are available (i.e., hair testing, scheduled breathalyzers, eye scans, nonobserved urine screens) they are not yet standardized and widely used to the point of meeting standards of care.

The evidence must be consistent (with no missed screens) and valid (with no out-of-range creatinine levels) for a minimum of 30 days. In addition, it is ideal for the period of abstinence to be lengthy enough to sufficiently demonstrate that the client has the ability to utilize the skills for a period of time during which stressors and other naturally occurring life events took place. For some client systems that is 30 days, while for others it may be two or three months, depending on the risk to others should the client relapse.

Elements That Put the Client at High Risk Are Resolved

William Cloud and Robert Granfield have done some excellent research about the phenomenon of spontaneous remission in those who were dependent upon substances (Cloud & Granfield, 2001; Granfield & Cloud, 1999). Through their work, they discovered that people who were successful in overcoming severe alcohol and other drug problems without outside treatment had several personal and environmental characteristics in common (Cloud & Granfield, 2001, pp. 159–160):

1. They tend to be high school graduates, many with college or more advanced degrees.
2. Most have vocational or professional skills, or otherwise are employable and are generally employed during their addictions. Of these, many are self-employed.
3. Overall, they tend to have the verbal skills that allow them to verbally express themselves and interact in various social settings.
4. They are often introspective, with an ability to self-evaluate their behavior and make appropriate plans and choices to solve problems.
5. During their substance dependency periods, many continue to have access to friends and meaningful relationships with others who do not have substance abuse problems.
6. The mental health of nearly all the people we interviewed in our studies was good. Among the few who had experienced mental health problems, such problems were not severe.
7. Most hold conventional pro-social values such as family life, the desire to be successful, the importance of a career, and a concern for how others perceive them.
8. Those who used illicit drugs like heroin and cocaine appear to be able to successfully straddle both the illicit drug subculture and the culture of conventional life.
9. Among those who have had contact with the criminal justice system, such contact tends to be in the form of DUI offenses or minimal legal infractions and incarcerations. They generally cannot be characterized as hard-core criminals.
10. Overall, through their recovery, they came to see themselves as part of a family and a community.

While clearly clients who are seeking services were not able to address their problems without the help of professionals, Cloud and Granfield's research holds clues as to many of the areas that should be addressed during treatment in order to better the odds of long-term success. For example, clients who are employed, who have resolved or stabilized any mental health symptoms, who are associating with friends who do not have problems with substances, who are able to think about how their actions might affect others, who can problem solve, and who have solid positive connections to their community and with others are at decreased risk even if they relapse in the future. It is prudent for therapists to be cognizant of these factors and to assist clients in exploring all of these factors in the context of their miracles prior to discharge.

Relapse or Child Safety Plan Completed

Relapse is a part of learning any new behavior. It is human nature to on occasion return to what is familiar and old hat. It takes time and effort to create new patterns and natural behaviors. Take driving a car, for example. When I first learned, it took all my attention to stay focused on keeping the car moving in the desired direction, let alone shifting into the appropriate gear without killing the engine. I was a bundle of nerves during each lesson for fear of making a fatal mistake. I did make plenty of mistakes, some more serious than others. They were all part of learning to drive. Now with decades of experience, I rarely think about the basic elements of driving or road manners. It is second nature. I still make mistakes on occasion, and because of the inherent risk of accident (both from my own mistakes and from the mistakes of others), I carry emergency equipment to address the situations that may occur.

Clients can fall victim to all-or-nothing thinking, putting them at elevated risk of heavy or binge use when they do slip. Using an analogy such as this with clients can be a very helpful way to normalize the mistakes they will make as they begin to address their substance abuse. Learning to drive is something that most clients have experienced, and most can now laugh about the mistakes and near misses they encountered during the experience. Once they realize that mistakes are part of learning, they can recover more quickly and prepare for the unexpected through creating an "emergency repair kit" (Pichot & Dolan, 2003, pp. 93–96) for the challenges that inevitably lie ahead. Part of this preparing is for clients to think about the potential risk to their children as well, and to think about what tools they will need to have in this emergency roadside repair kit to successfully care for their children. This may include a friend or family member who can care for the child or pick him or her up after school in the case of relapse. Regardless of the name of the plan (relapse plan, child safety plan, or emergency repair kit), all serve the same purpose of helping clients to be prepared for the normal bumps in the road of life ahead. This is essential to have in place prior to discharging a client from treatment.

Change Over 90 Days

In order for therapists to ensure that the work we do is sound, we have to depend on research. Believing we are making a difference alone is not sufficient. It is imperative that research becomes a part of day-to-day practice and guides our decisions with our clients. As mentioned in Chapter 1, evidenced-based practice is part of this effort to increase clinical accountability. This is a good thing as long as we define evidence-based practice as any form of treatment that has not been proved ineffective through research. Solution-focused brief therapy itself was created by carefully observing what worked and discarding what did not. There are many therapeutic practices that remain very promising and warrant further research. Unfortunately, adequate funding for all of the research that needs to be done can be challenging to acquire.

However, research is only valuable when the lessons learned are taken to heart by the therapists themselves and treatment is influenced as a result. One of these lessons is known as the 90-day rule. It is the concept that there is a minimum amount of treatment that is needed in order for client change to be lasting. According to the literature, that minimum is 90 days (National Institute of Drug Abuse, 2000b). Clients are at their highest risk of relapse within this first 90 days (Barnett, Branch, & Hunt, 1971), and additional resources during this time period serve to strengthen these new changes to ensure lasting results. This basic concept simply reminds us to ensure that clients have enough time while they have the support of treatment to fully incorporate the changes into their daily life—to make new habits that are tested by day-to-day challenges. This does not require weekly sessions throughout the treatment period; in fact, it is most effective if treatment is gradually decreased from weekly, to every other week, to even monthly as indicated by the clients' needs. Stepping out of treatment should be the next logical step regardless of how long the client has been engaged in treatment. Treatment frequency should be a fluid process that increases when difficulties arise and decreases when clients are doing well. Therefore, this should be the final factor when determining if treatment is ready to be finished.

Summary

Individual treatment and case management are integral parts of good client care in the substance abuse field. Whether the client is treated within an agency setting or by a private practitioner, the solution-focused therapist utilizes the same basic tenets for assisting the clients to envision and work from a place in which the problem is resolved—long term. In the following chapter we will explore how to effectively use solution-focused brief therapy in a group setting.

Endnotes

1. The case management we are referring to is that which is conducted by the client's therapist as a central part of treatment, for these services require a high level of therapeutic skills. We are not referring to the form of case management that is done by entry-level workers as a separate modality of care.
2. See Pichot and Dolan (2003) for a detailed discussion and examples of how to conduct this form of case management from a solution-focused stance.

6

Solution-Focused Group Therapy

Solutions develop when the therapist and client are able to construct the expectation of a useful and satisfactory change.

Steve de Shazer

Most of the original writing about solution-focused brief therapy was focused on working with individuals or families since this was the context in which the approach was originally developed. This can make it challenging at best to apply these foundational texts to the work with substance abusing clients since the majority of treatment with clients who have substance abuse problems is done in a group setting. In this chapter we will describe how to apply solution-focused brief therapy to a group treatment modality.

Introduction

Throughout the substance abuse treatment literature, one finds that group treatment is most frequently used. Not only is it the most cost-effective approach given the high number of clients needing services and the limited financial resources of the treatment agencies, but it has many clinical benefits as well. Since clients are frequently thought to be in denial about the gravity of their addiction, group settings are oftentimes seen as the most effective forum in which clients can receive direct feedback or confrontation from clients who are further along in the recovery process. In addition, it is oftentimes thought that clients are most likely to listen to the advice of other addicts before they will listen to a professional. It is this thinking that makes therapists who are in recovery themselves viewed as more effective in some treatment models. For example, this is the thinking behind the therapeutic community treatment models, in which clients who have successfully completed the treatment program frequently go on to become counselors for those who are new to the program (De Leon, 2004, p. 485). In approaches such as this, information and mentorship are highly valued and viewed as an integral part of treatment. Therefore, it is imperative when using this kind of model that clients learn to set aside their current way of thinking and follow the suggestions of others in order to conquer their addiction.

In addition, it is commonplace for many treatment groups to be viewed as a microcosm of the clients' world (Yalom, 2005, p. 33). This then allows therapists to use the interactions between clients to help them understand how the clients interact with those in their own lives, and therefore use the interactions with the fellow group members as a way to resolve external relational issues and learn more effective communication and coping skills. This allows the group setting to become a type of safety zone in which the clients can begin to understand themselves and explore more effective behaviors and ways of interacting within the world.

Education Groups

In the majority of substance abuse treatment centers there are two types of groups that are utilized: education groups and treatment or process-oriented groups (Khantzian, Golden-Schulman, & McAuliffe, 2004, p. 391). Both are viewed as highly beneficial in helping clients to better understand maladaptive coping strategies and to exchange these for more effective behaviors. Educational groups are oftentimes seen as the first step in treatment as clients learn about the process of addiction, medical complications caused by the use of substances, family issues, relapse prevention, and so forth. For example, motivational interviewing views this form of treatment as highly beneficial for clients who are in the precontemplative stage of change, for the therapist's role when working with precontemplative clients is to "raise doubt—increase the client's perception of risks and problems with current behavior" (Miller & Rollnick, 1991, p. 18). By providing the client with basic education, it is thought that the therapist is thereby able to increase the client's ambivalence about the current behavior and then move the client to the next stage of readiness for change. It is also in this setting that clients learn the basics that are commonly thought to be necessary in order to have lasting change.

Therapy Groups

Therapy or process-oriented groups are those that have the primary function to promote change in awareness and behavior. In their purest sense they are driven by the needs of the participating clients and not from an external source such as a curriculum. They can be either closed-ended (have a set number of sessions, and other clients are not permitted to join until a new series of sessions begins) or open-ended (different clients may be present during each session, and new clients may join at any point in the process). Open-ended groups are commonly viewed as more closely resembling a microcosm of life (Edelwich & Brodsky, 1992, p. 5) due to the constantly changing environment. The majority of substance abuse treatment groups are open-ended since this is the most cost-effective approach.

Therapy groups require a high level of skill to effectively run, since the therapist must be aware of basic group dynamics, ensure effective group norms, and also ensure that each client's needs are addressed. It can be challenging for treatment centers to ensure that clients' needs are truly being addressed due to the lack of preset agenda that is part of this form of therapy model. Because of this, there has been a recent push toward using more curriculum-based treatment approaches in both educational and therapy groups due to their prescriptive nature. The curriculum's effectiveness can be more easily researched to demonstrate its ability to obtain the desired outcome with clients, leaving less discretion to the individual therapists. These kinds of approaches can be very effective to ensure that clients have a basic level of treatment that covers specific elements, especially when the group is being led by a novice-level therapist who might otherwise miss crucial elements needed for recovery.

Support Groups versus Treatment Groups

Given the history of the field of substance abuse treatment, there is oftentimes confusion in both professionals' and clients' minds about the differences between a support group and a treatment group. According to Laban (1998), "There was considerable blurring between treatment and A.A., and this continues today" (p. 32). In order to effectively work with clients in a treatment capacity, it is imperative that we as professionals are clear about the differences, for the group norms and goals of each are very different. For example, it is commonplace for a client who finds Alcoholics

Anonymous helpful to come to a treatment group and begin exchanging telephone numbers or offering resources and mentorship to a fellow group member. While that behavior is very appropriate in the context of Alcoholics Anonymous or other support groups, it would most likely not be appropriate in the context of a treatment group. Let us take a more in-depth look at both of these types of groups.

Support Groups

There are many different kinds of support groups for those who are struggling with substance abuse-related problems. Alcoholics Anonymous is the most established and most recognized. From that organization came a plethora of other organizations that are based upon the 12 steps, such as Narcotics Anonymous, Crystal Meth Anonymous, Alateen, and Al-Anon, just to name a few. Over the years, additional support groups became available, such as Women for Sobriety, Rational Recovery, Moderation Management, and Save Our Selves, as well as countless others. All of these have an invaluable role in the recovery of those struggling with a substance abuse problem. There is definitely something to be said about being part of a group. According to SAMHSA (2006b), groups for substance abusers provide peer support, reduce isolation, offer family-like experiences, and instill hope.

In the majority of support groups, the groups are facilitated by one of the members rather than a mental health professional. This person not only facilitates the group, but also participates as a group member, sharing his or her own story and problems as well. Each person speaks about what he or she needs to address, and group members are simply there to offer support, ideas, and any other help they can. Everyone is welcome, and there is no prescreening to determine if someone is appropriate to be a part of the support group. In addition, it is common for group members to exchange phone numbers and to encourage each other to call any time of the day or night. There is a resultant sense of purpose and duty to help one another. Group members frequently tell their stories during the meetings, telling others of their experience, strength, and hope (Alcoholics Anonymous, 1976). It is by telling their stories that they remember the lessons learned and encourage others that change is possible. For some, a support group is all that is needed, while for others, a support group is more effective when combined with formal treatment or as part of a continuing care plan. Still others find that support groups are not helpful at all, for some find that "attendance at recovery-oriented meetings often triggers the very thing it is supposed to help stop" (Miller & Berg, 1995, p. 52). For those who find support groups helpful, they may participate in them for years, while others may find their need to participate in such a group more transient in nature.

Treatment Groups

Treatment groups offer many of the same benefits as support groups (such as a sense of belonging and being understood); however, they are different in many ways. First, treatment groups are always facilitated by a professional who is skilled in group leadership. This leader does not take part in the group process as a group member, but is present for the sole purpose of facilitating the group. This adds a sense of objectivity and allows the therapist to view the group itself as well as the individual clients as his or her responsibility. Second, clients are first screened to determine that they are appropriate for the purpose of the therapy group. This helps to ensure that all clients have something that they want to address in the group setting as well as ensuring that the clients will not be disruptive to the group process. Third, there is always the expectation that all clients actively work toward change when in a treatment group. While some groups may use a topic-based approach to facilitate a discussion, others use treatment plans or individual client goals as the agenda. Regardless of the format, all clients in a treatment group have been identified as needing to work toward some form of change by being a part of the group process. This serves to focus the clients on themselves during the group process rather than on each other. This results in a sense of taking responsibility for oneself in a treatment group rather than relying on the assistance of one another. The therapist is ultimately responsible for the welfare of each client, and clients are encouraged to call the therapist for assistance rather than to call one another. The ultimate goal of a treatment group is to resolve one's issues and to successfully leave treatment. Therefore, dependence on one another is discouraged, and independence and the ability to locate and use resources are encouraged.

While we recognize the valuable role that support groups play in the lives of many who are addressing substance abuse issues, our focus for the purpose of this chapter will be the treatment group. We will now take a more in-depth look at solution-focused group therapy and how we use this treatment modality to effect change.

Solution-Focused Group Therapy

As Linda Metcalf (1998) so eloquently wrote, "How simple the solution focused model is and yet how difficult it is when learning it to believe in its simplicity and flexibility" (p. 186). Nowhere is this more true than when learning how to apply solution-focused brief therapy to a group setting. When working with groups, it can be extremely challenging to remember to simply apply solution-focused brief therapy as it was originally designed, without succumbing to the belief that it must be somehow modified, or that components of it are somehow no longer applicable. It is our hope to help the reader understand that when working with groups, the solution-focused basics remain unchanged; the miracle question remains the foundation, and the work is done from a place in which the problem is resolved. The only difference is that the therapist is doing this simultaneously with multiple clients, and therefore must skillfully weave all of their miracles together while still retaining the profound respect for each individual that is the hallmark of solution-focused brief therapy. Simple, yet extremely difficult to master. When using solution-focused brief therapy in a group setting, there are five key areas in which solution-focused group therapy is unique:

1. The groups are treatment plan driven.
2. Clients are focused on themselves and their goals.
3. The group is seen as a place to work on individual miracles.
4. The clients gain unique benefits from working in a group setting.
5. The therapist takes a neutral and curious stance when addressing norms.

Let us explore each of these areas in more depth.

Treatment Plan Driven

When using solution-focused brief therapy, there is no need for formalized educational groups. All clients are viewed as unique in what they know, what they need, and how they best obtain information. Because of this, providing education in a group format is not consistent with this approach, for it is unlikely that a group of clients would find the same information helpful. I have also found it to be beneficial to have various informational pamphlets available to clients so that clients can readily access needed information as they see fit. Resource lists and other informational material can be very helpful to empower clients in finding information they need without having to attend structured educational sessions. When additional educational materials are needed, learning how to find and access these resources can be written into the client's treatment plan to help provide the client with the knowledge of how to find needed materials in the future. Once therapists hone their skills in truly listening to what individual clients say would be useful, therapists can readily identify what information the client is saying would be helpful, and can then empower the client to find this information in the most appropriate location.

Instead of using the group process to obtain needed educational materials, the focus in a solution-focused group setting is on helping the clients to obtain their individual miracles. There is an ancient Chinese proverb that says, "Give a man a fish, and he eats for a day. Teach him how to fish, and he eats for a lifetime." Solution-focused brief therapy follows this wisdom by constantly assisting the clients in learning how to fish rather than succumbing to the immediate desire to give them resources directly.

Focus on Themselves and Their Goals

Most human beings have a natural desire to help those around them who are in need. It is commonplace for clients to offer resources, suggestions, and ideas to other group members. While their intentions are well meaning, we have found it most helpful to encourage clients to focus on their own needs and solutions during the group process, and to allow the therapist to skillfully elicit answers from other group members. A critical element of effective solution-focused brief therapy is to assist the clients in evaluating the effectiveness of various behaviors for themselves. Learning this ability to think critically is necessary to ensure a successful future. Many of our clients come to us as a result of well-intentionally following other people's inaccurate advice or not thoroughly evaluating the potential consequences before they took action. Solution-focused brief therapy assists clients in developing critical thinking through the use of scales, difference questions, and relationship questions. It is our role as therapists to assist our clients in learning the necessary skills to fully evaluate their potential actions to determine if it will indeed be helpful in getting them to where they want to be in life. Because of this important clinical task, it is imperative that we teach clients in a group setting to allow their fellow group members to evaluate the effectiveness of potential behaviors without the input of others. By learning this skill, clients are then able to take this skill into their own life to avoid potential pitfalls.

Group Is Seen as a Place to Work on Individual Miracles

The foundation of all solution-focused work is the miracle question, for according to Steve de Shazer (1994), "The 'miracle question' is a way to begin constructing a bridge between therapist and client built around the (future) success of the therapy" (p. 95). Insoo Kim Berg (1994) goes on to say, "Answering these miracle questions will provide him with clues on what first steps he needs to take to find solutions" (p. 100). While other writers emphasize the importance of exceptions and group members' competencies (Metcalf, 1998) when using solution focused therapy in a group setting, we challenge the reader to look beyond this initial application of the approach to utilize the miracle question as it was truly intended: to assist the client to imagine a place in which the problems of today are resolved. By making the miracle question the foundation of solution-focused group work (identical to its use with individuals and families), the therapist is acting in accordance with the intentions of the founders of this approach. According to de Shazer et al. (2007), "It makes a difference whether or not the therapist assumes that clients have the capacity to create meaningful descriptions of what they want their lives to look like and how they want to be in the world. Asking the miracle question both implies and demands faith in the client's capacity to do this and the question needs to be asked in a manner that communicates that faith" (p. 39). By placing the miracle question as the central intervention, we are hereby expressing this faith in our clients, and they respond in kind.

Benefits From Working in a Group Setting

While our approach to working within a group setting is unique in that we discourage group members from giving suggestions and feedback to one another, we do find many benefits of utilizing this treatment modality. There is a healing element to learning that one is not alone in one's struggles and problems. Likewise, it is useful to watch as other group members discover solutions and gain excitement as positive change becomes the norm. We liken solution-focused group process to parallel play in young children. Each is playing independently but is enjoying one another's company. In addition, each is quietly observing what the other is doing and how that might be something he or she might try while each remains focused on his or her own independent activity. It is common to hear clients state that they plan to try something that was learned in the group setting. While the goal is not to intentionally teach other clients what to do, there is a helpful secondary gain of clients overhearing and becoming curious about other client's solutions. For clients who have difficulty imagining alternative behaviors, such a setting can be just the environment they need to jump-start their own solutions.

Lastly, working within such a group environment has the powerful benefit of increasing the clients' hope that change is possible. By becoming witness to other clients' painful situations transforming into exciting futures, clients cannot help but become hopeful that such changes are possible for them as well. These eyewitness accounts are much more powerful than any statements or stories that we as professionals could ever give. As Berg and Dolan (2001) state, "Hope is the greatest gift we can offer our clients" (p. 85). We could not find it more fitting that in solution-focused brief therapy groups, this hope is offered from client to client.

Neutral and Curious Stance When Addressing Norms

Yalom (2005) states that it is the therapist's job to recognize and prevent factors that jeopardize group cohesiveness. This safe environment must be present in order for clients to feel comfortable to talk openly and to truly explore possible solutions. Edelwich and Brodsky (1992) go on to state that "a group can function effectively only in an atmosphere of discipline and respect for the purposes of the group" (p. 10). This can be a challenging proposition since many clients who have been externally mandated into substance abuse treatment services initially present as angry and frustrated that they have to participate at all. Because of this inherent challenge, many texts instructing how to effectively work with the "resistive client" in a group setting are now commonplace and considered to be valuable for group facilitators.

Solution-focused group therapists agree that this basic supportive and respectful environment is key to any effective client change when utilizing this treatment modality; however, we do not find it helpful to assume that we know the motivation behind the disruptive behavior when it occurs. Because we take this not-knowing stance when we facilitate a group, the therapist assumes a very curious attitude when addressing situations as they arise. Clients' comments or behavior might be addressed in a group setting if it can be done in a genuinely respectful way, or it might be done by politely asking the client to follow the facilitator out of the room for a more private interaction. Regardless of where the therapist decides to address the issue at hand, the therapist's focus remains on what the client is needing and what he or she would find most helpful, rather than instructing the client as to what the client should or should not do in the group setting. We have found that focusing on what the client needs most frequently resolves the disruptive behavior. We will take a more in-depth look at how we address norms in the following chapter.

Group Skeleton

In order to fully understand how to effectively apply solution-focused brief therapy to a group setting, it is helpful to understand the basic outline or skeleton (see Figure 6.1) from which the therapist works (Pichot & Dolan, 2003, pp. 48–49).

Let us take a look at each step in more detail using portions of a transcript of a group session I facilitated working with three clients, who were all externally mandated for services.

1. Ask an introduction question. Invite group members to say their names and answer the introduction question.

Teri: So is it OK if I spend some time getting to know you guys a little bit?
Group members: Yeah [all nodding in agreement].
Teri: Alright. [Looking to all group members; ready to begin group] I guess my first question would be: Who are you? What I mean by that is: What is most important to you? How would you describe you?
Judy: OK. I always go first. Umm ... OK ... I am Judy ... to describe in words ... outgoing, a caring people-person. What is most important to me right now is my child, my baby.
Teri: OK.
Judy: A couple weeks ago we made symbols, and I have to show you. I know you guys are probably sick of seeing it but I have to show you anyway [she passes an item over].
Teri: Oh, that is wonderful [making a purposeful decision to allow this since it is directly related to a previous treatment group discussion,

---

Group Skeleton

1. Ask an introduction question. Invite group members to say their names and answer the introduction question.

2. Group leader silently identifies common themes from group answers and finds a broader theme that includes all the common themes. This is done through silently asking self questions that assist the therapist in hearing what is important to all of the clients.

3. Group leader reflects (aloud) similarities among group members' responses, summarizing common themes until all are included, and then suggests one broad, inclusive theme.

4. Group leader asks the group's permission for the group to address the theme identified in step 3 unless there is another (emergency) issue that needs to be addressed.

5. Ask miracle question (or similar future-oriented question) based on the theme identified in step 3.

6. Get as many details as possible about the miracle question (or similar question asked in step 5).

7. Listen for exceptions, and follow up by getting as many details as possible. If no exceptions are identified, move on to next step.

8. Ask scaling question to determine clients' current level of progress toward their goals.

9. Referring to previous scaling question, find out what the clients have done to reach and maintain current level of progress.

10. Find out where on the scale (step 8) the clients think others (probation officer, caseworker, children, spouse or partner, pets, employer, etc.) in their lives would rate them and what the clients are doing that would cause this rating.

11. Ask group members what role this conversation (steps 1 to 10) regarding the group theme plays in working toward their miracles. (How was this conversation helpful in getting closer to the miracle?)

12. Based on their responses to steps 1 to 11, invite the clients to assign themselves homework.

13. Give group members feedback.

Figure 6.1 Group Skeleton

but immediately directing the conversation away from support group-like conversation]! So what does this represent?

Judy: My baby.

Teri: What is his name? [Seeking to connect with the client before asking more direct questions about purpose and relevance]

Judy: Tony. The other side …

Teri: [Turning the item over] Oh!

Judy: Should look at it first because that's ... he was 1 pound 6 ounces when he was born, and if I didn't do drugs, he would have been a "chunky monkey."

Teri: And now he is a "chunky monkey" even though ...

Judy: Yeah ... he is now. [Smiling. Clearly proud of her accomplishments]

Teri: And so, having this ...

Judy: Helps me. Helps me get through day by day, and keeps me focused.

Teri: OK. So being focused keeps you going.

Judy: Exactly!

Teri: Because Tony is most important.

Judy: Exactly!

Teri: OK. Very helpful. Thank you. And you ... [Turning to the next client]

Sam: Hmm. I'm not quite as good at this.

Teri: That's OK. You have lots of time to practice.

Judy: I've been here longer than you [laughing, trying to encourage Sam].

Teri: That's OK. You have an angel on your calf there to protect you. Who are you?

Sam: [Smiling at the reference to his tattoo] That's a teenager rebellion thing.

Teri: Yeah? You still there or have you moved on?

Sam: No. I've moved on.

Teri: Where are you now?

Sam: I don't know. I'm past that, but I don't know how to explain where I'm at. I just need to get this stuff out of the way.

Teri: So this isn't where you are [motioning to the tattoo]. Are you where you want to be?

Sam: No. I'm here.

Teri: OK. Fair answer [careful not to push too much]. So, this is your past [motioning to the tattoo]. You're here now. What's important to have in the future?

Sam: I don't know ... I just don't know. I'd just like my own place. Stuff like that.

Teri: And what would that tattoo look like?

Sam: [Looking up for the first time and directly at me]

Teri: If you had one on the other calf. You know ...

Sam: Hmm. Maybe ... I don't know [looks back down to the ground]. Then I would know what to do.

Teri: That's fair. And how about you? [Turning to the third group member]

Bob: I'm an outdoor person ... somewhat of an adrenalin junkie. Fun to be around, but I have a tendency to be quick tempered at times. Umm ...

Teri: What's important to you?

Bob: What's important to me is to just try to be a good person. Try not to be so impulsive. Try not to be so ... I have my moments of being like really an asshole. Try not to be an asshole all the time to people.

Teri: Uh hum.

Bob: And just to find some moderation in my life. Everything I do with almost ... I can't say with an addiction. I can't do anything in moderation. It's either 100% or nothing. So I need to find that in-between. My whole life has been that way. I'm a Libra, and Libra's have a hard time balancing. It's either this way or that way. My life has been pretty much a roller coaster.

Teri: Would you like to find that balance? Would that be something that would be helpful, or ...

Bob: Oh yeah, I mean ... I've been finding it for a while now.

Teri: OK. Have you found it or are you finding it? Where are you?

Bob: Well ... for a long time there I thought I found it, but I kind of had a relapse in the last couple of weeks. I really overextended myself with work and stuff. Turned out to be a very bad thing for me because I got mentally and physically exhausted. My family kind of went downhill. My mom ... she's been watching my kid, and I worked like 21 days straight and didn't get to spend a lot of time with Susan. My mom is 72 years old and is a diabetic. I mean, she's not feeling too good ... [Settling in the chair for a long conversation]

Teri: Hang on a minute. Can I interrupt you? I lose my questions pretty easy.

Bob: OK.

2. Group leader silently identifies common themes from group answers and finds a broader theme that includes all the common themes. This is done through silently asking self questions that assist the therapist in hearing what is important to all of the clients.

The theme is at times a word, such as *coping*, and at other times more of a phrase or concept, such as "balancing what is on your plate." The keys to identifying a theme is that it must come directly from what is most important to the clients at that specific point in time, and it must be a solid fit for each and every client. If it does not fit each client, it is too narrow, and the therapist must mentally step back and see what would be a concept that is inclusive of all of the clients. At this point in the group, all of the clients have expressed who they are and what is important to each of them. We are approximately six minutes into the two-hour group, and it is time to begin my transition from the introduction to the working phase.

At this point in the group, I have all that I need to know to begin to develop my theme. This can be a challenging step in the process since the group facilitator must both mentally organize what the clients gave while continuing to lead the group. I usually find it helpful to begin to summarize parts of what I know while I continue to develop the theme within my own head. This helps me to remember what I know while I continue to search for how to organize the remaining parts. In this example, I have a sense that each client does have something concrete that he or she wants to be different; however, I am aware that I do not have a word to succinctly summarize what they want, which will make it very difficult for the clients to follow along. Having some way to quickly reference what it is that they told me they want will be important to quickly connect each client into our work throughout the session. Here is how I gather those missing parts:

Teri: We will come back to that because I really want to get to what you're talking about there. But, what I'm curious about is if you had to pick one word that is most important to you, what is it?

Bob: Maybe consistency or stability.

Teri: OK … OK … so consistency or stability. [Turning to Judy to re-engage her in the conversation] Focus.

Judy: Focus [confirming that focus was what was most important to her].

Teri: [Turning to Sam to re-engage him] And getting through, but you're not quite sure what it is.

Judy: And what do you call self-esteem … I'm trying to work on? … Confidence!

Teri: Confidence. OK. Is there a word, Sam, that's coming to you that's like this that is something that you want?

Sam: Responsible.

Teri: Responsible … OK.

3. Group leader reflects (aloud) similarities among group members' responses, summarizing common themes until all are included, and then suggests one broad, inclusive theme.

Teri: So tell me again … Responsible [to Sam], confidence [to Judy], and … [Motioning to Bob to fill in the blank. This is done very purposefully to help Bob connect to a single word or phrase since he tends to talk in stories, which can be too distracting for group work.]

Bob: Umm … What did I say? … Stability!

Teri: Stability. OK. Remember those. Is that OK?

Group members: [All nod in agreement.]

4. Group leader asks the group's permission for the group to address the theme identified in step 3 unless there is another (emergency) issue that needs to be addressed.

Teri: Those are big things! So let me ask you this: Would this be helpful to talk about, or is there something more important to talk about today? Like you talked about relapse and stuff … Would that be important to go back to, or if we talk about these things …

Bob: You know … I just got way into my work and other things suffered and … [Returning to storytelling]

Teri: But if you had what we are talking about here, would that make these relapses and stuff go away? [Refocusing him on what he said he wanted]

Bob: I think they went away by the last time I went to class. I told the therapist that I was on the verge of something … you know. Getting drunk or getting high … because I was just so exhausted.

Teri: Yeah … and when you are stable, you won't have those.

Bob: Yeah! [Suddenly connecting to how focusing on what he said he wanted would make a difference]

Teri: So if we could give you this gift of stability, these other things will go away.

Bob: Yeah! I went to court and they said I could have my girl back at anytime, and after that a lot of things fell into place and it's like this one guy that I was working with …

Teri: Is it OK if I cut off some of your stories?

Bob: OK. [Not offended at all]

Teri: Is that alright? If there's a story that is really important … 'cause I don't want to be rude.

Bob: OK.

Teri: Part of my style is to … 'cause I have to keep three people's stories together …

Bob: Yeah. OK.

Teri: OK. Back to my question. If we worked on confidence, responsibil-
     ity, and stability, would this be a worthwhile group? Or is there
     something more pressing that you showed up today to get?

The therapist's acknowledgment of Bob's use of the word *relapse* and
checking in to see if it would be more helpful to directly address this is
a good example of the therapist being cognizant of more emergency or
urgent issues. Should Bob have stated that it would be helpful to address
the relapse or had another client mentioned an urgent matter, the therapist would have then incorporated it into this group's theme of "things the
clients want to have more of." For example, relapse could have easily been
incorporated by adding "the ability to stay on the path" as a verbal way to
connect Bob into the theme. In this case, none of this was needed, for Bob
was comfortable working on stability.

**7. Listen for exceptions, and follow up by getting as many details as pos-
sible. If no exceptions are identified, move on to next step.**

While this step is listed in the skeleton as step 7, many parts of the
skeleton are not a linear process. The group therapist is constantly challenged during all parts of the group process to listen for exceptions and to
determine when it would be most helpful to follow an offered exception.
The key to following up on exceptions is for the therapist to always do so
in a purposeful fashion and to then remember where he or she was in the
group process once the exception has been explored. In this transcript, I
decided to follow an exception that a client offered at this point in the skeleton, so I moved this step out of order for the purpose of this example.

Judy: Well, one thing we talked about last week. We had two homework
     assignments. One was to live your miracle day, which I did not
     do. Didn't plan ahead, and didn't do it.
Teri: OK.
Judy: And the second thing was to … where my problem with confidence
     is … to let yourself be vulnerable and how do you deal with that
     vulnerability. How to without doing the usual … turning to
     drugs, or how do you … do you know what I'm saying?
Teri: Yeah. Let me make sure I …
Judy: I did do that!
Teri: Wow! How did you do that? [Not really sure where this will lead, but
     it seemed like an important exception to follow]

Judy: Well, I set it up. It wasn't really real because I didn't get any call from friends I shouldn't be hanging out with. I didn't get any tests, but I just set up with my sister. She called me and was like, "Do you want to go get high?" I set it up ahead of time. I told her sometime this week, I want you to call me. My sister has nothing to do with drugs. She's not ... she's like a person I look up to.

Teri: So it was like a trial run.

Judy: It totally was. Because last time I was truly tested, I did not pass, so I didn't have a test this past week, so I wanted it set up for me.

Teri: And so how did you do?

Judy: I did good! I said, "OK. I'll call you back," but I didn't call back. I called my boyfriend, and I said, "My sister wants to go get high. I need someone around me to keep me from doing it." So he said, "OK. Let's go play pool." So he picked me up, and we went and played pool and just talked about the pros and cons of if I did get high. What would I lose? What would I gain? Stuff like that.

Teri: Oh! Sounds cool! I have about 10 questions in my head, but I'm going to put them on hold for just a second. Would this be helpful now? Because I want to be sure that today's group is helpful for all three of you. Not just two and not just one. Like we talked about getting these qualities. Would that be helpful? [When working in a group setting it is important not to work too long with an individual client, since it runs the risk of losing the attention and interest of the other group members. At this point, I am purposefully returning to the group skeleton, by gently directing the group members back to step 4 to determine if it would be helpful to everyone to proceed with the theme.]

Group members: [All nod]

Teri: For real? OK. So here's my question ...

5. Ask miracle question (or similar future-oriented question) based on the theme identified in step 3.

Taking the time to thoroughly engage each client prior to asking the miracle question is key. This section demonstrates the therapist's continual efforts to walk beside the clients to determine their potential response to the miracle question, address their concerns, and then to develop a yes set to ensure the clients are comfortable and willing to think in a different way. Being careful to hear and engage each client during this stage will prevent clients from voicing disagreement to the miracle question at a later time during the intervention (when it would be disruptive to the group process).

Teri: Now you may have heard this question before, but I promise that if you guys really poured your hearts into this question, you would be done with treatment. I can't stress this enough. This is like the magic bullet.

Group members: [Smiling, and starting to become engaged again]

Judy: Uh oh! [Said in a playful tone]

Teri: Do you guys believe in magic bullets?

Judy: No, but I believe in magic doors! [Playfully referring to a modification of the miracle question used with that group before, as the other group members joined in the lighthearted laughter (Pichot & Dolan, 2003, p. 81)]

Teri: OK. Good! OK ... You guys have heard of the miracle question? [Nods from the group members] You guys willing to go through it with me?

Sam and Bob: Yeah.

It is important to note here that it is because of the careful preparation for asking the miracle question that the clients are now very comfortable to move forward with the intervention. Without this, the clients might have stated no to this question, presenting a conundrum for the therapist. Prevention is the key here.

Judy: I always have trouble with this question.

Teri: And that's OK ... That's OK. Are you willing to go through it with me?

Judy: Yes ... Yes. [Here is the yes set.]

Teri: Because it's such a powerful question, and I guarantee that if you do it in your heart, even if it takes you 10 times, this is a question that can never be done too many times. OK? But if you get stuck, let me know. So, here's the question: Are you guys all going home after this tonight?

Group members: Yeah.

Teri: OK. Here's the question. So I want you to imagine that when you go home tonight and go to bed, this miracle happens. And this miracle is that you get this trait we are talking about ... you are stable. You have that stability [to Bob]. You have that confidence [to Judy]. And you are responsible [to Sam]. Not too much, just as much as you want. Can you picture it [to all]? What this trait would look like? So here's the catch: You were asleep, and so you don't know that you got this miracle. So my question is: When you first wake up, what are the first small, itsy bitsy signs that let you know that something's different? That this miracle happened even before you put your feet on the ground, or maybe before you open your eyes?

6. Get as many details as possible about the miracle question (or similar question asked in step 5).

Judy: The only thing I can think of before I even get out of bed would be … umm … a feeling of relief.

Teri: Yeah? So you have this sense of relief. What else would be different that would let you [to the group as a whole] know something's different … you have that confidence, or you have that responsibility, or stability?

Judy: I hate this question.

Teri: I know, but it's so important [said with a mix of compassion and encouragement].

Since the therapist had discovered during step 5 that this client has difficulty with the miracle question, this is not a surprise. Because this has already been addressed and the client has already agreed to walk through this intervention despite her struggles, this does not become a distraction here. A simple acknowledgment is all that is needed. Should this step not have been taken, this would have required more work by the therapist at this point to address this concern, risking a distraction for the rest of the group.

Bob: I would probably wake up with a little more focus.

Teri: Yeah?

Bob: Yeah!

Teri: What would you be focused on this morning?

Bob: Umm … Just everything in general. I'm usually so scatterbrained …

Teri: But on this morning …

Bob: My thoughts are clear about what I gotta do without my uh … self-doubts, insecurities, and other things interjecting into my thought process.

Teri: OK. That would be a lot!

Bob: Yeah!

Teri: That would be a huge difference.

Bob: Yeah! It's just lately it's been real rough for me because I've been so close to getting my kid back, and so scared like I've done all this work, but I'm scared to death!

Teri: So on this miracle day, instead ...

The client steps out of the miracle day on many occasions during this transcript, but is easily refocused by the therapist. When working with a client such as this, it is imperative that the therapist notices as soon as the client steps out of the miracle day and resists the temptation to follow the client away from the miracle day toward coping questions. Because the therapist notices the meandering, she can easily refocus the client back on what will be different on this miracle day. Later on during this transcript, the client begins to self-correct with no prompting from the therapist.

Bob: I'd be focused ... the insecurities are gone, and I could focus on what needs to be done and stay there.

Teri: OK.

Bob: Not overwhelmed myself ... so I don't ... you know ... do something in excess to get away from something.

Teri: Umm hmm. You have these clear thoughts.

Bob: Yeah! There's none of the doubt or any of these other things I have been having lately.

Teri: OK.

Bob: How I'm going to deal with being a single father ...

Teri: Almost sounds like you have more self-confidence.

Judy: I was going to say ... self-doubt would be completely gone. [Talking about herself]

Bob: Yeah!

Teri: Yeah ... So does that relate?

This is a nice example of the therapist linking the clients' words together while still encouraging each to work on his or her own miracle. This linking creates the relevance that is needed to ensure that all of the clients continue to listen and work on their own miracles even when another client is speaking. This keeps all of the clients engaged and creates a comfortable pace for the group through allowing and facilitating client interrupting and interacting in a respectful and purposeful manner.

Bob: Yeah. I've never felt this way my whole life until just after my last court date. It's like I can get her back anytime now but ...

Teri: That's a lot of pressure ...

Bob: It's almost like ... have I been lying to myself? Is this really what I want? I've worked so hard for this, but now it's here ... and are you going to be able to deal with it?

Teri: So on this miracle day you would have that confidence that you can deal with it. Is there anything else you [looking to Judy] would add to this since you both are in a similar ...?

Judy: Confidence, but for a different reason.

Teri: Exactly.

Judy: I would say the self-doubt would be gone.

Bob: That self-doubt just drains you of all your energy.

Teri: So you would have more energy? [To Bob]

Bob: Yeah!

Teri: Is that what you are saying?

Bob: Yeah! I would! I would because I just spend all this energy. I spend 16 hours at work and only get 10 hours of work done, and look back and think, "What did you do all day?" It's like all day, I'm just thinking of stuff all day and then I'm exhausted. It's like ...

Teri: So on this morning, you would be waking up and have all this energy.

Bob: I'd have all this energy. I've got energy. I'd be focused, I'd be self-confident.

Teri: How about you [to Sam]? You are lying there in bed. What's different?

Sam is a nice example of a client who would most likely not speak if the therapist did not provide an opening for him. He is willing to participate, but responds best to the therapist making a turn for him.

Sam: I'd be thinking of things that I could do.

Teri: OK. That sounds sorta similar. That focus. Is that on track or not?

Sam: That's part of it.

Teri: OK. So help me understand.

Sam: Just thinking. I'd be like lying there and important things would just ... you know ... be there, so I can get things done.

Teri: Do you mean like prioritizing? Is that it?

Sam: That's a good word for it.

Teri: OK. So just knowing that this is most important. I don't know if you guys are seeing it, but it seems like there are some things in common. You [to Judy] started the group talking about this focus.

Judy: Umm hmm.

Teri: And you [to Bob] are talking about clear thoughts. [Bob nods.] And you [to Sam] are talking about this ability to prioritize. Do those fit?

Bob: Yeah! If I could stay focused, I could prioritize, but right now everything in my life is just chaotic. In chaos.

Teri: Yeah. So this miracle would be a pretty big deal? What would be different in your life if you [to Sam] were able to prioritize?

Sam: Umm. Just things would fall into place. Things would get taken care of.

Teri: Hmm. What would be different about you this morning that would allow you to follow through with it? You know in your head, and you're clear on how you would prioritize, but what would be different when you put your pants on … going through your morning?

Sam: I have no idea.

Teri: Yeah? I know I have a lot of questions. [Sam smiles, clearly connected despite his difficulty answering.] Let me ask you this. Who notices first thing? Who is around?

Some clients are more aware of what others would notice or what others are doing than of their own internal process. This is common with adolescent clients, but can also be found with adult clients. When clients have a difficult time speaking from their own perspective, it can be useful to ask questions about what others would notice. This provides a useful way to continue a meaningful conversation and better match how the client thinks. Sam is a nice example of this. However, in order to keep the group members united, the shift to relationship questions needs to include everyone.

Bob: My boss would notice first thing. She sees me first thing in the morning.

Teri: Yeah? Anyone notice sooner? A cat? A mouse in the house?

Bob: Probably my dog. I have a dog.

Teri: Dog? You have a dog?

Bob: Umm hmm. He'd probably notice.

Teri: OK. How about you guys [to Judy and Sam]. Who would notice first? Anyone you live with?

Judy: Hmm.

Sam: Dad.

Teri: OK. So, dad [to Sam], dog [to Bob], and Judy?

Judy: My son. But he is only seven and a half months, so …

Teri: If a dog can notice, a seven-and-a-half-month-old child will notice.

Judy: I would be so focused that I would have time to spend with him in the morning.

Teri: Wow!

Judy: Instead of rushing and getting ready and telling him I have to do it because he is not fast enough.

Teri: So he would definitely notice.

Judy: Because I don't get time to spend with him in the morning and that's the best time to spend with him; he's all groggy … just waking up.

Teri: Yeah … So you have time for him.

Judy: Time.

Teri: So what would you do with your time with him?

Judy: Snuggle … definitely … talk, try to get him to say words.

Teri: So you would teach him things.

Judy: Teach him things definitely.

Teri: Wow! Does he learn better in the morning?

Judy: Yes. More active in the morning.

Teri: So you notice these things.

Judy: Yeah. More active in the morning. Umm … I don't know. I think just the general aura of happiness because it's not always there. This day you would just be filled with joy. It's the day you've tried to go to no matter how long you have tried and you've reached it. So …

Teri: So you'd have some time, you'd have some joy. What would your dad [to Sam] notice?

Sam: I was on time.

Teri: On time for …

Sam: School.

Teri: School. So you are getting ready, or what would he notice that makes him say, "Wow! Sam is going to get out of the house on time today!"

Sam: Sit down. Having coffee with him. Waiting to leave.

Teri: Would that be different? Sitting down, having a cup of coffee with your dad?

Sam: Yeah [smiling].

Teri: Yeah? You're smiling [laughing]. I saw that. What would he think of that?

Sam: He would probably think something was wrong! [Both laughing]

Teri: So what difference do you think it would make for him? If you had a few moments with him. What difference would it make for you or him to just slow down and have a cup of coffee?

Sam: He'd appreciate it.

Teri: Really?

Sam: Just to have the time ... since I don't get to spend a lot of time with him. He'd appreciate it.

Teri: What difference would it make for you?

Sam: It'd be OK ... that I got to spend time with him.

Teri: Are you guys pretty close?

Sam: Well ... we are guys ... I mean ... [Talking for the first time with his head up and appearing completely engaged]

Teri: Well yeah. [Laughter by all]

Judy: As close as guys can get.

Teri: But you want that ... in a guy way ...

Sam: In a guy way.

This part of the transcript during which the miracle question is fully explored is very long, and it constitutes the majority of the two-hour group. During this working phase, it became apparent that Judy and Bob's children are the most important people in their lives and that Sam's changes would positively impact his relationship with his mother. All three clients were hoping to make a positive change within these relationships, which resulted in a natural shift in the conversation to the concept that each client wanted to give a gift to these important people—the gift of being a better person. The following are excerpts taken to illustrate the remaining six steps (please note that step 7 was taken out of order and has already been illustrated).

8. Ask scaling question to determine clients' current level of progress toward their goals.

Teri: So I'm wondering on a scale of 1 to 10, 10 being that you have given this gift to your mom [to Sam]. She doesn't worry at all, and she's totally confident that you are the most responsible son she could ever dream of having ... and the two of you [to Bob and Judy] have given this gift to your children. You are totally this kind of person you were mentioning that you want to be. OK? That's a 10. And a 1 is you've never even thought of giving this gift. Where would you say you are?

Judy: 8.5.

Teri: OK.

Bob: Three weeks ago I would have given myself a 9.

Teri: OK. And today?

Bob: About a 7.
Teri: OK. Sam?
Sam: 7.

During this part in the skeleton, it is important to only collect the clients' numbers and save any explanation for the next step. If this is not done, the group can become tangential, and clients can even begin to change their numbers based on what other clients are saying. The therapist's goal is to simply collect the numbers while communicating that there are no wrong numbers.

9. Referring to previous scaling question, find out what the clients have done to reach and maintain current level of progress.

Teri: So you guys have done a lot of work already. Why are you as high as you are?
Bob: Well, I'm at a 7 because I regressed.

Bob's response is very common. Clients are accustomed to justifying why they aren't higher or farther along. It is important that therapists quickly clarify that we are looking for something very different. We want to know why he is as high as he is. This creates a significantly different conversation. One that is more positive and hopeful in nature.

Teri: OK. I guess my question is: So why are you as high as you are? Why a 7 and not a 6?
Bob: Because I haven't totally lost it.
Teri: Yeah?
Bob: It's still there. I caught myself instead of having a relapse, but uh …
Teri: So you put the breaks on as you were sliding.
Bob: Yeah! 'cause I lost a lot of ground.
Teri: So what are those brakes? How did you do that as you were sliding down?
Bob: I actually … thought before I reacted.
Teri: Is that new?
Bob: Yes.
Teri: Wow!
Bob: Usually I'm just so impulsive when I feel that way. I just do and do it, but for once in my life it's someone other than myself. And the thing I thought of was, "If I do this, I could lose Susan."

Teri: Yeah?

Judy: That's exactly what I did this week! Exactly!

Bob: Because when you were talking earlier that's just how my week has
         gone ... was just like your story that you were talking about ear-
         lier, and I wanted to jump in with you 'cause it was kinda like
         that. What she had said, and I wanted to put my little ... in to ...
         but mine was true.

Judy: Yeah, and mine was fake.

Teri: With someone calling you about drugs? [To Bob]

This interruption by joining the conversation and directing it through
asking a question is crucial. Without it, the group would have drifted into
a support group-like setting, and the purpose and focus gained through
the miracle question would have been lost. By the therapist jumping in, the
therapist can easily retain control of the interaction and redirect toward
the questions at hand at the appropriate time.

Bob: No ... it was pretty much my own self. Just being emotionally burned
         out physically and emotionally. I had so many thoughts ...
         When was that? ... About two to three weeks ago ... about get-
         ting drunk or getting high, and that was because I was so tired.
         I was so emotionally just whatever ... and I wanted to either get
         drunk or get high ... something, but instead of reacting impul-
         sively, I decided to do ... take it into other methods of dealing
         with it.

Teri: And how did you do that? How did you think first and remember
         about Susan first?

Bob: We've gone through a lot here ... [Referring to his work in treatment]

Teri: But it's in here [motioning within]. So what did you do?

Bob: I really think I used a lot of skills I learned in this class.

Teri: How did you remember?

Bob: Because I have my emergency roadside repair kit [referring to a relapse
         prevention exercise we had done in a previous group (Pichot &
         Dolan, 2003, pp. 93–95; Johnson & Webster, 2002)]

Teri: You do?

Bob: Yeah. I remembered a lot of things on it. My last homework assignment
         to myself was that I needed to work on my tools. Again, I could
         feel myself slipping, and before I wouldn't have even noticed.

Teri: So that was new ... You noticed.

Most group sessions are a mixture of established and new clients. This interaction is a nice example of how the therapist can simply validate work the client has done in previous sessions, while remaining focused on the work at hand. There is no need to explain to the other clients to which exercise the client is referring. This interaction is purely about Bob and what he has learned. The group members can easily follow Bob's message, that he is making progress. During an interaction such as this, the therapist wants to help the client to determine what he is doing to sustain the changes. Any additional attention given to the previous exercise by the therapist would only send the message that the key was something that we as a professional did. Alternatively, we want the client to identify what he or she did and internalize the change. In this example this was done by highlighting that the client "noticed."

Bob: Yeah. Instead of impulsively going out and getting drunk or high, I thought about the consequences first.

Teri: So that's huge!

Bob: Yeah! I've regressed, but I caught myself [smiling]. I know! I caught myself, and that made me feel really good.

Teri: One more question before I pick on Sam since he thinks I forgot him again. [Playfully responding to the fact that Sam was beginning to appear disengaged] I want to know: What did you learn from this slip that has been the greatest gift?

Bob: That I do have self-control ... maybe not in all aspects, but in a lot of aspects that I didn't have before.

Teri: Yeah? OK. That's an important thing to know about yourself. It's important to remember that in every slip, there are amazing lessons to learn. It sounds like you found yours.

Bob: I did.

Teri: So [turning to Sam] why are you a 7 and not a 6?

Sam: Because I can cope with stuff a lot better. I don't know exactly why I came up with that number. I just know I'm not where I'd like to be, but I'm not doing totally bad.

Teri: So what lets you know you are not doing as bad as "totally bad?"

Sam: Just ... I don't know. Just like my mom is not totally stressed out. I'm still not doing everything, but I'm not totally bad. I talk to my mom now. I used to only talk to her through my dad.

Teri: So this talking to her directly is part of being a 7?

Sam: [Nods]

Teri: What difference does it make to her to talk to her directly?

Sam: Do you mean face-to-face?

Teri: Either way. Just for her to hear from you and not through your dad.

Sam: I think it's a mom thing, but I think it makes her feel good.

Teri: OK.

Sam: She sorta backs off more at a 7.

Teri: So she sorta backs off more as you move up the scale and take charge, become more responsible?

Sam: Yeah.

Teri: I want all of you to imagine that it's next time you are here, and you are higher on the scale. I don't know if it's a half point or a whole point, but you are higher. So you are giving more of this gift to your mom or to your child. What is different that lets you know you are a little higher?

Consistent with solution-focused brief therapy, we ask the client to imagine a place in which the problem is a little more resolved and then to look back from this place when moving up the scale. This prevents us from slipping back into problem-solving thinking.

Judy: Less doubt for me.

Teri: OK.

Judy: I had a lot of doubt. Always worrying about screwing up when I first started coming here.

Teri: So it would be just a little less.

Judy: It's less and less. It used to be … every day that I worried. Now it's maybe once a week, but it's like I'm growing the confidence, so it's like not in my head.

Teri: So what will be in your head … taking up all the space?

Judy: It wouldn't have anything to do with any of this!

Teri: OK. Fair. [Everyone takes a moment to enjoy Judy's humor.]

Judy: I think it would be about learning how to be a good parent because I don't know how to be a good parent. I'm just learning as I go, but I think it would be learning from how my parents raised me … wanting to do stuff different.

Teri: That's like what you were saying [to Bob].

Bob: Pretty much, yeah.

Judy: I think about that all the time. What can I do that I didn't get to do with my parents?

Teri: So you would be thinking, "How could I give to my child the things that I didn't get?" Isn't that what you were saying? [To Bob to highlight the similarities between what both were saying]

Bob: Uh hum.

Judy: How can I improve on what I know? How can I make it better for him? I would also be thinking, "How could I improve myself at work and at home? How could I improve myself with my family and with those I love?"

Teri: So that would be more of what you will have when you are higher?

Judy: Yeah! I'd say about a 9.

Teri: 9.

Judy: Yeah. I can't imagine what 10 would be like ... well, I guess I can since we just went through it ... but I think I'm there. I really can't see myself getting better. I can only see myself going down, and I need to stop thinking about that.

Teri: So how about you guys [to Bob and Sam]. You are higher than you are now. What would let you know?

Bob: Mine would be a little more emotionally stable.

Teri: And how would you know?

Bob: Well, I would feel the way I feel right now without all this self-doubt.

Teri: So what would be there instead?

Bob: There would be some confidence. But see my confidence ... where I'm having the doubt is in being a parent ...

Teri: So where would you think you will be next week?

Bob: Next week? Hopefully I'll be back up to a 9.

Teri: OK, so at a 9, what is going on for you that lets you know, "Yes, I'm a 9."

Bob: Well, I'm getting back on the routine I was on before three weeks ago.

Teri: OK.

Bob: Because I'm not overworked. I have more quality time. I'll be having more time for myself.

Teri: OK.

Bob: 'Cause the last three weeks I haven't had one minute for myself.

Teri: So that goes back to taking that time. Like all of you were talking about ... [to the entire group] slowing down and taking the time. [Back to Bob] So, at a 9, you will have more of that.

Bob: Yeah, but I'll still have the self-doubt of being a parent and the only way I will get over that is by ...

Judy: Being a parent.

Bob: Just experiencing it because every day is going to be a new experience for me.

Teri: So you have an idea of what this 9 is going to look like.

Bob: Oh yeah!

Teri: OK. So it has more of the routine, it sounds like you are very realistic that you will still have some of those doubts, but ...

Bob: But it won't be so much on my mind since I won't be so disoriented 'cause I won't be so tired. I will be able to think more rationally because I'm not disillusioned. I'm not tired. I'll be back on my old routine.

Teri: So it sounds like that's key ... slowing down and taking care of yourself.

Bob: Yeah. Because if I don't take care of myself, how can I take care of anything else?

Teri: I'm going to interrupt you since I want to check in with Sam. So [to Sam], it's next week ...

Sam: Umm hmm ... I'll be higher no matter what next week because I don't have to go to school.

Judy: Sweet!

Teri: Remember ... this scale is about this gift to your mother ...

Sam: She will be higher since she doesn't have to worry about it. I don't have to worry about it.

Teri: OK. So there's a chunk that goes away. So is there anything else that will be different? It sounds like that piece is sorta like gravy. It's going to happen no matter what.

Sam: Yeah.

Teri: So imagine you are higher, what would let you know?

Sam: Probably because I had a good week.

Teri: How did you pull that off?

Sam: Just got my stuff taken care of. That's all I can say. I got my community service done.

Teri: So you prioritized? ... I don't want to put words in your mouth.

Sam: That's kinda what I was getting at.

10. Find out where on the scale (step 8) the clients think others (probation officer, caseworker, children, spouse or partner, pets, employer, etc.) in their lives would rate them and what the clients are doing that would cause this rating.

Because the clients had such a wealth of meaningful things to discuss during this group session and readily identified so many things that they wanted to be different for themselves, I did not find it necessary to interrupt the flow of the working phase of group to ask the clients this question or to explore this concept using a scale format during this group. In addition to having things that they wanted to achieve for themselves, they appeared acutely aware of how their own behavior was currently impacting those they love. Through our conversation about what gift they would like to give to their loved ones, what difference this gift would make, and so forth, the clients were already demonstrating that they were thinking from a systems perspective and that they saw the potential benefit that their current and proposed changes would make on those whom they love. As long as the group therapist is purposefully aware of the necessary steps and is making all decisions in a purposeful fashion, it can be very effective to use the steps in a more fluid fashion. In doing so, not every step will be included in every group. Should the group members have told me that they had achieved all the changes that they wanted to make, I would have spent the majority of the group session exploring step 10 in order to assist the clients in thinking from a broader perspective. In this case, it was not necessary.

11. Ask group members what role this conversation (steps 1 to 10) regarding the group theme plays in working toward their miracles. (How was this conversation helpful in getting closer to the miracle?)

When working with clients in a group setting, we build the theme around what is most important to each client that day. This is always directly connected to their larger miracles, but is oftentimes a smaller component. This step in the skeleton is essential in assisting the clients to connect the work that was done that day back to their larger miracle, thereby ensuring they see purpose in the work done.

Teri: So how was group today helpful in getting you closer to your miracle?
Bob: It made me look a little bit deeper into what I value most … between work, family, my daughter. Let me vent some of my insecurities and get some input from you guys. The last few weeks have been rather shitty, so it feels good just to let it come out.
Teri: So how are you better once it's out?
Bob: Because if I keep it inside, it just stays there and it doesn't get any better, but when I let it out, I can hear myself say it.
Teri: Oh! Is it sorta like doing your laundry? If it stays in the hamper it never gets clean?
Bob: Uh hum.

Teri: So if you get it out, you can see what needs to be cleaned.

Bob: Exactly! If I keep it within myself, it isn't as real.

Teri: So you did some sorting tonight.

Bob: Yeah! I've been doing some sorting since Saturday. I've been reprioritizing my life and what's important.

Judy: I've realized tonight that I have less self-doubt.

Teri: Wow!

Judy: That means to me that I am getting more confident.

Teri: So you have more confidence, and you [to Bob] have more self-control. See how much you learned about yourselves by sorting? And you [to Judy] even made it through the miracle question.

Group: [Everyone laughs at the playful reminder of how difficult the question was initially to Judy.]

Teri: And there was something good at the end! Your life.

Judy: That's what the miracle is.

Teri: How about you, Sam?

Sam: Just gets me back on track. Helps me know what's important. Gets my head on straight.

12. Based on their responses to steps 1 to 11, invite the clients to assign themselves homework.

During the course of the treatment session, clients have uncovered many things that they will be doing differently in the future. They are hopefully now viewing the solutions and themselves in a different light, making finding something that they could do differently now a natural next step. When I work with clients individually, I find it helpful to simply ask them at the end of each session what would make sense to them to work on between now and next time we meet. It is common for clients to identify something that directly relates to our previous conversation to assign themselves as homework. When working with a group, I find it is most helpful to have some form of homework sheet that allows the clients to take a moment and pick something that is meaningful. Oftentimes it is something that they spoke about directly; other times it is an idea that they heard from a group member that they would like to try. This homework sheet also provides a way to reflect back on previous homework tasks they have given themselves, and allows them to see their own progress. (See Chapter 9 for a sample form.)

13. Give group members feedback.

Teri: Before we wrap up for tonight, I wanted to share my thoughts with you. I have been very impressed by the hard work that each of you did. I could tell that each of you was talking about things that were very meaningful and dear to your hearts. For example, these gifts. There was a connectedness that each of you showed with your mom [to Sam], to Tony [to Judy], and to Susan [to Bob]. Each of you mentioned how much each of these people would notice and, in turn, what a difference it would make to you.

Judy: Even a seven-and-a-half-month-old.

Teri: Yes! Even at seven and a half months old! I was struck by how powerful that conversation was and how all three of you know in your hearts that you have to be vulnerable and that this self-doubt is a sign of caring, not a sign of failure. The best parents are the ones who are not afraid to say they don't know ... and [to Bob] how you knew that taking a few steps back isn't necessarily a bad thing ... that important lessons come from slips. You are a better person today because of it. Now sometimes I like to give homework in addition to what you assigned yourself. Today is one of those days. I want you to notice when you give this gift. How did you do it, and what difference does it make? So you never forget how your hearts are joined with that person you love.

Traditionally in solution-focused brief therapy, the therapist takes a break near the end of the session to meet with the team (if the therapist has the luxury of working with a team) or simply to gather one's thoughts and to come up with compliments and ideas of possible experiments (de Shazer et al., 2007, p. 11). While it is most helpful for the therapist to step away from the clients for a moment to create this feedback (for it creates a sense of anticipation in the clients), we realize this is not always possible in all settings. This form of feedback plays an important role in solidifying the lessons and connections that the clients discovered during the group process. By summarizing them and letting the clients know that these lessons and connections were heard and found valuable, the therapist enables the clients to leave the session with the most salient points fresh in their minds. In this example, the additional noticing homework assignment helped to move the work in the session into the clients' daily lives, making it meaningful and likely to positively impact their world.

Summary

Applying solution-focused brief therapy to the group setting is one of the most challenging endeavors. There are many client stories and voices to keep straight, while remembering to effectively address group dynamics and remain true to the approach. It is a skill that takes time and persistence to truly master. Having a solid understanding of the basic skeleton can be very helpful, much like having a road map when navigating a new destination. Unfortunately, despite a road map's usefulness, it can only take the traveler so far when the unexpected occurs. A wise traveler comes prepared for the unexpected and is able to act with fluidity and knowledge when challenges arise. In Chapter 7 we will discuss some of these possible unexpected elements and possible tools to have on hand to increase your confidence as you practice applying this approach to the wonderful world of group therapy.

7

A More In-Depth Look at
Working With Groups

> Complaining about our problems is one way in which we build and maintain
> social relationships. We risk creating a tragic life story for ourselves.
>
> **Gayle Miller and Steve de Shazer**

Working in a group setting can be quite challenging. Although the process
is easily understood, therapists frequently find that the application is difficult. In this chapter we will provide an in-depth look at several elements
of solution-focused group work, and provide the reader with additional
tools to help effectively use this treatment modality.

Group Themes

Why Bother Finding a Theme?

In order to effectively work with multiple clients at one time utilizing solution-focused brief therapy, it is imperative that the therapist have some way
to meaningfully link the clients' conversations together. In family work,
the family members' shared family goal is this meaningful link. However,
when working in a group setting, the therapist's intent is to assist each
client to achieve his or her individual miracle. This necessitates identifying a ligature among a group of individuals who have differing goals.
Without this unifying factor, the work will be analogous to individual
work, with the other clients functioning as audience members until it is
their turn to participate. Without a link, clients who are more accepting
of participating in the group process will well-intentionally turn to more
supportive behaviors as a means to participate, such as giving advise or
making compassionate statements, and even asking additional questions

about problem elements that a solution-focused therapist would otherwise wisely ignore. Clients who are angry that they are mandated into such a setting will oftentimes become distracting, questioning why they have to be present when the conversation at hand has nothing to do with them. This apparent lack of relevance will fuel their discontent.

The solution to these kinds of problems is to help each client find relevance in every group interaction. Therapists who are using problem-focused approaches oftentimes seek to find this relevance by grouping clients who have similar problems together, believing that therefore their solutions must be similar as well. However, consistent with the basic tenets of solution-focused brief therapy, we seek to find this common thread through the clients' solutions or desired paths. The key then becomes for the therapists to train their ears to hear the common elements about which the clients are speaking during each group session. While the individual clients' miracles will remain fairly consistent from session to session, the individual aspects of the miracles about which they are currently focused will constantly change, depending on the specific nature of their focus during each interaction. For example, a client's overall miracle may be to regain custody of her children and to obtain control over her life and her decisions. This is a very broad goal, as miracles oftentimes are. During one session the client's focus may be on parenting. During another session it may be on obtaining employment or a place to live. Yet during a third session, the client's focus may be on building friendships or setting limits with others. While the client's personal miracle remains the same, the client's focus is continually changing, depending on her life circumstances and what is important to her on each particular day. Because of this, how each client fits into the larger group theme will vary from session to session, and requires purposeful listening on the part of the solution-focused group therapist.

Finding the Theme

Hearing the group theme takes time to perfect. It is imperative that the identified theme is sufficiently broad so that it encompasses each client. Consistent with solution-focused brief therapy, the theme should fit what the clients are truly saying, rather than attempting to get the clients to fit a theme that is too narrow or simply not a good fit for all group members. The theme does not have to lend itself to a specific label (such as "relationships"), but is oftentimes a broader concept (such as "something they want more of"). I used to encourage therapists to label the group theme with a word or phrase so they could clearly communicate it. However, over the years I found that this limited how they sometimes thought of themes, so I now say that it is sufficient as long as the therapist knows the theme is present and can clearly identify and communicate it within the client conversations.

My family enjoys completing puzzles, and one day I discovered a puzzle that was a perfect example of this principle of themes within a group setting. It was a puzzle of a tiger. However, upon closer inspection, I discovered that each blotch of color within this puzzle consisted of miniature pictures of individual tigers in various poses and settings. Each tiny picture was perfect and complete on its own. Individually they were independent of one another. However, when one stood back and glanced at all of the individual pictures side by side, a larger image was unmistakable. At the time, my mother and I playfully joked about how difficult completing such a puzzle would be, for the temptation would be to become overly absorbed into the individual pictures and lose sight of the large image. How true this is when working with groups as well. However, with time, therapists are able to train their ears to hear the uniqueness of each client's story while remaining cognizant of where that client's story fits into the larger image of the group's developing theme.

Another helpful way to think about themes for those who are more kinesetic is to think about the feel of each individual client's focus as each answers the check-in question: Is the client frustrated, mellow, excited, and so forth? For example, one client may be talking about having a difficult day due to not getting the desired results at a recent court hearing. A second client may then speak about being disappointed about not getting a job. Lastly, a third client tells of having to learn to control his toddler's tantrums. Using this example, each client has a sense of frustration or struggle. This desire to learn to better cope with this frustration or struggle can then serve as the group's theme, while the individual clients deal with their individual solutions to this frustration. In another example, one client might talk about putting in three applications for jobs, a second about attending parenting classes, and a third about completing some community service hours. In this example, the feel is mellow and that of plugging along and doing what needs to be done. This then can become the group's theme. It will serve as a common thread that weaves among them throughout the group's conversations.

A common mistake that I have discovered that therapists make that results in an inability to hear the group's theme is having either too much or not the necessary information from each client during the check-in phase of group. It is important to remember that there are two objectives during the check-in period. The first is to hear what is at the client's heart, and the second is to determine if there is something that occurred that needs to be addressed (i.e., relapse, crisis). It is this first objective that is imperative to finding a group theme. The therapist needs to collect only enough information to determine what is most important to each client at this very moment. With time, therapists are able to feel or instinctually know when they have found what lies at the heart of each client. There is a solidness and depth at the moment that content is shared by the client. Once the therapist has heard what is most important to each client, the theme is always present, waiting to be discovered. If the therapist collects too much information during check-in, the theme can be easily lost in the clutter of information. Once the theme is found, the therapist then works in a purposeful way to continue to link the clients throughout all parts of the group process.

Keeping the Group Members Linked

Nail versus Screw

Therapists who are familiar with utilizing solution-focused brief therapy oftentimes initially take a more individualized approach when asking the miracle question and discovering the specifics of this important day with clients in a group setting. This can be compared to a skillful craftsman carefully tapping an individual nail into the desired place. While this is very effective for the individual client who is the focus of the therapist's attention, it can be damaging to the group norms and create significant problems later on. We have found that it is more effective to take a circular approach when working with clients in a group setting, such as that of the careful turning action required when moving a screw into position. With each twist and turn, the screw travels uniformly to a deeper level within the wood. Similarly, a solution-focused group therapist travels around the group, including all group members, during each element of the miracle question. By doing so, the group members travel through the miracle question (or other similar future-oriented intervention) as a group. This allows them to relate to each other during all portions of the intervention as well as gather and apply useful ideas that they glean from one another. This creates a sense of relevance in the conversation to all clients, which retains their engagement even when the therapist's focus is on a different group member.

Pacing

While the pacing in an individual solution-focused session is oftentimes slow (allowing for clients to take their time to think through the questions to determine the most accurate answer), the pacing within a group session is more often expeditious. This is necessitated by the likelihood of clients interjecting during quiet periods as they work on their own miracles and share how they would answer the question at hand. Although the therapist may be asking a question to an individual group member, in truth, the therapist is really inviting all of the clients to think about each question and apply it to themselves as well. This interrupting and spontaneously answering questions by all group members are wonderful elements of the group modality and serve to add energy and enthusiasm to the group process. These factors further serve to demonstrate relevance and encourage all group members to use the conversations to their benefit.

However, this quicker pace also requires that the therapist takes an active role to direct this energy to ensure that the meaning of the questions and the direction under way is not thwarted by the interruptions and multiple voices. If the client who is the focus of the therapist's questions would be prevented from gaining the full benefit of the question by another group member's interruption, the therapist must skillfully pause the interrupting client and finish the work at hand. The therapist must continually evaluate the involvement level of each client to ensure that each client is sufficiently engaged during each conversation while not becoming intrusive to the work of others. It is a delicate balance for sure.

Speaking in Turn versus Jumping In

When ensuring to include all of the group members, there are two different options. The first is to go around the circle and ask each client to answer in turn. The second is to ask group members to jump in and volunteer their answers as they are comfortable. Under ideal circumstances solution-focused therapists utilize this second approach, for it trusts the clients' timing and desire to participate. Not all clients need to answer every question, and not every client finds it helpful to participate verbally.

This individual preference is something that is important to respect and nurture. For example, clients can be given paper and pen to participate nonverbally, or a variety of other tools can be used to increase the clients' comfort level and match the individual client's style of participation. By allowing clients who are less talkative to volunteer when they have something meaningful to add, the therapist creates a nice balance between the talkers and those who are quieter. The key is ensuring that each client is getting something out of participating in the group process regardless of the level of verbal participation.

During times in which the group energy is low and clients are not readily volunteering to jump in, the therapist can create this element by putting words to nonverbal participation. For example, when the therapist notices that a group member is nodding in apparent agreement as another group member is speaking, it can be very effective for the therapist to skillfully interject and offer words to the group member's nods. The therapist might say, "Paul, it looks like you relate to what Wendy is saying." Once the client confirms that this indeed is what his head nods meant, the therapist can then redirect to the original client or toward the group as a whole, as most appropriate. This simple action role-models to the clients that interjections are welcome and demonstrates that others are simultaneously working toward their own miracles. It can also send the powerful message to clients that the therapist is truly noticing each and every client, even those who are not currently speaking. Lastly, it can also have a very positive effect for clients who have not yet seen the relevance of other people's conversations to them. When I see a client who is not very engaged when other clients are speaking, I find that it can be very helpful for me to jump over to the nonengaged client and ask a question or two about how the current conversation relates to what he or she is working on. This simple action invites the client to think about others' conversations in a new way, one that illuminates the relevance.

This tool of offering words to group members' nonverbal actions is very powerful, and can serve to pave the way for clients who are more soft spoken. When I see a client who is clearly engaged while another client is speaking, and yet who rarely jumps in, I find it very effective to create a verbal opening for the client. I might say, "Susan, it looks like you are doing a lot of thinking over there. How does this relate to you?" As a result of such well-timed questions, clients oftentimes are more likely to begin jumping in once they have a positive experience of speaking in this way.

On occasion, it is necessary for therapists to go around the circle and ask the clients to answer in turn. This approach slows down the process and institutes a more orderly feel. This can be very helpful when a group member or two are taking up more than their share of the group time and this lack of balance is starting to have a negative impact on the group norms. It can also be helpful when group members are more tangential and the group leader is having difficulty maintaining focus and direction. By slowing down the group process in this way, the therapist can gently let group members know they need to "wait their turn." While the end result is a decrease in the amount of energy and enthusiasm, at times this is precisely what is needed in order to maintain an effective environment.

Ways to Actively Work in the Group Setting

So far in our discussion of group work we have mentioned the use of the miracle question. While we believe this is the most effective tool in suspending clients' disbelief so that they can explore a place in which the problem is resolved, it is just one of four categories in which work can take place in a group setting. Let us take a look at all four methods as well as when they are most effective.

Going to the Other Side of the Problem

The first method is to simply take the client to the other side of the problem. Ideally when working with clients there is something that the clients want to be different. When this is readily identified, the best intervention is something that takes them to the other side of the problem, a place in which the problem is resolved. The most powerful intervention to attain this is the miracle question since it is tied to the daily cue of sleeping. It is something that each of us does on a daily basis, and provides the wonderful reminder of the possibility of change every time the client wakes up in the morning. Other interventions that have varying degrees of the components of the miracle question are the magic door, possessed time machine, therapist casting a spell/giving a gift, fast forwarding to the end of a session, magic wand, trait shopping, and the call from the future (Pichot & Dolan, 2003, pp. 81–89). All of these interventions have at their core the idea of helping clients to achieve something that they do not currently have or to increase the amount of a desirable quality, skill, or trait that they currently have.

When working with clients who come to treatment wanting something that they do not have or wanting to increase the amount of something that they currently have, there are four scales that can serve to measure the necessary progress and also to provide insight to the therapist about where to best target the intervention:

1. Progress toward obtaining this quality, trait, or skill (10 equals that they have what they want)
2. Other people's perception of the client's obtainment of this quality, trait, or skill (10 equals that they believe the clients have what they want)
3. Confidence of maintaining this quality, trait, or skill (10 equals that they have complete confidence they can keep what they have obtained)
4. Other people's confidence of the client's ability to maintain this quality, trait, or skill (10 equals that they have complete confidence that the clients will keep what they have obtained)

Clients may be at varying points on any of these four scales. However, an intervention such as the miracle question that takes the clients to a place in which they are a 10 on whichever scale is necessary can be very effective.

While many of our clients readily identify something they want to be different (even if it is just that they want someone else to have the necessary confidence in their skills), over the years I have discovered that there are three other categories of clients that frequently populate substance abuse treatment groups that do not have anything that they would readily like to change. This has forced me to identify other ways of working with these clients.

Solidify Work Already Being Done

True to the model of solution-focused brief therapy, some clients have already done a substantial amount of work prior to coming to treatment. This concept of presession change (de Shazer et al., 2007, p. 5) can be a powerful place to start for clients who view coming to treatment more as a formality. Other clients may have made substantial changes while in treatment; however, their referral sources continue to have concern that these changes are still so new and might not yet be permanent. With some of these clients increasing the client's referral source's confidence through the use of the miracle question or other future-oriented question can be a frustrating experience since the clients may not be able to identify anything they will be doing differently in the future. For both of these groups, any attempts to move forward and explore something that will be different in the future may not be effective. Sometimes, clients in this group may interpret such attempts as discounting the positive changes they have achieved. It is at times like this that the most effective intervention is simply to solidify the changes they have made.

Clients oftentimes view themselves as a victim of circumstances. This is true regarding negative events as well as successes. According to our clients, these things just happen and are independent of anything the clients have done. How often we have heard clients say that they just "did it." Or that the change "just happened." This brings us to our second method of facilitating change, for it is precisely in these incidences that it is imperative that we help clients identify what they did to create the change, for without this knowledge they could not recreate this positive change if needed in the future. By using Insoo Kim Berg's two-step complement (Pichot & Dolan, 2003, p. 26), the therapist can verbally highlight changes that the client would otherwise overlook. This question, "How did you do that?" then becomes the key element for the entire group, working to purposefully pick apart each and every choice, decision, and response to help the clients to increase the odds of being able to recreate these positive outcomes in the future. This kind of working contains the same purposefully slow movement that one sees in the effective use of the miracle question. The therapist follows each and every lead offered by the clients to explore how they knew this would be a good decision, what let them know it was a good decision, and how did they remember to do this. The in-depth answers to these questions are key to assisting the client in taking responsibility for these effective actions rather than crediting chance. By understanding what led to these kinds of effective decisions, the client then gains the ability to make purposeful decisions in the future. This kind of group intervention has a way of empowering clients and letting them know that their previous changes were not in vain. As a result of such groups, I have discovered that some clients then become motivated to make additional changes and are able to identify something they would like to change or have more of. While not the goal of this kind of group, it is a wonderful by-product.

Learning Lessons and Answering the Question "So What?"

The third way of effectively working within a solution-focused group setting is to assist the clients to explore the differences as a result of, and the significance of, the changes that the clients are making. This is a particularly effective strategy when clients are readily able to identify changes that they are making and how they are achieving these. At times clients can become so absorbed in making the necessary changes (specifically when the changes are required by an external source) that they do not take the time to explore what, if any, positive benefits they are experiencing as a result. This can be especially true in substance abuse treatment regarding remaining substance-free. In many agencies, this is a requirement. It is also frequently a requirement of the clients' referral sources. Yet how many times have professionals really taken the time to ask the clients how their lives are different (positive or negative) because of this? Daring to ask the clients "So what?" if you will, can be just what is needed to help them explore if these are changes that they want to continue even after the external mandates are lifted. Unfortunately, it is often just assumed that of course the clients' lives are better as a result. However, if clients do not identify clear benefits and connect these benefits to actions they are purposefully taking, the behaviors are unlikely to continue in the future, for the clients will see no benefit of expending the effort.

By asking the clients in a respectful and curious manner, "So what?" the therapist is able to gently challenge them to have purpose and meaning behind their actions. The therapist's tone and verbal padding are crucial to the success of asking such a question, for by asking this question the therapist is inviting the clients to explore previously unexplored territory. Such a venture into the unknown can be perceived as intrusive if the clients do not truly understand the intent of the question. Here is an example of how this can be successfully done.

Client (C): So, things have been going really well. I've been clean now for six months and drugs aren't even a thought any more.
Therapist (T): Wow! It sounds like you have been doing a lot of work!
C: Well, it was a lot of work, but it isn't any more.
T: Is this something that you want to continue?
C: I have to. It's not really an option.
T: OK. I have what might initially sound like a silly question, but it is something that I think is really important. Are you OK with me asking such a question? [Creating a yes set to better the odds of the client feeling more comfortable going into a new way of thinking]
C: I guess so.
T: OK. Well, it sounds like you have been doing what you need to do.
C: Yes.
T: And it is no longer a struggle for you.

C: Yes.
T: So, I'm wondering [speaking very slowly and deliberately] ... so what?
   ... How does this change your world to be doing all of these
   great things?
C: It makes a huge difference!
T: Really! Tell me about that.

Conversations such as this with clients within a group setting have a powerful way of firing up clients and motivating them to continue the changes, not because they have to, but because they now realize they want to regardless of any external mandate. This provides the ability for clients to stand up for their choices within their own environments, bettering the odds of lasting change. This intrinsic change from "have to" to "want to" is a crucial element of effective treatment, and this in and of itself has the ability to decrease the clients' risk of relapse.

A slight variation on this approach is to assist the client in exploring the lessons that the client learned by going through difficult times. For example, clients frequently come to group and report that they used substances. They are oftentimes quick to say that they are no longer engaging in this behavior, and seem to want to put the unpleasant incident behind them without much ado. However, in rushing past these incidents they are forgetting to explore the success that also came with the slip. The very fact that they are in group speaking of the incidents testifies to the reality that the clients were able to cease the substance use. While clients' natural tendencies are to focus on the slip, a skilled solution-focused therapist will instead focus on the stopping behavior and on the lessons that the clients learned by surviving the undesired behavior. This refocusing on the lessons learned has a deepening effect as the clients discover that these mistakes have meaning and value that was previously overlooked and disregarded.

Reviewing and Planning Ahead

Lastly, it is common to encounter clients in substance abuse treatment groups who have successfully completed their initial treatment goals, and their goal is now to demonstrate to the referral source that they can sustain the changes long term. These clients need to demonstrate that they can regularly attend groups, provide urine screens, and cope with the day-to-day struggles without reverting back to substance use or other destructive habits. Therefore, our fourth way of effectively working with clients in a group setting is to assist the clients to verbally complete a review of what has occurred between now and last time they were in group in order to explore how they handled day-to-day challenges: What worked? How did they know to do what they did? What lets them know they made the best decision? What difference did their decisions make? How did they remember to make the decisions they now agree were effective? This teaches the clients how to effectively evaluate their own lives, make necessary adjustments, and move forward.

Once the clients have identified what worked during the past period of time, the therapist then asks the clients to imagine that it is the next time that we are meeting. We then ask them to think back from that future place to explore how they handled what came their way, how they remembered the skills and tools they needed, and how they successfully navigated through the difficult spots. This part of the intervention assists clients in taking responsibility for their future actions, helping them understand that what happens to them is most often a direct result of the choices that they make. This way of working with clients also gives the clients a structured way of planning ahead, setting goals, and working toward the attainment of their goals.

The Use of Analogies

As solution-focused therapists we seek to challenge our clients to think about themselves and their decisions in different ways, ways that illuminate the solutions to their, at times, overwhelming problems. It is not up to us to find the solutions, only to pose purposefully worded questions to invite clients to search in places previously ignored. Analogies have a powerful way of taking the ordinary and demonstrating the similarities between the known and the unknown. The use of analogies can be just the needed tool that provides the necessary bridge for the client to understand the previously baffling dilemma.

While analogies themselves are not one of the core solution-focused interventions, they remind us that one can readily identify Eriksonian influences throughout solution-focused brief therapy (de Shazer, 1988, p. 139). Yes sets, the consulting break, and analogies are a few examples of this. Analogies, similes, and metaphors are used throughout solution-focused literature to both teach therapists this approach and work with clients (Berg & Steiner, 2003; Dolan, 1998; Pichot & Dolan, 2003). Steve de

Shazer (1988) wrote about his original training in Erickson's work and how he further expanded this work by using such interventions "without any deliberate efforts to induce trance" (p. 139) through his work in solution-focused brief therapy. He goes on to write that through such interventions, the clients "become more receptive to what the therapist says" (p. 139).

I am oftentimes asked how one can learn to use analogies with clients. Unfortunately, I believe the use of analogies is not something that is learned, but something that is noticed. By noticing what is occurring around us, we can discover similarities to our lives and the situations at hand. It is no different when working with clients. Once therapists become more comfortable using solution-focused principles, concepts, and interventions, they can free their brains to just "be." It is only from this place of being and noticing that analogies are formed. I have yet to meet a therapist who has not been able to improve his or her ability to use analogies as a result of this noticing.

Analogies are especially helpful when working with clients who are concerned that the therapist may be forming an opinion or judging them. Analogies have a way of relaxing clients' defenses and inviting the client to take whatever message is most fitting (White & Epston, 1990). For example, a client I was working with spoke about the difficulty of saying goodbye to her child after the regularly scheduled, supervised visits. Although they both had a wonderful time during their short visit together, she told of the tears and cries from her child when it came time for the visit to end. As we spoke, she confided that she even questioned if their time together was doing more harm than good since the painful goodbyes seemed to overshadow the good. I was working with my therapy dog that day, and after the client received a short visit with my canine partner, I spoke about how I know that someday my beloved pet will die. I told her that I knew that when I decided to open my heart to him. That day will be incredibly hard, but even though I know that day is coming, each moment we have together is well worth the impending pain. It is a small price to pay for our wonderful time together. I then asked her if she thought it was wise to get pets for children knowing that they will most likely die before the child. She quickly said, "Oh yes! That is just a part of life." I went on to explain that she knows her child the best, and it is up to her to decide how to most appropriately teach him that pain is a normal part of life. Does she want to teach him to focus on the pain or to focus on the joy? It is up to her to decide the answers to this question. As she left that night, she simply said, "Thank you for the dog thing." This simple analogy provided a clear path in her mind between the known and the unknown and allowed her to think about her difficulty in a new and different way.

Let us take a look at two other analogies that have come to me at various times when working with groups. Our purpose in giving these examples is not for you to take and use them as written, but to stimulate your creativity to see how analogies can be helpful in various situations to assist clients to move from the known to the unknown.

Playpen Analogy

Clients who are in need of substance abuse treatment are oftentimes court involved. They have myriad legal mandates and find these to be quite intrusive. It is not uncommon for clients in these circumstances to see their externally mandated restrictions as something that is unique to them. It was during one of these conversations that the playpen analogy was formed. I began by talking about how we, as loving parents, oftentimes purchase small enclosures for our children to allow them protected space to play. When observing some children in playpens (or play yards as they are now sometimes called), we see that some play contently, seemingly unaware of the limits on their freedom. Other children seem obsessed with the restrictions. Otherwise entertaining toys become boring, as the child yells and screams at the very concept of mesh walls. As our children grow, the "playpen" becomes bigger. We may require that the children remain in various rooms to play under supervision or allow them to play within the confines of backyards. Adolescents may be asked to telephone home at various times as a way of keeping tabs of their welfare. All of this is done for the safety of the child. Even as adults, we live within a playpen. There are laws that limit how fast I am allowed to drive, rules at work that limit my clothing choices, and so forth. Just like the child in the literal playpen, I can either choose to play happily within these limits (i.e., turn the radio up and sing as I drive within the posted speed limit) or yell and scream about the injustices of the limitations and risk the consequences. When I have used this analogy with my clients, they seem to quickly discover that the goal in life is not to free oneself from all limitations, but to learn to find happiness within our playpens. It is not something that I tell them, but something they discover sometime during the conversation. As a result, their way of thinking becomes more productive, and they more readily search for and find solutions.

New Coke versus Coke Classic Analogy

Another common thought among many court-mandated clients is the concept that all they need to do is get back to how things were before they found themselves in this trouble. They see the changes that they are currently making as something that they have to do for now and long for the day that they can revert back to their old way of being. While it is oftentimes true that the clients were doing many things that worked prior to their legal difficulties, they are oftentimes painfully unaware that the decisions that they were making are what resulted in their current problems. It was during such group conversation that I thought of my New Coke versus Coke Classic analogy. When I present analogies, I find it most effective to just be genuine and let the clients know that our conversation made me think of something that might initially seem a little odd, but to please bear with me as I share what is in my head. I have yet to have clients say they have no interest in learning what I am thinking. Being a person who enjoys Coca-Cola products, I told them about this company's decision in 1985 to create a new and improved version of Coca-Cola in order to better compete against their rival, the Pepsi-Cola Company. Unfortunately for the company, this sweeter version (unofficially named New Coke) was not well received. Sales plummeted and Coca-Cola scrambled to find a new marketing plan. In an effort to revive its image, Coca-Cola reintroduced its original formula, but with new marketing, labeling it "Coke Classic." The public was soon very happy, and Coca-Cola sales skyrocketed.

While Coca-Cola did return to its original product, it had to make some changes to its packaging and marketing in order to obtain the desired success. This analogy has a wonderful way of validating that the clients do have a good "product" to which they can return. However, it further challenges them to think about changes in "packaging" or "marketing" that might be needed in order to remain successful. I have found it very helpful to ask clients to imagine they are at some point in the future, and they have fine-tuned their product, packaging, or marketing. What changes have they made, and what did they decide to keep? This always results in a spirited conversation as clients take the analogy in directions I had never considered as they integrate their own way of thinking and discover their unique solutions.

As I hope we have demonstrated, analogies are a fun method to invite clients to think in different ways. They provide the invitation for clients to apply known information to their current dilemmas, while allowing the therapist to avoid an expert stance. In the following section, we will explore additional ways that the solution-focused group therapist can skillfully address unproductive group thinking, inappropriate behaviors, and the unexpected while empowering the clients and minimizing the need for taking back the expert role from the clients.

Group Norms

According to Edelwich and Brodsky (1992), "It is the agency's responsibility to establish clearly defined group norms. Some of these are uniform for all groups; others allow the leader some flexibility in setting norms for particular groups" (p. 22). This sentiment is also reflected in Yalom's (2005) work. While having a few written group rules (i.e., be on time for group, no eating during group) can be very helpful, it is impossible to put into writing every expectation. We would suggest no more than 10 written rules that consist of the most common behavioral culprits. For example, it is impossible to fully identify a group theme, and therefore have a solid foundation for the group's work, when clients arrive after check-in has been completed. It is also very difficult to remain focused on the tasks at hand if clients' cell phones or pagers continually ring and need to be addressed during a group session. Procedural rules that address these kinds of potential distractions can be very helpful in providing basic guidelines. However, having more than 10 of these kinds of rules can be overwhelming and is most often unnecessary.

Despite the written rules, there will be additional situations that need to be addressed. For example, I once was at a park and observed a sign that said, "Please do not throw the picnic table into the lake." Clearly there had been previous problems with this behavior, which resulted in the perceived need for the posted sign in addition to the previously listed park rules. However, it would be impossible to post signs for each and every possible behavior that would be inappropriate. Such is the case with groups as well.

When I work with therapists who are new to solution-focused brief therapy, they are oftentimes surprised when I teach them about addressing norms in a group setting. They frequently tell me that they believe that this kind of intervention does not fit with solution-focused brief therapy since the client is the expert in this approach and the therapist is to follow the clients' lead. When I have then gently questioned how they would maintain the group environment as a safe place in which to work and still allow these kinds of behaviors to continue, they are at a loss. They readily understand the importance of ensuring a safe environment, and yet they do not clearly understand how solution-focused brief therapy allows for this. Those who do address group norms most often do so by resorting to group facilitation skills they learned in school, thereby utilizing a more problem-focused mindset in order to resolve this apparent conflict. However, it is imperative that solution-focused therapists understand that solution-focused brief therapy states that the clients are the expert on themselves. However, the therapist still remains the expert of the process and on how behavioral change works. Therefore, it is our role as therapists to skillfully address ineffective client behavior and create an environment in which the clients can do their work. While we accomplish the same goal of group safety as our problem-focused counterparts, our methods and thinking behind our actions are very different. For example, remaining true to the basic tenets of solution-focused brief therapy, we prefer to focus the clients' energy on what is effective rather than on what is not. In addition, we want to take the least intrusive approach to address behaviors that may have a negative impact on the group as a whole or on individual group members. We have found that we have a more positive outcome when we are able to trust our group members' intentions while still gently redirecting their behavior. Since this concept of addressing norms from a solution-focused mindset is relatively unwritten about in solution-focused literature, we have taken the opportunity to discuss various group situations throughout this chapter and how these might be handled from a solution-focused mindset in more depth. Let us take a look at how this is done.

Continuum of Interventions

It is helpful to think of the ways in which a therapist can intervene with clients regarding behavior and norms on a continuum from least intrusive to most intrusive. Least intrusive interventions include purposefully ignoring, verbally connecting the clients to each other, or asking direct questions about something unrelated to the troublesome behavior. On the most intrusive end of the continuum is asking the client to step outside of the room to talk. In the middle are a full range of interventions, including asking the client to do something different as a help to the therapist, asking the client to directly stop the behavior, giving information, or giving the client other directives, just to name a few. As a general rule, we have found that if the behavior occurred in front of other clients, it also needs to be addressed on some level in front of these other clients. This ensures that the other group members know that the therapist is aware of the behavior and is working to address it. This then ensures that the group environment remains a safe place to discuss difficult issues, for the group members know that the therapist will act on their behalf. The therapist should always choose the least intrusive intervention whenever possible. This ensures that clients are not put in an embarrassing position when this could otherwise have been prevented. The therapist can then move up the continuum, gradually using more intrusive interventions if necessary to address the issue.

Watching for Snowballs

Anyone who has played in the snow has learned that snow readily sticks to itself. It is this basic concept that allows children to begin with a tiny ball of snow and then roll it over the ground to collect more in order to create a huge snowball suitable for making the perfect snowman. Should a person form a snowball and roll it down the hill, it will soon become very large and unwieldy despite the initially very small and simple mass. Similarly, group norm difficulties always begin with very small and manageable behaviors that most often readily respond to very low-level interventions. Should the therapists not notice or choose to ignore the inappropriate behavior, they risk being met with very damaging group norms that may or may not be mendable despite the use of the most highly intrusive interventions. Therefore, it is imperative for the therapist to understand the value of quickly addressing group norms even when the most effective approach is not yet known, for time is of the essence.

There are many behaviors that are only deemed potential norm problems by the reaction of other group members or the engagement of the client in the group process. For example, should a client take out a nail file and begin to quietly file her fingernail during a group, this may or may not be problematic. These kinds of seemingly innocent behaviors can only be understood within the context of the setting. When I work with therapists regarding group facilitation, I prefer that the therapist role-plays the potential norm issue, for it is in seeing all of the nonverbal clues as well as the reactions from other group members that the behaviors take on meaning and illuminate the most appropriate response. Let us say that the client previously mentioned had been intently listening to other group members' conversation and then quietly reached into her purse for the nail file. No one other than the therapist appeared to even notice as the client quietly filed a bothersome part of her nail before gently dropping the file back into her purse. In this case, it is not a potential norm issue since the client is actively engaged and is sending the message to everyone that she is listening and respectful. However, let us now say that the client had previously been staring at the poster on a wall of the group room and not giving her fellow clients any attention when they spoke. Then the client picks up her purse and rummages for a nail file. She then drops her purse back on the ground with a thump, and proceeds to sit back to file her nails, still seemingly unaware of the verbal content of the group members. Several clients glance in her direction due to the continued movement and noise she is causing. In this situation it must be addressed, for although she may be listening to others, it is not evident by her actions. In addition, the other group members' glances communicate that they are distracted by this client. Ideally, the therapist would have been aware that the client was initially staring at a poster and not very engaged in the conversation. The therapist would have made verbal connections between her and the other clients to help engage her in the group conversation. Should the client continue to show signs that she remains disengaged, it would be most effective to gently intervene as soon as the woman reached for her purse since this signals that the lower-level interventions were not effective. Rather than saying to the woman, "Judy, you are not allowed to get anything from your purse during group" (focusing on the negative behavior), it would be most effective to respond to the client's apparent disengagement to the group conversation and actively invite her appropriate participation. The therapist might do this by quickly switching the group's attention to Judy and saying, "Judy, it looks like we are losing you over there. You mentioned during check-in that you are staying clean. I'm wondering what differences you have noticed as a result." By acknowledging the obvious (the client is not engaged), the other group members are assured that the therapist sees what they are seeing as well. The therapist then redirects Judy to something more appropriate. Therapists who are new to this approach oftentimes tell me that they do not intervene in this manner at this point in time since they do not know what to say to the client. Therefore, they do nothing. My response is that they need to simply invite her to participate in any way they can. It is too risky to wait until the therapist has formulated the perfect question. Just jump in and ask her anything that is focused on what she wants or that she is doing well.

Most clients will discontinue their current behaviors when the obvious is stated, the group's focus is on them, and they are invited to actively participate in a structured way. Should the client continue by picking up her purse and looking for an item despite the therapist's low-level intervention, the therapist should then move up the continuum and use increasingly intrusive interventions. For example, the therapist might say, "I'm sorry. Just a minute please [to the client she is currently working with]. Judy, I need your help here. I have such a difficult time concentrating, and I am having a difficult time focusing with the movement on your side of the room. Would you be willing to set your purse back down? It would really help me a lot. Thank you." By making the issue the therapist's, the client is much more likely to feel comfortable despite the very direct intervention. Should the client now continue this disruptive behavior, the therapist has ruled out that Judy is doing this because she is simply unaware of the distraction she is causing. If it continues, the therapist should either take a break (allowing time for the therapist to talk directly to Judy privately and see what is going on resulting in her disengagement in group) or ask for a moment with Judy in private outside the group room. In either case, the solution-focused therapist's conversation with Judy should be from a place of concern and curiosity and not reprimand, for the therapist trusts that Judy has a good reason for this behavior, although it cannot continue in a group setting. The therapist may decide that Judy would benefit more from sitting in the waiting room quietly working on her treatment plan or other written assignment, or should schedule an individual session to address the issues at hand. The client should only return to the group setting if the client's inappropriate behavior will stop and she is able to become engaged in the group conversation and benefit from participating.

Should the therapist not take these steps and allow Judy to continue these seemingly innocent behaviors unaddressed, the safety of the group would be compromised. While the therapist might not see any fallout from this during this session, it would certainly build just like our snowball rolling downhill. Group members will lose trust in their facilitator to intervene and keep the environment productive, they might begin to cross talk in support group-like fashion, and most likely, they will begin to talk on a more superficial level. Should the therapist only begin to address these continued behaviors weeks after this snowball is well developed, it is likely the group members will challenge the therapist's authority to redirect. While a highly skilled therapist can address these norm issues and rebuild a working environment, it can take its toll on both the therapist and clients.

Over the years I have discovered some common norm problems that frequently trip up therapists who are new to this approach. These norm patterns are very easy to recognize once the therapist is aware of their potential due to the clients' predictable behaviors or statements at the early stages of these snowballs. Let us take a look at five of the most common ones and how to address them.

Common Norms to Watch For

"I Don't Agree"

The first is characterized by a client stating "I don't agree" to the therapist's explanation. While on the surface it seems rather benign, it signals a much greater problem that will become very contagious if left unaddressed. There are many aspects of facilitating a group that are not up for discussion. These may include procedural rules or how the therapist interacts and addresses another group member. Issues determining the therapist's actions are oftentimes the result of factors that are not appropriate to be shared with other clients. It is imperative that clients have a basic level of trust in the therapist, that he or she is working for the benefit of each group member even when others are not privy to all the facts of the case. This general level of trust is necessary to protect each client's confidentiality and to allow the therapist to make sound decisions based on solid education and the solution-focused tenets. When clients respond to an explanation of the therapist's decision by stating "I don't agree," they are signaling that there is a larger trust issue between the client and the therapist. Until this larger issue is resolved, this damaging norm will cause havoc within the group setting, for it sends the message to others that the therapist is not acting in group members' behalf, and therefore should be questioned and not trusted.

The first thing that must be determined before taking action is if this is an individual client's concern or if it is a group issue. This is easily accomplished by carefully noting the response of other group members. We will address how to handle it if it is a group issue in the next section. If the group members remain quiet and do not engage even nonverbally with the talking client, it is an individual issue. If it is deemed to be an individual issue, it is best handled promptly through the use of a higher-level intervention by simply saying, "OK. Let's go talk more outside, so I can better address your concerns." This is one of the few times we would suggest moving directly to the highest level of intervention due to the damage that addressing this individual issue publicly would otherwise cause. Once alone with the client the therapist should explain that there are frequently many relevant factors that are not appropriate to discuss with the client. The therapist might then use a medical analogy to try to help the client move from the understood to the unknown. For example, the therapist might talk about going to a physician for a condition. The doctor has significant training in the most appropriate dosages for various medications. The doctor has to weigh the pros and cons of the medications to determine the most appropriate course of treatment. While the patient would be wise to question the doctor to better understand his own situation, it would be foolhardy to question the doctor's judgment when treating another patient, for the initial patient is not privy to the lab tests and other forms of evidence that resulted in the prescribed course of action for the second patient. In addition, the patient most likely lacks the medical expertise to competently weigh all relevant data. The therapist could then bring the conversation back to the client and state that the client has every right to question why the therapist is making decisions about him; however, this should be addressed in a private setting and not in the group since it would be inappropriate for the therapist to bring in confidential information in a public setting that is necessary to fully answer the question. The client should only return to group once the trust has been rebuilt in the therapist's actions and an agreement has been reached that the client will question the therapist in the appropriate private setting. In addition, the client needs to be accepting of those times in which the answer is not appropriate to be shared with him in order to protect another's confidentiality.

Curious versus Complaining

The second common norm issue is easily recognized by its involvement by more than one client. It may include the statement "I don't agree," but is voiced by multiple clients and is most likely about procedures or group rules. More broadly, it is hallmarked by clients complaining about external limits in a group setting. Because it is clearly a concern of multiple clients, it must be addressed in the group setting. If the clients' complaints are about something outside of the therapist's control (i.e., "the system" or their referral source), the therapist should validate the frustrations and then redirect to how they are coping with things that are beyond their control. It is imperative that the therapist retains control of the group conversation and does not allow cross talk to turn the group into uncontrolled complaining. For example, the therapist might say, "Now hold on a minute [interrupting the complaining and regaining verbal control]. That does sounds frustrating! There are so many things that are beyond your control right now. That has to be tough. So, I'm wondering what is helping you get through all these mandates even when you don't agree. What helps you remember why you are doing this in the first place?" This way of addressing the concerns reminds the clients that group is the ideal setting to learn to better cope with the frustrations of their situations. Should the clients continue to complain, the therapist might have to use a higher-level intervention. For example, "Now hold on [said with a playful tone, but clearly stopping the complaining]. It's clear to me that there is a lot you don't agree with. Unfortunately, what you guys are talking about, I can't help change either. It's important to me that you get something out of group, and I'm not hearing we can solve those difficulties. The only thing I can help with, regarding it, is to help you learn to better deal with the struggles." This sends a clear message that the conversation is not productive, but it stops short of saying the clients are not allowed to discuss it. Instead, it again redirects the clients to a conversation that would be helpful. However, should this intervention be ineffective, the therapist will be forced to directly say this.

At times, the clients complain directly about decisions within the power of the therapist or agency. It is important that the therapist does not compromise the decisions due to these complaints, but remains focused on the clients and what is going on with them. In most instances, the clients are viewing the rule solely from their perspective and are unaware of the necessity of this rule. It can be tempting to quickly jump in and explain the sound logic behind the decision to the clients only to be met with increased frustration and hostility. Instead, it is most effective to determine if the clients are really curious as to the explanation or are simply complaining. It is relatively common for clients to make statements such as "I don't know why they won't let us smoke. It's so dumb!" and yet not truly be interested in the rationale behind the decision. A Chinese proverb once said, "There is nothing more worthless than the answer to the unasked question." It is very true when addressing this norm issue. Offering the answer when clients truly are not curious is like throwing gasoline on a small fire. It will quickly erupt in a more difficult situation, since clients oftentimes view the explanation as defending. It can be a very effective strategy on the part of the therapist to give hints that an explanation exists, but then wait to see if the clients ask directly. For example, the therapist might say, "I know it must be frustrating, especially since most of you rarely run into why the rule was originally made. It probably doesn't make any sense." This alludes to an explanation, but validates their point that it does not make sense. Clients who are truly interested will then ask for the explanation. If the clients do not ask, the therapist should proceed as above by inviting the clients to explore how they cope with rules that do not make sense or those with which they do not agree.

"We" Thinking

This third common norm is easy to spot and oftentimes walks hand in hand with the fourth norm, which we will describe next. We thinking is present any time clients speak for one another or for the group as a whole. It can signal that other damaging norms are already in place (such as lack of trust). However, this norm is fairly easy to address when caught in its early stages. The therapist's goal when addressing this norm is to understand what the individual client's thoughts and perspectives are and then move on to invite the others to share their individual thoughts directly. If left unchecked it can progress into the damaging group phenomenon called group think (Janis, 1972, p. 9), in which group members lose their ability to think and act independently and rely on the opinions of others to validate what is true or best. Solution-focused brief therapy trusts that each client is the expert on himself or herself. This requires that the therapist actively cultivates an environment in which the clients continue to think only for themselves and gain the ability to evaluate decisions and actions based on what the individual client believes is best. All of the therapist's questions work to this end. Anything that threatens this key element must be immediately addressed. The following interaction demonstrates how this can be done.

T: So what have you been doing that has helped you?
C: We have all been doing all kinds of things [looking around the room for validation].
T: Now hold on a minute. I will hear from each of them in a minute. Right now, I want to know what you have done.
C: But they have done good.
T: I know. But I want to hear what you think are the most important things you have done.

In this example, the client has good intentions by speaking for others. However, the therapist would have prevented each client from determining what are the best things each has done, and therefore preventing each from practicing this self-evaluation should she have allowed the client to speak for other group members. By remembering that clients have good intentions, therapists can then carefully pad their response in a way that redirects each client's attention back on himself or herself.

"Us Against Them" Thinking
Because many substance abuse treatment clients are externally mandated and have legal involvement, many come to therapy believing that the "system" is against them. Some view themselves as being unjustly treated, and project this onto their treatment provider as well. As previously mentioned, effective therapy requires a degree of trust in the treating professional. While most clients are initially reserved, it does not take much time for most to learn that the solution-focused therapist is nonjudgmental and there to help. However, this norm issue does rear its ugly head from time to time and must be promptly addressed. A common phrase heard when this norm issue is present is: "You guys ..." An astute therapist will quickly interrupt and clarify, asking, "Hold on ... 'you guys?' Who are you referring to?" Should the client state that it is believed that the therapist is part of the system, it is imperative that this be corrected. It can also be helpful to invite the client to ask questions to check things out to avoid any need to assume how the therapist will act and think.

Hints that this norm issue is present may also appear during group breaks or other times when the clients are interacting without therapist facilitation. This norm can be the direct result of therapists becoming so task focused that they do not take a few minutes to sit with the clients in the waiting room to look at pictures of their children or engage in other casual conversations with the clients. When professionals only make time to run into the treatment room and immediately begin work, clients quickly surmise that the professional is not personable. Clients may begin to stop more casual, enjoyable conversation as soon as the therapist arrives, which will result in the clients acting one way with each other and another when the therapist is present. This can then progress to the clients following agency rules when the therapist is present, and not following them when in the therapist's absence. When the therapist then addresses the rule breaking, this only serves as additional proof in the clients' eyes that the staff is against them. It is a vicious cycle. It is important to remember that "when clients believe you are interested in them and want to work with them, they are more likely to cooperate and work with you to make changes" (Berg, 1994, p. 52). By taking casual moments and showing interest in them as people, this interest and care is communicated and leads to a more casual transition into the work together. Talking about appropriate topics (weather, children, movies) and then making a clear transition into group (i.e., "OK. Let's get started with group") demonstrates to clients that they can be themselves regardless of whether the therapist is in the room, minimizing the risk of this damaging norm.

In training new therapists, this can be an uncomfortable idea for many. They are comfortable during a treatment session, but struggle with how to interact in a manner that is appropriate and yet more casual. While in problem-focused approaches the therapist may serve as a mentor and self-disclosure in many areas (including past history of substance abuse) is common, this form of counselor self-disclosure and mentorship is not consistent with the basic tenets of solution-focused brief therapy (Pichot & Dolan, 2003), for it is based on the idea that similar problems will lead to similar solutions. In solution-focused brief therapy, clients are encouraged to find their own solutions. The therapist's experience will only serve as a distraction and may give the false impression that the therapist's solutions are best for the client. Because of this, solution-focused therapists do not share significant personal information. It has been our experience that clients readily understand and appreciate our reasons for not disclosing our personal histories once our rationale is disclosed. However, there are many common factors that are neutral and appropriate to discuss. For example, I work with a therapy dog, so my love of animals is clearly apparent to my clients. This serves as a wonderful conversation opener with clients about pets and love of dogs. I have discovered that the key to casual conversations with clients is to disclose a small amount (i.e., "I love dogs" or "I love the warmer weather we are having"), and then gently turn the focus back on the clients through casual questions. Even such superficial conversations such as "What cute shoes!" can make a world of difference in helping our clients feel more comfortable and see us as people working with them rather than against them.

Clapping

This leads us to the fifth common norm issue: clapping. As human beings, we are conditioned to clap as a sign to others that we appreciate what they have done. It is a form of praise. Clients oftentimes clap when my therapy dog catches a bone off of his nose, and he finds the clapping (and well as the bone he caught) a welcome reward for a job well done. When clients clap in response to an achievement of another client, it is well-intentioned praise. However, when we return to the basic tenets of solution-focused brief therapy, the therapist's job is to encourage the clients to evaluate themselves. Too often their reliance on the assessment of others is precisely what led to the lack of judgment and current problem. Group therapy should be a place where clients continue to be encouraged to evaluate their behaviors for themselves to determine if something they did was truly worthy of praise. When clients are allowed to spontaneously clap for one another, they unintentionally deprive group members of this opportunity to evaluate for themselves. In addition, they can mistakenly believe that something they did was meaningful simply because others deemed it so.

When spontaneous clapping is present in a group setting, it is indicative that group members are working from a support group mindset rather than a treatment mindset. It is a simple problem to solve when caught early. Here is an example of how this can be done.

C: I had a very good week. I finally got a job! [Spontaneous clapping]
T: Now hold on a minute [compassionately stopping the clapping and turning again to the client]. Is this a good thing?
C: Oh yes. I have been working very hard to get this job.
T: So it is the one you wanted?
C: Yes, it has perfect hours, and will work great with my schedule!
T: OK. [Turning to the group] It sounds like this is a clappable occasion. Let's give her a round of applause.

Once the therapist has ensured that the client has made a full evaluation of what she did and determined that this was a significant achievement, clapping is allowed. It can serve as a nice reinforcement to the client's internal assessment. By initially, directly stopping the spontaneous clapping and demonstrating that only the client could determine if the rest of us should clap, a powerful message is sent to the other clients as well that clients will evaluate their own decisions, and we will then join in the celebration.

When All Else Fails

Learning effective solution-focused group facilitation is a daunting task. It is challenging enough to have to think on one's feet when working with 1 client, let alone 12. Because of this, it is imperative that therapists remember to use this approach with themselves during the learning process. Just like with our clients, we would not expect them to jump from 1 to 10 on a progress scale. We would also never want clients to become discouraged and quit when they determine they are only a 3 rather than the desired 10. Similarly, therapists need to continually evaluate themselves on a 10-point scale, 10 being that they have mastered solution-focused group facilitation and 1 being that they would not recognize a solution-focused group if they saw one. Rather than succumbing to the temptation to try to analyze why one is not higher on the scale, we invite therapists to explore what makes them as high as they are. What worked, and how did you get through?

When I was a child I took piano lessons. Being a shy child, I found preparing for recitals overwhelming and scary. During my practice sessions, I would quickly become discouraged when I could not get my tiny fingers to hit the correct notes in the scripted tempo. I would then stop playing in a huff, believing that the song was ruined and that continuing was pointless. My teacher was so patient. She rarely took a stand, but I remember her saying on one occasion, "You can't just quit. You are going to be playing in front of all those people. I don't care how badly you mess up. You are to keep your fingers moving and finish the song. You are to then get up and politely bow." That expectation to keep playing despite my mistakes made a significant difference not only in my music but also in my adult life. Quitting was no longer an option, so I was challenged to make the best of what I had. Even after mistakes, I ended my performance with confidence and a focus on the parts that went well. After each recital, my teacher was not one to just let me forget my performance, never to play that song again. She patiently helped me review, and even encouraged me to master the rough patches so that I learned from my mistakes. These are lessons that have stuck with me for decades, and lessons that I now teach new therapists. No matter how poorly they think the group is going, they are to simply finish the recital. They are to do their best. After the group is over, there will be time to learn from what went well and to remember lessons that were temporarily forgotten in the heat of the moment. It is by just finishing the recital that they will slowly move up the scale and gain confidence and skill.

Summary

Solution-focused group therapy can be a powerful treatment modality. Within the context of group, clients receive support and ideas from their fellow group members. However, as with all helpful modalities, there is the potential for problems if the therapist is not aware of potential pitfalls and problems. By being skilled at hearing the group theme, the group therapist can ensure that clients find relevance in all conversations, and by understanding the four different ways to work within the group context, therapists can ensure that group is beneficial for all involved. Adding the playful spirit of analogies can help therapists bring concepts to life and assist clients in moving from the known to the unknown. And lastly, having a solid understanding of the early warning signs of damaging norms can prevent the group from heading off course. In Chapter 8 we will explore additional applications and practice issues of substance abuse treatment, including working with adolescents and other populations.

8

Additional Applications and Practice Issues

> Expertise lies in the manner in which the conversation is conducted, not in the
> ability to convey a venerated body of information.
>
> **M. Bobele, G. Gardner, and J. Biever**

Throughout the previous chapters we have explained in detail the basics about both substance abuse treatment and solution-focused brief therapy, more advanced considerations of the approach, how to conduct thorough and credible evaluations that are consistent with solution-focused brief therapy, and how to use the approach in both individual and group settings. In this final clinical chapter we will address additional applications and practice issues that come into play when using solution-focused brief therapy in the field of substance abuse treatment, such as how to address traditional substance abuse treatment elements, working with adolescents, co-occurring disorders, and cultural considerations.

Traditional Substance Abuse Treatment Elements

As therapists become more knowledgeable and skilled in the use of solution-focused brief therapy, it is commonplace for some black-and-white thinking to initially take hold when they are faced with some of the more traditional substance abuse treatment elements. Encounters with traditional substance abuse treatment elements are expected when one works within the agency settings. Many treatment agencies continue to recommend that clients attend support groups such as Alcoholics Anonymous as part of treatment and aftercare, and state regulations commonly mandate lists of topic areas that must be covered during treatment. However, even when working in a private practice setting, therapists are likely to encounter clients who are actively involved in 12-step programs such as

Alcoholics Anonymous, or those who hold true to the belief that addiction is a disease. As a supervisor, I have found it commonplace for less experienced solution-focused therapists to initially think that these components are not compatible with solution-focused brief therapy, or even begin to discourage these practices. It is at times such as these that I have found it imperative to help these well-intentioned therapists to broaden their view of solution-focused brief therapy to see how its basic tenets lend themselves to being inclusive rather than exclusive. As a solution-focused therapist, I am an expert on the process of change. This allows my clients to be the experts on themselves and on the content of their solutions. It is a human quality to listen with an ear to quickly identify that with which we do not agree. Instead, this approach challenges us to listen with a neutral ear, trusting that the content simply is, without judgment. This neutrality allows us to then trust our skills to create change by applying this approach to what the client brings. Let us take a deeper look at how this would apply to two of the most common elements of traditional substance abuse treatment.

12-Step Recovery Programs

As with many things, I have found that it is wise to become educated on various cultures (the 12-step programs are a culture in and of themselves) in order to allow me to skillfully use the language of a specific culture when I am interacting with someone who strongly embraces it. This allows me to move within the culture verbally and to easily adapt my questions to be more congruous and respectful. This also provides me with a profound respect and appreciation for the culture itself, which is required in order to truly see the similarities and how elements of both can be true. For example, my favorite passage of the "Big Book," the term used to describe the primary text (Alcoholics Anonymous, 1976), is: "When I focus on what's good today, I have a good day, and when I focus on what's bad, I have a bad day. If I focus on a problem, the problem increases; if I focus on the answer, the answer increases" (p. 451). My second favorite passage is: "When I stopped living in the problem and began living in the answer, the problem went away. From that moment on, I have not had a single compulsion to drink" (p. 449). These passages oftentimes surprise professionals who only have a cursory knowledge of the 12-step programs, for they echo the underlying tenets of solution-focused brief therapy and reflect the universal truth that whatever one focuses on gets bigger. It is passages such as these that form a bridge of commonality between the 12-step programs and solution-focused brief therapy.

Similarly, the Alcoholics Anonymous slogan "One day at a time" can initially be thought to be incongruent with solution-focused brief therapy's vision of the future. Clients on occasion may initially balk at the idea of thinking about their goals and plans for the future since they may view that as being foolhardy. Similarly, clients may have difficulty with the wording that the problem that brought you here is resolved, since many who are active in the 12-step programs believe that they will always be an alcoholic or addict. The experienced solution-focused therapist understands that when clients hesitate or express these concerns, it is simply an indication that the therapist is not using culturally sensitive language or is not taking small enough steps, for the miracle question is simply about tomorrow, not weeks, months, or even years into the future. Clients who find even tomorrow to be too large of a step can best be fast forwarded only to that night as they lie down to sleep. Here is an example of how a therapist might recover from a verbal blunder and change to more culturally sound language:

Client (C): I don't want to do any of that future stuff. I need to live my life one day at a time to stay sober.

Therapist (T): I completely agree. Living your life day to day is the best answer for you right now. Would it be OK if I asked you some questions about your day?

C: Sure. I just get too overwhelmed with that miracle question since all I know for sure is that I'm sober today.

T: OK. Fair enough. So I am going to ask you a strange question. Is that OK?

C: Yeah.

T: I want you to imagine that it is at the end of the day, and you are lying there in your bed thinking, "I am proud of how I handled today. I am moving in the right direction. Alcohol was not an issue for me today." What did you do today that let you know that you handled it well and that you are heading where you want to go?

By reframing the goal to be that "alcohol was not an issue today" and by only forwarding to the end of the day, the therapist is consistent with the beliefs of the client, thereby allowing the client and therapist to work hand in hand toward imagining a place in which the problem is resolved, just for today.

Lastly, it is common for clients who are active in the 12-step programs to believe that they have a disease and that they must abstain from all substances. Many solution-focused therapists who are new to this field initially struggle with this idea since the literature suggests that many people do completely recover from substance dependence, and some go on to drink in a controlled manner (Cloud & Granfield, 2001; Davies, 1962; Davies, Scott, & Malherbe, 1969; Granfield & Cloud, 1999; Sobell, Sobell, Toneatto, & Leo, 1993; de Shazer & Isebaert, 2003). However, it is important for us to also understand that this is not the case for other clients. Some clients do need to discontinue their use completely, and it is helpful for some to view themselves as a recovering addict or alcoholic for life. Part of solution-focused brief therapy is a complete acceptance of the path that each client chooses. Consistent with our earlier definition of the client (that of the entire client's system), this suggests that we should be accepting of this path regardless of who within the client's system is mandating abstinence (i.e., regulation, agency, legal system, or client), trusting that the clients can and will make good decisions should their system change in the future. This neutral stance and this lack of investment as to the etiology of addiction are key in solution-focused brief therapy. This neutral stance and ultimate faith in the client allow the solution-focused therapist to operate fluidly within disease-based as well as harm reduction models of treatment.

Required Topics

When working within an agency setting, it is commonplace for therapists to be mandated to address various topics with clients as part of treatment. This requirement may stem directly from state or federal regulations, or it may be internally required by the agency. Regardless of who is mandating the content, it is imperative that the therapist look beyond the requirements to the intent. In the majority of cases, the intent is to ensure that all clients have a solid grasp of a preidentified body of knowledge prior to discharge. By viewing the requirements in this manner, it becomes more apparent how a solution-focused therapist can easily work within this requirement. For example, in work with pregnant women, it is common for regulations to require that clients understand the potential negative impact of substances on the unborn fetus, proper nutrition, the importance of prenatal care, child development, and so forth. When one looks at the intent of this regulation, it has merit regardless of one's theoretical approach.

Listening to Clients

When working from a solution-focused approach, we do not assume that the clients have or do not have the required knowledge. Instead, we listen to the clients as they speak about their miracles, paying specific attention to the required content areas to assess what knowledge the clients already possess. If the client does not readily address the required content, the therapist then asks direct questions to invite the client to describe the area in question. For example, if the client did not volunteer information about her knowledge of the potential negative impact of substances on the unborn fetus, the therapists might ask, "I'm wondering what you did to ensure that your baby was so healthy?" A question such as this invites myriad answers, such as "Well, I didn't do drugs, that's for sure. I also ate right, got enough sleep ..." The therapist can then follow up on each of these answers, asking how the client knew to do these things, and so on.

Three Levels of Learning

As one learns new information, there are three general levels of learning. In the first level, the person is able to repeat the information back in a parroting fashion. Technically, this is the only level of learning that regulation oftentimes requires, and this can be easily met through a lecture format. During the second level of learning, the person is able to not only repeat the information back, but also paraphrase the information, demonstrating that the person understands the content enough to change the wording while retaining the meaning. Lastly, in the third level of learning, the person is able to not only repeat it back and paraphrase the information, but also apply the information and use it in a personal context. It is this level of learning that is the true test of understanding and is naturally achieved through solution-focused brief therapy, for the clients demonstrate the knowledge by describing how they will be applying it in their miracle.

Providing New Information

So you may be wondering, "That sounds great, but what do you do if the client does not have the knowledge or maybe has incorrect information?" A novice solution-focused therapist might mistakenly think that it would be inappropriate to ever give advice or provide information when using this approach since one of the foundational tenets is to trust that the clients hold their own answers. This would be incorrect. For example, if a client believes that one can get HIV from touching a door knob, it would be short-sighted for a therapist to leave that belief unchecked. The correct information needs to be provided so that the client can make informed decisions. The key difference is that solution-focused therapists simply give the information and then resume allowing the clients to be the experts of how that information will impact their lives. Even ideas and suggestions are presented in a more tentative, suggestive form rather than the traditional advice format (de Shazer et al., 2007). I have also found it very helpful to have many kinds of brief, educational brochures and resource materials readily available in the office waiting room. This allows clients to browse at their leisure, taking whatever content areas they think would be useful. The therapist can then bring this into the therapy session by noticing what the clients chose and complimenting them for wanting to gain more knowledge.

Documentation

The final step when working in this fashion is to ensure that there is thorough documentation. This is necessary in order to demonstrate that the client does indeed have the required content and knows how to effectively apply it. Without this step, it might mistakenly appear as though the solution-focused therapist did not meet the requirements, for the material will not have been presented in the easier-to-audit method of generic educational sessions or lectures. Working in this format does put the burden of proof onto the therapist to provide documentation that the regulations were met, for the clients will most likely never realize that an educational topic was covered and will think the session was solely based on their needs and agendas.

Working With Adolescents

Professionals typically either love working with adolescents or hate it. It can be a challenging population with which to work due to adolescents' in-your-face stance, challenge of the status quo, and at times outlandish presentation. Personally, I enjoy this population since I know there is less room for error, thereby testing my skills. If my question was poorly worded or was redundant, an adolescent will quickly tell me (frequently with an eye roll for effect), and if I am not truly listening or hearing what is at an adolescent's heart, that will be made clear as well. There is simply less need to guess or assume; however, that also requires a thicker skin.

Before taking a closer look at working with adolescents, it is important to understand how consistent the underlying concepts behind solution-focused brief therapy are with how the human brain naturally learns. One of the first toys I can remember playing with as a child was a six-and-a-half-inch-diameter plastic red-and-blue ball with yellow shaped pieces (I now know that toy was called a Shape-O Toy by Tupperware™). The goal when playing with this toy is to match the yellow shapes to the similarly shaped holes in the ball, thereby learning shape recognition as well as developing coordination and dexterity. When watching a child play with this toy, it soon becomes apparent that the child does not usually become overly frustrated when the triangle does not fit into the square hole. The child may make a few attempts to force it in the square hole, but then readily moves to explore a different hole. When the triangle hole is discovered, the child simply memorizes that the triangle did indeed fit into that hole, making the discovery of the correct hole more expeditious after several repetitions. The child somehow naturally knows that it would be less effective to memorize all of the many holes into which the triangle does not fit. Solution-focused brief therapy mirrors this basic learning principle of inviting clients, regardless of age, to simply focus on what fits.

When working with adolescents it is important to understand their developmental tasks. It is a time in which their role is to challenge what they are told and what they know in an effort to discover who they are, what they believe, and who they want to be, thereby allowing them to differentiate from their family of origin (Werner-Wilson, 2000). This results in their necessary desire to suspend external limits, challenge the norms, and look to their peers and to themselves to reevaluate their reality. Because one of the fundamental tenets of solution-focused brief therapy is to look to the clients to find their own solutions, this is a natural fit for this developmental stage. The inherent systemic nature of solution-focused brief therapy provides a reality check for the clients, while the client-as-expert stance empowers the clients to develop critical thinking and develop their own answers within their context. However, there are two important elements to remember when working with adolescents to increase success: understanding the power of the parent/guardian and using the "imaginary audience."

The Power of the Parent/Guardian

Working with an adolescent is frequently akin to working with a mandated or court-ordered client. Adolescents rarely wake up and decide they want to meet with an unfamiliar professional and talk about personal matters. This is usually mandated by a parent or guardian. As a general rule, we have found that adolescents by and large do what is required by their parents (it is important to note here that we said they do what is *required*, not necessarily what the parent *wants*). Therefore, similar to working with a court-ordered adult, it is imperative that it is clear what the referral source (the parent, in the case of adolescents) is actually requiring and will therefore take action to enforce. This may mean that it would be prudent on occasion to work with the parent to help clarify this as well. When doing this, we have discovered that many parents really do not have firm beliefs about alcohol or marijuana use as long as the child is attending school and is not involved with other illegal or disruptive activity. Therefore, adolescents who have parents with these views are less likely to discontinue their alcohol and marijuana use all together; it is not required. By discovering the parents' proverbial line in the sand, the therapist can then work in a more congruent manner with the adolescent.

Following this principle that adolescents typically will do what is required by the parent, we have found it important for the parents to have all of the relevant information so that they can make sound decisions. It is commonplace for parents to believe that their child is less involved in substance use than is reflected by the evaluation testing instruments. We have had adolescents court-ordered into treatment due to possession charges only to be told by the parents that "kids will be kids" and say that they believe the courts are overreacting. By ensuring that the parents understand the data collected during the evaluation process, the parents can then make an educated decision regarding treatment and goal setting.

Imaginary Audience

A normal part of adolescence is a form of self-consciousness that has been referred to in the literature as having an imaginary audience (Elkind, 1967). When working with adolescents, it is common to discover that they can have a difficult time answering questions that are reflective in nature (i.e., What would be different about you?), while they have minimal problems answering relationship questions (i.e., What would your dad say was different about you?). Being cognizant of this developmental fact when working with an adolescent can make interventions more effective.

When adult clients answer the miracle question, they frequently first answer with something that they observe to be different within them (i.e., "I would feel peace"); however, adolescents frequently answer within the context of others (i.e., "My dad wouldn't be banging on the door because

I had overslept"). Because the general wording of the miracle question is intentionally very broad (i.e., What would be the first thing you would notice?), there is no need to modify the question for work with adolescents. In fact, this broad wording allows for adolescents who have developed the ability to be reflective to answer in kind, thereby allowing the client to choose either an internal or external path. However, should the client choose the external path, it is most helpful to honor this while continuing to focus on the client.

T: So I'm wondering, what are the first things you notice, even before you open your eyes?

C: Well, my dad wouldn't be banging on the door because I'm late.

T: Wow! Would that be different?

C: Yeah [laughing]! I hate mornings.

T: So what is different about you on this morning that lets him know that he doesn't have to bang on the door? [This response honors the external reference while focusing the client on what is different within her, thereby allowing the client to explore her own behaviors and thoughts in a developmentally consistent fashion.]

C: That I was up.

T: And what difference does that make for you to begin your day without your dad needing to bang on your door?

C: It makes a huge difference. I can start my day off in a good mood.

Had the therapist not been cognizant of the appropriateness of the client's initial reference to her father, the therapist might have mistakenly tried to refocus the client onto herself by asking, "Since we can't change your father, what would you notice was different about you?" This response would have sent the message to the client that her answer was incorrect and would most likely have resulted in the stereotypical adolescent answer, "I don't know." Another beginner's error would be to forget that the desired focus is on the client's change in behavior, and therefore ask more about the father (i.e., "So what else would your father have noticed?"). This choice would have led to a more superficial path and bypassed the potentially rich conversation of assisting the client in exploring what she is doing to create this change in her father's behavior. We have discovered that our adolescent clients have no problem answering questions about their own behaviors as long as the therapist respects and understands that their answers will oftentimes be within the context of others.

Co-occurring Disorders

It is commonplace for clients who are experiencing difficulties with substances to also have a co-occurring mental health diagnosis. According to a report to congress by the Substance Abuse and Mental Health Services Administration (2002), "42.7 percent of individuals with a 12-month addictive disorder had a least one 12-month mental disorder" (p. 3). It goes on to say, "61 percent of individuals with bi-polar disorder also had a substance abuse disorder (more than five times as likely as the general population)" (p. 3). This increased correlation is precisely why there has been an increased focus on mental health assessment and appropriate treatment provision when the ASAM Patient Placement Criteria was revised in 2001 (Mee-Lee, 2001). Clinicians must be skilled in treating both substance abuse and mental health disorders to be optimally effective in this field.

Diagnoses and Labels

Since solution-focused brief therapy assists clients in looking beyond their current problems to a place in which the problems are resolved, it effectively addresses substance abuse and mental health disorders simultaneously. In its purest form, there is no need for the use of diagnoses or labels, for those are used to describe problems. This does not mean, however, that solution-focused therapists are oblivious to the presence of a mental health disorder. Contrarily, they choose to look beyond the diagnoses and labels to assist the client in identifying and taking ownership of a life in which both problems are resolved. While diagnoses and labels are not viewed as clinically necessary in solution-focused brief therapy, they are seen as necessary for communicating with problem-focused professionals and to secure payment reimbursement.

The Use of Psychotropic Medications

There is no doubt that psychotropic medications serve an invaluable role in treating many mental health disorders, and their use is consistent with solution-focused brief therapy. However, there is a key difference in how a solution-focused therapist views psychotropic medication, and that is that the clients are viewed to be the experts regarding whether the medication would be helpful in assisting them in working toward their miracles. Should a client initially state that medications would not be helpful, this would be respected. However, in working toward the client's miracle, the therapist would consistently look for indicators that the client is making progress and that each person within the client's system agrees. If at some point the client does not appear to be making progress, this will be explored through the use of relationship questions.

T: So, I'm wondering where on our scale would your wife say you are, 10 equals that you are living this miracle and that she has no concerns and 1 is that it is the worst it has ever been.

C: I would say about a 4.

T: OK. What does she see that lets her know she is a 4 and not a 3?

C: Well, she is noticing that I am able to get up in the mornings and get to work. That impresses her.

T: Wow, so she is higher than you placed yourself on that scale a few minutes ago. What does she see that you don't?

C: Well, she doesn't know that I still hear voices. They don't scare me now, so she doesn't know they are still there.

T: Wow! That sounds different that you are no longer frightened by them.

C: Yes, but I really want them to go away.

T: I can understand that. I'm wondering, if we were to think back to your miracle day, were you hearing voices on that day?

C: No. They were completely gone.

T: How did you manage that?

C: I think I was back on my medication.

T: So taking medication helps?

C: Yeah, I hate to take it, but I now see it does make a difference.

T: Hmm.

C: I think I'll call Dr. Smith and see about getting back on it.

It is a common occurrence for clients to come to their own conclusion that medication would be helpful when they are held accountable for change in a respectful manner (M. C. Cabie, personal communication, June 28, 1996). Clients truly want to achieve their miracles, and when the therapist respectfully invites the clients to explore what will be different when the mental health symptoms and other current problems are resolved, they are oftentimes more than willing to acknowledge that medication may be the best alternative. Because this decision comes from the client, the client is more likely to comply with their medications despite some of the unpleasant side effects.

Cultural Considerations

No discussion about any therapeutic approach would be complete without describing the importance of being culturally sensitive and ensuring that our methodologies are culturally relevant. Because solution-focused brief therapy rests steadfastly upon the expertise of each client, the solutions that the clients generate are always culturally appropriate. Families who depend upon extended family members seamlessly incorporate these loved ones into their miracles, while religious clients readily incorporate religious tenets and practices into their solutions. A therapist with the most advanced training could never have suggested a more culturally aware plan than that created by the clients themselves. It serves as a fitting reminder that the clients are the experts on themselves, while the therapist is only the expert on the process of change and asking purposeful questions. It is the therapist's role to listen carefully and respectfully to each and every solution, trusting the wisdom it holds.

Summary

Paradoxically, the underlying tenets of solution-focused brief therapy lend themselves to working well with clients who are strong believers of the 12-step programs, the disease model of recovery, and many other cultural groups, for the foundation of solution-focused brief therapy is that of faith in the clients and their solutions. This faith requires that the therapist remain neutral and skillfully work within the context that the clients and their systems provide. This neutral stance allows the therapist to work effectively with more traditional substance abuse treatment components, adolescents, co-occurring disorders, and myriad situations. In Chapter 9, we will provide some sample forms and handouts that we hope will be helpful as you apply the concepts learned in our book with your clients and settings.

9

Forms and Handouts

> When the future, expressed in terms of goals, is drawn in specifics, i.e., in behavioral terms, and the goals are ones established by the client, then doing something now (in the present) to obtain those goals makes sense.
>
> **Steve de Shazer**

Introduction

Paperwork and the completion of myriad forms is a necessary evil for all therapists. While it is not something to which most therapists aspire, most come to terms that paperwork is necessary in order to provide evidence that purposeful work was done during the time together and that standards of care were met. The majority of client files are never subpoenaed into court or reviewed by outside sources; however, an experienced clinician knows too well that one never knows which client will come to some ill fate, requiring the file and the content of the therapy sessions to come under scrutiny. Nowhere is this more true than when working with substance abusing clients in an agency setting. Throughout my career working with the highest risk clients, I have had countless clients die from car accidents, medical complications, suicide, homicide, and the like. Each required soulful review of the file to ensure that each client received the utmost level of care and that the therapist did not overlook warning signs.

In private practice settings, insurance companies require clear documentation that their dollars were well spent. Audits can occur at random, and a wise therapist keeps adequate records that demonstrate standards of care were met. In this chapter we will review three types of ongoing documentation that would be prudent to include in client records: client issues lists, treatment plans, and homework sheets. They serve to assist a problem-focused reviewer in clearly understanding how a solution-focused therapist is meeting standards of care, while allowing the therapist the flexibility to provide solution-focused services unencumbered to the client.

Client Issues List

The identification of client problems or issues[1] is a standard practice in problem-focused approaches. This provides the therapist with the necessary information to formulate diagnoses and determine the most appropriate course of action. Over the years, it has become standard practice to include a list of all of the identified problems in the clients' charts. This allows the therapist to readily glance at the list to ensure that treatment is sufficiently addressing each area of concern. While a specific list of problems is not a stated requirement of standards of care, therapists are required to prove that they did not overlook any problem that would readily be identified by a jury of their peers should client care come into question. The simplest way to demonstrate to an outside reviewer that all problems (many therapists now use the term *issues* in an attempt to move away from the more negative term *problem*) were identified is to include a formal list. This is now standard practice in most agency settings as a tool to limit liability and provide easy chart review by clinical supervisors.

When working from a solution-focused stance, I have found it imperative to include an issues list in each client file. The use of solution-focused brief therapy is rarely understood by most reviewers and is even met with suspicion at times. Because of this, I have found that the reviewers are assured that clients are receiving excellent care when they can easily see that we have not minimized issues that standards of care would identify as problematic. I have learned that it is best to translate my solution-focused work into problem-focused language when I work with or am accountable to other professionals, and the client issues list serves as an invaluable tool in this end.

The first step when completing a client issues list (see Figure 9.1) is to brainstorm a list of issues that all members in the client system would identify (this would include the regulation ring of the system as discussed in Chapter 2). This may include child welfare concerns, legal involvement, past or current mental health symptoms, medical issues, parenting concerns, and so on. It can be helpful to step into a regulatory agency's shoes to think from a broader perspective of what should be included. A well-formulated list also includes any issues that arose from the evaluation testing and the American Society of Addiction Medicine Patient Placement

Client Issues List

Client: _Susan Smith_   Client Number: _123456_

	Date ID	Who ID	STAGE	Disposition	Issue
1	4/30/07	Client	Action	Child Welfare	Client history of substance abuse resulting in caseworker concern
2	4/30/07	Client	Maintenance	Resolved	Client's husband committed suicide
3	4/30/07	Client	Action	Probation	Legal charges resulting in probation involvement
4	4/30/07	Client	Action	Physician	Client is pregnant and in need of prenatal care
5	4/30/07	Caseworker	Contemplative	Child Welfare to refer client	Client report of past diagnosis of "Borderline Personality Disorder" and "Depression" resulting in possible need for treatment.
6	4/30/07	Client	Maintenance	Resolved	Client history of physical and sexual abuse
7	4/30/07	Client	Action	Food Stamps	Lack of employment resulting in financial stress and need for additional assistance.
8	4/30/07	Client	Action	Substance Abuse Treatment Agency	Unresolved grief resulting in conflict with partner
9	4/30/07	Client	Action	Substance Abuse Treatment Agency	Children have extensive developmental needs that are currently unaddressed
10	4/30/07	Client	Pre-contemplative	Declined	Client smokes tobacco
11					

Figure 9.1   Sample Client Issues List

Criteria, Second Edition, Revised (ASAM PPC-2R). This demonstrates to a reviewer that these issues were taken into account during the treatment planning phase. (It is important to note that a solution-focused therapist does not use the testing directly when creating treatment plans unless the client identifies that an issue noted in the testing would be useful to address in that manner. The issues are simply listed on the issues list to demonstrate to a potential reviewer that the therapist is aware of them.)

The second step is to then step into the client's shoes to determine which of these issues the client would agree are of concern. If the client would agree that a specific issue is a concern, then the word *client* would be listed under the "Who ID" (or who identified the issue) column. In Colorado, at the time of this writing, standards of care are to use motivational interviewing (Miller & Rollnick, 2002)[2] terminology. Therefore, we have included a column to translate our work into this language for the reviewer. As you can see in Figure 9.1, issue 5 was identified by the client's caseworker (meaning that the client does not fully agree that she has any mental health issues). Therefore, the identified stage of change is listed as contemplative since this client is open to the caseworker's suggestion to complete a mental health evaluation, although she is not convinced it is needed.

The third step is to determine what professional agency is responsible for ensuring that each issue gets resolved. This is then written in the "Disposition" column. Sometimes standards of care require that issues be identified even though there are no current symptoms, in order to demonstrate that the therapist is aware of the history and the resultant potential impact on the client's current behavior. The therapist would then write "resolved" as the disposition (see issues 2 and 6). The stage of change in these cases would be maintenance. In these cases, the client would be listed under the "Who ID" column to indicate that there are no professionals who are expressing concern regarding this past issue. Other times clients and those within the client's system state that the identified issue is not something that needs to be changed (these would only be issues that are required to be identified by the regulation ring). An example of this would be tobacco use (see issue 10). Colorado identifies tobacco as a substance of abuse, so this should be included on the issues list. However, most referral sources do not require clients to make changes in this area. Should a client decline making any changes in this area, it would be listed as "declined" and the stage of change would be precontemplative. Since we learned about the tobacco use from the client and there are no professionals who are insisting that the client address this issue, we would list "client" in the "Who ID" column.

Having a single form that lists all of the agencies involved in the client's life (those listed in the "Disposition" column) serves an important role of informing the therapist about who is involved in the client's system. Releases of information should then be gathered according to the client's comfort level in order to work from a systematic approach throughout the client's treatment episode.

When working with a client to formulate this list, it is imperative that the client's voice be paramount. This means that the majority of issues listed should be those that the client identified and wants to be different, and are thereby listed in the action stage of change. This provides a foundation for the solution-focused therapist and client to work together to create a treatment plan. In our example the client disclosed to the therapist that it would be helpful for her to be able to talk with her partner and children about areas of sadness they had recently experienced. She also identified that she would like to better understand her children and how to relate to them. The therapist then translated the client's wishes into problem-focused language (see issues 8 and 9) and listed the substance abuse treatment agency as the disposition. (It is important to note that a problem-focused therapist might assume that the client's current difficulty in dealing with grief is connected to her prior experience with her previous husband's suicide. A solution-focused therapist would make no such assumption. Using a list such as this allows the solution-focused therapist to acknowledge that this past suicide event is known, but to separate these two issues and remain focused on the client's current issue as described by the client. Without such a list, a problem-focused reviewer might erroneously believe that the therapist was not aware of this information and did not take this past history into account.) Let us now look at how these treatment plans would be written to allow a problem-focused reviewer to understand the work that will be done.

Treatment Planning

Writing solution-focused treatment plans can initially seem like a daunting task. How can a therapist write a list of specific tasks that a client is to do while still holding true to the basic tenet of solution-focused brief therapy of allowing the client to be the expert on the solution? The key to this dilemma is for the therapist to write broad steps that are still specific and measurable,[3] but that guide the clients to discovering their own solutions. Ideally, the steps would build upon each other, with the client's answers providing the direction for subsequent steps. Let us first begin with understanding client objectives.

The format that I have found to be most compatible with solution-focused brief therapy uses two objectives to break the larger goal into two smaller components: a thinking component and a doing component. Solution-focused brief therapy (similar to most approaches) begins with a thinking or cognitive type portion. This cognitive portion includes the miracle question and has the desired outcome of assisting the client to imagine life without the problem. Other positive outcomes of this cognitive piece are for the clients to become more aware of what they are doing that is working, and perhaps become encouraged that the miracle is occurring on occasion. This serves to shift the clients' focus to the solution rather than being preoccupied by the problem. Lastly, by imagining life without the problem, clients gain clues of what behaviors they will have begun doing in order to resolve the problem. This insight provides the foundation for the next objective.

Solution-focused brief therapy then has a second component: action. Once clients identify what they are currently doing that works, it is natural for them to consciously engage in these behaviors more frequently. Likewise, once they become more aware of behaviors they will be doing once the problem is resolved, they readily begin to engage in those as well. These two normal processes (the thinking and the doing) readily lend themselves to clear steps that can be used to break down each of these objectives. As you can see from Figures 9.2 and 9.3,[4] the treatment plans take on a similar feel, while remaining individualized to the clients' desired outcomes. Client language is incorporated into the treatment plans whenever possible (for example, the phrase "openly and honestly" in Figure 9.2) to make the plans client-friendly and a natural extension of the work that will be done during the sessions.

As the therapist naturally utilizes solution-focused brief therapy during group or individual sessions by asking the client the miracle question, the client in turn completes the first step of the first objective (the client will identify how her life will be different when …). Noticing assignments and difference questions are an integral part of a solution-focused treatment plan. Scales can also be added to the second objective as needed, allowing clients to regularly measure their progress in any given area. Each plan is customized to the language of the client's desired goal. Written assignments can be used for clients who find that medium helpful, while noticing and verbally telling group members or the therapist can be used for others.

Homework Sheets

As clients identify what will be different once the problem is resolved, they readily begin to identify small, tangible activities that they can do between sessions to get them closer to their goals. We have found it valuable to capture these specific tasks and record them. Not only do they serve as valuable evidence for reviewers that our clients are active participants in creating and working toward change, but they also help motivate clients to follow through once they have committed in writing to accomplishing a specific task. The homework sheet (see Figure 9.4) is a basic form that

INDIVIDUAL TREATMENT PLAN #1
Client Issue's List # 8

Client Name: Susan Smith   Client #: 123456
Responsible Counselor: Samantha   Date: 4/30/07

GOAL: The client will identify and practice the skills necessary to increase her ability to communicate "openly and honestly" with her boyfriend and children about grief and loss. (Action)

SHORT TERM OBJECTIVE: The client will identify the skills necessary to increase her ability to communicate "openly and honestly" with her boyfriend and children about grief and loss.

DUE DATE: 7/16/07

CLIENT'S STEPS:

1. The client will identify ways in which her life is different when she has the ability to communicate "openly and honestly" with her boyfriend and children about grief and loss x 1. (MQ)

2. The client will identify skills that she currently uses that help her to communicate "openly and honestly" with her boyfriend and children about grief and loss 1 per week x 6 weeks.

3. The client will notice times when she is able to communicate with her boyfriend "openly and honestly" about grief and loss and will identify the skills she used to assist her in doing so, 1 x per week x 6 weeks.

SHORT TERM OBEJCTIVE: The client will practice the skills necessary to increase her ability to communicate "openly and honestly" with her boyfriend and children about grief and loss.

DUE DATE: 7/16/07

CLIENT'S STEPS:

1. The client will share with the group the answer to her miracle question x 1.

2. The client will practice the skills necessary to increase her ability to communicate "openly and honestly" with her boyfriend and children about grief and loss and report her progress to the adult group 1 x per week for 6 weeks.

3. The client will notice the difference it makes for her when she is able to communicate "openly and honestly" with her boyfriend and children about grief and loss, daily.

4. The client will notice the difference it makes for her boyfriend and children when she is able to communicate "openly and honestly" with them about grief and loss, daily.

COUNSELOR STEPS:

1. The counselor will facilitate groups 1x per week x 6 weeks.

2. The counselor will monitor the client's progress 1x per week x 6 weeks.

3. The counselor will meet individually with the client on an as needed basis.

4. The counselor will meet individually with the client following the 6-week period to assess her progress and need for additional treatment services.

_____   _____   _____   _____
CLIENT SIGNATURE   DATE   COUNSELOR SIGNATURE   DATE
■■

_____   _____
DATE CLIENT COMPLETED GOAL   COUNSELOR SIGNATURE

Figure 9.2 Sample Treatment Plan 1

allows clients to record in their own words their desired goal and each step they identify as the sessions progress. This fluidity allows the client assignments to be much more specific than would be possible on a pre-made treatment plan, for clients can modify and hone their assignments based upon the outcome of previous tasks. The top of the form provides a space for the clients to write their goal in their own words. This provides

INDIVIDUAL TREATMENT PLAN #2
Client Issue's List # 9

Client Name: Susan Smith	Client #: 123456
Responsible Counselor: Samantha	Date: 4/30/07

GOAL: The client will explore and implement what she needs to do in order to address the developmental needs of her children and the child she is expecting. (Action)

SHORT TERM OBJECTIVE: The client will explore what she will need to do to address the developmental needs of her children and the child she is expecting.

DUE DATE: 7/16/07

CLIENT'S STEPS:

1. The client is to describe how her life will be different when she has the confidence that she can address the developmental needs of her children and the child she is expecting, x 1. (MQ)

2. The client will discuss in the adult group what she is currently doing to address the developmental needs of her children and the child she is expecting, x 1.

3. The client will discuss in the adult group what she is doing in her miracle day when she has the confidence in her ability to address the developmental needs of her children and the child she is expecting, x 1.

SHORT TERM OBEJCTIVE: The client will implement what she needs to do in order to address the developmental needs of her children and the child she is expecting.

DUE DATE: 7/16/07

CLIENT'S STEPS:

1. The client will gain knowledge about child development so she can be educated about what she needs to be aware of for her children and the child she is expecting, on-going.

2. The client will discuss in group what she is doing to help her son cope with his belief that he needs to care for her while she is pregnant, 2 x's per month for 8 weeks.

3. The client will continue to address the developmental needs of her daughter and share with the adult group what she is doing that works well, 2 x's per month for 8 weeks.

4. The client will discuss with the group what difference it makes in her life when she is confident in her ability to address the developmental needs of her children and the child she is expecting, x 1.

COUNSELOR STEPS:

1. The counselor will facilitate group 2 x's per month for 8 weeks.

2. The counselor will monitor the client's progress 2 x's per month for 8 weeks.

3. The counselor will assess the client's progress at the end of the 8 weeks to evaluate the need for further treatment.

_____   _____   _____   _____
CLIENT SIGNATURE   DATE   COUNSELOR SIGNATURE   DATE

_____   _____
DATE CLIENT COMPLETED GOAL   COUNSELOR SIGNATURE

Figure 9.3   Sample Treatment Plan 2

excellent feedback for the therapist as to how accurate the treatment plans truly are. If the client's written goal is significantly different from the formalized treatment plan, it would be wise for the therapist to update the treatment plan to be more in line with the client's own words. The homework sheet also allows a space for the clients to change their mind and create a new treatment goal at any point. The clients then write what they would like to assign themselves for homework at the end of each session.

TREATMENT CONTRACT/HOMEWORK SHEET

Client's Goal:_____

_____

Modified Goal:_____

_____

Homework:
1:

_____

2:

_____

3:

_____

4:

_____

5:

_____

6:

_____

7:

_____

8:

_____

9:

_____

10:

_____

Client Name_____
Client Number _____

Figure 9.4 Sample Homework Sheet

Having all of the assignments on the same page allows clients to reflect upon previous assignments to determine if they are satisfied with their progress and to be reminded of how far they have come. Once treatment is finished, these homework sheets become attached to the treatment plans in the clients' files since they work in partnership to guide/demonstrate the agreed upon plan for treatment.

Summary

Paperwork is a necessary part of good client care. While regulatory agencies and standards of care dictate what type of information must be present in client files, there are creative ways to ensure that problem-focused reviewers can readily understand and respect the work done by solution-focused therapists. While we have provided you a few examples, the possibilities are endless.

Endnotes

1. The terms *problem* and *issue* can be used interchangeably; however, we prefer the term *issue* when required in chart documentation in an effort to help remind the solution-focused therapist that the identification of such items is primarily to help translate the solution-focused work into problem-focused language.

2. It is important to note that motivational interviewing builds upon the original work of Prochaska and DiClemente (1984), Prochaska, Norcross and DiClemente (1994), and Prochaska and Norcross (1999). In Miller and Rollnick's (2002) work, they focus on utilizing Prochaska, DiClemente, and Norcross's stages-of-change model to increase motivation in clients who are struggling with substance misuse. Although the stages-of-change model was created by Prochaska, Norcross and DiClemente, we refer the reader to motivational interviewing since the field of substance abuse uses this as a foundational text, and because the goal of writing the stage of change here is to demonstrate to a potential reviewer that the therapist is familiar with Miller and Rollnick's work in increasing motivation in this population.

3. It is important to note that solution-focused brief therapy adheres to all the components of well-written treatment plans. While reviewing the basics of writing sound treatment plans is outside the purpose of this text, treatment plans should be measurable, specific, written in terms of something positive rather than the absence of something negative, and so on (Berg & Miller, 1992).

4. Special thanks to therapist Lee Culbertson for sharing the concepts from an actual client case for these treatment plan samples.

Appendix: Resources

We have included an annotated list of our favorite texts on this subject and those we believe may be most beneficial for additional reading. Enjoy.

Alcoholics Anonymous World Services. (1976). *Alcoholics anonymous* (3rd ed.). New York: Author.

- This volume was written by the founders of Alcoholics Anonymous (AA) originally in 1939. This book is the fundamental and basic text for AA. It provides guidance and direction for those dealing with an addiction and how to move toward recovery. The book begins with the founder's story of recovery and provides steps and motivation for those trying to achieve and maintain sobriety. A large portion of the book contains individual stories of those in recovery. These stories are intended to "represent the current membership of Alcoholics Anonymous more accurately, and thereby to reach more alcoholics" (pp. xii).

Beck, A. T., Steer, R. A., & Brown, G. K. (1996). *BDI-II Manual*. San Antonio: Psychological Corp., Harcourt Brace.

- The *BDI-II Manual* describes the development of the Beck Depression Inventory. Chapters on administration and scoring and psychometric characteristics are included. This manual can only be obtained by purchasing copies of the BDI-II.

Beck, A. T., Steer, R. A., & Garbin, M. G. (1988). Psychometric properties of the Beck Depression Inventory: Twenty-five years of evaluation. *Clinical Psychology Review, 8,* 77–100.

- Beck, Steer, and Garbin give a report of the psychometric properties of the Beck Depression Inventory (BDI) between the years 1961 and 1986. The reported internal consistency for the BDI is .86 for psychiatric patients and .81 for nonpsychiatric subjects. The BDI is reported as discriminating between subtypes of depression as well as differences between anxiety and depression.

Berg, I. K. (1994). *Family based services: A solution-focused approach*. New York: Norton.

- This book is intended for clinicians working in the child welfare system. Berg describes how to identify client resources in a way that can be used to empower families who are involved with the system. Some of the topics covered by the book include: developing cooperation with clients, goal setting and contract making, how to conduct a family session, reporting child abuse while maintaining a therapeutic relationship with the client, and special problems that arise in child welfare. Emphasis is placed on the uniqueness of solutions and families.

Berg, I. K. (1995). Solution-focused brief therapy with substance abusers. In A. Washton (Ed.), *Psychotherapy and substance abuse: A practitioner's handbook* (pp. 223–242). New York: Guilford.

- This chapter gives step-by-step procedures for using solution-focused brief therapy with substance abusers. Berg stresses the need to switch from problem solving to solution building when working with this population. The role and importance of highlighting clients' exceptions is discussed. Berg writes to an audience that is new or unfamiliar with the model and encourages further readings of the literature on solution-focused brief therapy.

Berg, I. K., & de Shazer, S. (1993). Making numbers talk: Language in therapy. In S. Friendman (Ed.), *The new language of change: Constructive collaboration in psychotherapy*. New York: Guilford.

- Berg and de Shazer begin by discussing different views of language. The use of scaling questions is then described in detail. Scaling is presented as a way in which to construct a helpful way of talking given that the client and the therapist can never really understand each other's words. Cases are given to illustrate their interventions.

Berg, I. K., & Dolan, Y. (2001). *Tales of solutions: A collection of hope-inspiring stories*. New York: Norton.

- This book is a compilation of stories about how small changes in seemingly hopeless situations led to large changes for people from around the world. These stories are categorized into chapters based on solution-focused principles and interventions such as the miracle question, finding exceptions, scaling, going slowly, and so forth. Berg and Dolan offer commentary to highlight and expand the collection of hope-inspiring stories.

Berg, I. K., & Gallagher, D. (1991). Solution-focused brief treatment with adolescent substance abusers. In T. C. Todd & M. D. Selekman (Eds.), *Family therapy approaches with adolescent substance abusers* (pp. 93–111). Needham Heights, MA: Allyn and Bacon.

- In this chapter the authors discuss adolescent substance abuse from a developmental and a solution-focused lens. Berg and Gallagher provide key intervention strategies for using solution-focused brief therapy with an adolescent substance abusing population. A case example is given to guide the reader through the interventions. The authors stress the importance of clients developing goals that are salient to them.

Berg, I. K., & Miller, S. D. (1992). *Working with the problem drinker: A solution-focused approach*. New York: Norton.

- Berg and Miller provide a nontraditional approach to working with the problem drinker. They discuss their five-step model, which includes the following chapters: "Developing Cooperative

Client-Therapist Relationships," "Developing Well-Formed Treat-
ment Goals," "Negotiating and Cooperating: Goals and the Client-
Therapist Relationship," "Orienting Toward Solution: How to
Interview for a Change," and "The Components, and Types and
Delivery of Treatment Interventions." Case examples are also
included to illustrate their approach.

Berg, I. K., & Reuss, N. H. (1998). *Solutions step by step: A substance abuse
treatment manual.* New York: Norton.

- Berg and Reuss's focus is on how to use clients' past strategies of success to aid in building solutions for the future. The book includes two
  sections. Part 1 describes a detailed look at how to use solution-focused
  brief therapy with substance abusers. Part 2 includes several chapters
  that cover specific treatment situations (e.g., chronic relapsing clients,
  women with substance abuse issues, etc.). Throughout the book the
  authors give helpful tips from the field of substance abuse treatment.
  Questions are also stated and answered by the authors from a solution-focused perspective. In addition, a video was created to illustrate
  the interventions from the book and can be purchased separately.

Berg, I. K., & Steiner, T. (2003). *Children's solution work.* New York: Norton.

- This book is written for those who already understand solution-
  focused brief therapy and those who want to gain a greater confidence of applying the model to working with children. Berg and
  Steiner give step-by-step suggestions to working with children and
  parents. In the first part of the book the authors discuss why they
  believe that solution-focused brief therapy is helpful when working
  with children and their families. A section on learning to prepare
  for working with children is also given. Next, the authors answer
  questions they have been asked over the years about using the solution-focused model with children. Finally, they give support and
  suggestions for clinicians who find themselves at an impasse.

Bertalanffy, L. von. (1968). *General system theory: Foundations, development, applications.* New York: George Braziller.

- This source is a fundamental foundation for all systems-oriented
  therapeutic models. The author writes this book in an attempt to
  address the scientific community in a manner that broadens its view
  of general systems theory. A chapter is included on the application
  of general systems theory to the fields of psychology and psychiatry. Original citations are provided, and von Bertalanffy widens the
  view of the application of systems theory.

Budman, S. H., & Gurman, A. S. (1988). *Theory and practice of brief therapy.* New York: Guilford.

- This book provides a description of brief therapy, why it is utilized,
  how to make it effective, and special consideration for brief therapy.

The authors provide a chapter for five common presenting concerns for therapy and how they are addressed in a brief format. These presenting concerns include loss, developmental concerns, marital or family conflict, symptomatic presentation, and personality disorders. The authors also provide information on brief group therapy and considerations for termination. Case examples are provided to illustrate the brief therapy model.

Cloud, W., & Granfield, R. (2001). *Recovery from addiction*. New York: New York University Press.

- Cloud and Granfield present a range of information related to traditional and nontraditional approaches to the treatment of addiction for individuals interested in recovery or for their friends or family members. The authors present the pros and cons of traditional treatment methods and 12-step groups, as well as other emerging treatment options. The authors outline environmental considerations and things to consider when selecting a treatment approach. Additionally, Cloud and Granfield present ideas and considerations for how to overcome addiction individually, without the assistance of groups or other treatment options.

DeJong, P., & Berg, I. K. (2008). *Interviewing for solutions* (3rd ed). Belmont, CA: Thomson Brooks/Cole.

- The focus of DeJong and Berg's book is to describe how they interview clients in a solution-focused manner. They describe their interviewing approach as solution building and contrast it to the traditional methods of problem solving. Topics such as interviewing involuntary and crisis clients are discussed. Outcome research on solution-focused brief therapy is also presented. Interviews from the authors are given to illustrate solution-building language. To complement this book, an *Instructor's Resource Manual*, *Learner's Workbook*, and videotape are available.

Department of Health and Human Services Substance Abuse and Mental Health Services Administration. (1999). *Brief interventions and brief therapies for substance abuse* (TIP 34, DHHS Publication SMA 99-3353). Rockville, MD: Center for Substance Abuse Treatment. Retrieved on December 13, 2007, from http://www.ncbi.nlm.nih.gov/books/bv.fcgi?rid=hstat5.chapter.59192

- This book is part of SAMHSA's Treatment Improvement Protocol (TIP) series and covers the issue of brief interventions and brief interventions with substance abusers. Various types of brief therapy are presented and offered as tools for substance abuse clinicians. Theory and application of the models are presented in a very reader-friendly manner. This document is published by SAMHSA and is available online.

de Shazer, S. (1982). *Patterns of brief family therapy*. New York: Guilford.

- De Shazer uses *Patterns of Brief Family Therapy* to describe the evolution of his model at the Brief Family Therapy Center (BFTC) in Milwaukee, Wisconsin. A philosophical explanation of the foundations of the center's work is given in detail. A discussion of change sets the tone for the book. The author continues by describing key influences to the work at the BFTC, such as Milton Erickson, the Mental Research Institute, and the Milan Group. Procedures are included with case examples to illustrate the work.

de Shazer, S. (1985). *Keys to solution in brief therapy*. New York: Norton.

- This book uses the analogy of a skeleton key to illustrate therapy. The author states that solutions occur through keys instead of locks. Skeleton keys work in various locks and thus represent how solutions do not need to fit the complexity of the lock. The book emphasizes that the details and history of a client's problem are not important. The focus is to help clients discuss how they will know that their problem is solved. de Shazer also talks about the therapeutic relationship as being cooperative in nature. Many case examples are given to illustrate various topics throughout the book.

de Shazer, S. (1986). An indirect approach to brief therapy. *The Family Therapy Collections, 19*, 48–55.

- This article uses a case example to illustrate prescribing the symptom to a family that presented for therapy with a daughter experiencing stomach pains. The therapist prescribed the symptom of predicting who else in the family would have a stomachache. After the third session the mother thanked the therapist for saving their marriage. While the therapist was not aware of the marital problems, this example shows the usefulness of indirect approaches. The author describes in detail how indirect interventions can be useful in creating solutions.

de Shazer, S. (1988). *Clues: Investigating solutions in brief therapy*. New York: Norton.

- In this book, de Shazer takes an in-depth look at what happens during a therapeutic interview. Main concepts of solution-focused brief therapy are addressed and discussed in *Clues*. Principles such as "the solution always comes before the problem" and "nothing always happens" are discussed. Several chapters focus on the development of a theory of solution. Many case examples are given to illustrate concepts of the model.

de Shazer, S. (1991). *Putting difference to work*. New York: Norton.

- In this book de Shazer continues to discuss the nature of therapeutic interview as a conversation. He stresses the disconnect between problems and solutions in order to create more options for solution development. This book uses narratives and essays to discuss general labels such as *therapy*, *family therapy*, and *brief therapy*. The emphasis is more on describing and thinking about therapy versus how to do therapy. Part 1 covers structuralism, poststructuralism, and constructivism. The second part of the book deals with topics such as language games, therapeutic change, and the concept of exception.

de Shazer, S. (1993). Creative misunderstanding: There is no escape from language. In S. Gilligan & R. Price (Eds.), *Therapeutic conversations*. New York: W. W. Norton & Co.

- In this book chapter the author describes three related issues: therapeutic conversations, the use of language, and viewing therapy as conversation. de Shazer begins by explaining the difference between therapy is conversation and therapy as conversation. Next, a philosophical discussion of word meaning and usage is covered. Finally, the author discusses the definitions of therapy and conversation. At the end of the chapter, Stephen Gilligan gives a commentary on de Shazer's writings.

de Shazer, S. (1994). *Words were originally magic*. New York: Norton.

- *Words Were Originally Magic* describes in depth the use of language. de Shazer explains how his approach is poststructural and highlights other philosophical nuances of solution-focused brief therapy. Part 2 of the book discusses the differences between problem-talk and solution-talk. de Shazer does a nice job in this section using clinical excerpts to illustrate how he employs language to achieve specific goals with his clients. Overall, this is a wonderful book that describes in detail how solution-focused brief therapy is a unique clinical approach.

de Shazer, S., & Berg, I. K. (1992). Doing therapy: A post-structural revision. *Journal of Marital and Family Therapy*, *18*, 71–81.

- This article by de Shazer and Berg aims to discuss the importance and meaning of language within a therapeutic setting. Wittgenstein's concept of "language games" is discussed along with "private language" and constructivism. de Shazer and Berg write about poststructuralism and the role of language in therapy. Case material is used to illustrate their stance.

de Shazer, S., Berg, I. K., Lipchik, E., Nunnaly, E., Molnar, A., Gingerich, W., et al. (1986). Brief therapy: Focused solution development. *Family Process*, *25*, 207–221.

- This article begins by describing the history of brief therapy. The authors then go on to describe their work at the Brief Family Therapy Center (BFTC). They state that they are most interested in solutions and how they work. Seven principles of their work are given and described. The differences between complaints and solutions are described in order to highlight how the work at the BFTC differs from other brief therapy approaches. Case examples are given to illustrate their work. Next, the authors describe the format of their therapy sessions in detail. Lastly, the authors describe how they follow-up with the clients and their evaluation of client progress.

de Shazer, S., Dolan, Y., Korman, H., Trepper, T., McCollum, E., & Berg, I. K. (2007). *More than miracles: The state of the art of solution-focused brief therapy*. New York: Haworth.

- *More Than Miracles* is a comprehensive version of recent developments in solution-focused brief therapy. This book begins with an overview of the basic principles and premises of solution-focused brief therapy. Several chapters give case examples that illustrate how these solution-focused principles and techniques can be employed in therapy, and are accompanied by explanatory commentary and descriptions from the authors. Additionally, this book addresses how emotions are utilized in solution-focused brief therapy, and concludes with a chapter that answers common questions and misconceptions about the model.

de Shazer, S., & Isebaert, L. (2003). The Bruges Model: A solution-focused approach to problem drinking. *Journal of Family Psychotherapy, 14,* 43–52.

- Co-authors de Shazer and Isebaert describe a new program with problem drinkers in Bruges, Belgium. The Bruges Model for the treatment of problem drinking is described in depth. Both inpatient and outpatient treatment are offered using this approach. One main feature of this model is that the client is given a choice between abstinence-based or controlled drinking. A four-year follow-up on the model was conducted and is reported in this article. Results show that out of 118 inpatient and 72 outpatient clients, 84% of the inpatient clients and 81% of the outpatient clients reported maintaining their goal of either controlled drinking or abstaining from alcohol.

Dolan, Y. M. (1985). *A path with a heart: Ericksonian utilization with resistant and chronic clients*. New York: Brunner/Mazel.

- Dolan's *A Path With a Heart* is a practitioner's guide for therapists working with resistant and chronic clients. A sequential progression of the chapters requires one to read them in numerical order. Dolan begins by describing Ericksonian utilization and moves toward using hypnosis with chronic and resistant clients. The last chapter of the book applies Ericksonian utilization in group settings. Dolan discusses using the client's resources to obtain therapeutic change.

Dolan, Y. M. (1991). *Resolving sexual abuse: Solution-focused brief therapy and Ericksonian hypnosis for adult survivors*. New York: Norton.

- Dolan provides specific and practical techniques that enable clients not only to resolve past sexual abuse but also to form a clear map of functional, healthy behaviors and perceptions to replace trauma-based coping behaviors. She offers specific strategies for addressing and treating the following issues related to sexual abuse: post-traumatic amnesia, self-mutilation, sexual dysfunctions, memory problems, and many other symptoms. Emphasis is placed on the survivor's natural resources and behavior.

Dolan, Y. (1998). *One small step: Moving beyond trauma and therapy to a life of joy.* Watsonville, CA: Papier-Mache.

- Dolan writes this book for survivors of trauma who are interested in finding joy in life again. This book is divided into four parts. Part 1 is centered on the idea of appreciating what is happening in the present. Dolan provides numerous creative ways of relaxing and enjoying the here and now. Part 2 outlines thoughts and methods for moving toward a positive future perspective. Part 3 provides a way of honoring the events of the past and the impact of those events while actively overcoming these experiences through coping strategies and altering expectations. Finally, Part 4 outlines methods for developing support groups, gives ideas for group exercises, and provides resources for survivors to consider.

Donley, R. J., Horan, J. J., & DeShong, R. L. (1989). The effect of several self-disclosure permutations on counseling process and outcome. *Journal of Counseling and Development, 67,* 408–412.

- This article reports the findings of a study conducted on the effects of counselor self-disclosure. College seniors with deficient job-interviewing skills were assigned to one of the groups. Two kinds of counselor self-disclosures were used, along with two groups not using self-disclosures. Results indicated that counselor self-disclosures are not particularly helpful to clients.

Duncan, B. L., Hubble, M. A., & Miller, S. D. (1997, July/August). Stepping off the throne. *Family Therapy Networker, 21,* 22–33.

- The authors describe two cases in which they focused on listening to the client and inviting his or her participation. They discuss research findings on what is helpful in session and tie the results into their work. The authors share that through their years of clinical experience they have learned first and foremost the value of their words with clients, instead of techniques or models.

Eakes, G., Walsh, S., Markowski, M., Cain, H., & Swanson, M. (1997). Family-centered brief solution-focused brief therapy with chronic schizophrenia: A pilot study. *Journal of Family Therapy, 19,* 145–158.

- This article presents the results of an outcome study on using solution-focused brief therapy with families and clients diagnosed with schizophrenia. This study used a traditional experimental design with a control group receiving traditional outpatient therapy. The Family Environment Scale was given to both groups before and after treatment. Significant differences were found on the following subscales of the Family Environment Scale: active-recreational orientation, expressiveness, moral religious emphasis, and family incongruence.

Erickson, M. H., & Rossi, E. (1979). *Hypnotherapy: An exploratory casebook*. New York: Irvington.

- Erickson and Rossi begin this book by providing a step-by-step look at hypnotherapy and a specific view of the utilization approach to hypnotherapy. The authors outline several indirect forms of suggestion, and transition to a description of trance induction and suggestion; this is followed by a discussion about posthypnotic suggestion. Individual chapters have been dedicated to case studies that showcase the use of hypnotherapy in reducing pain and discomfort, reducing symptoms, revivifying or retrieving forgotten memories, increasing ability to cope, and transforming identity and increasing potential. The authors include in several of the chapters exercises for the facilitator to utilize in order to practice achieving the attitudes and skills needed to perform this work.

Erickson, M. H., Rossi, E., & Rossi, S. (1976). *Hypnotic realities*. New York: Irvington.

- Milton Erickson, along with Ernest Rossi and Sheila Rossi, co-author a book that talks in depth about inducing clinical hypnosis and forms of hypnotic suggestion. Erickson discusses various ways in which psychotherapists can use persuasion in session with or without induction of trance. Chapters share a common format that includes the following: a description of Erickson's induction of clinical hypnosis, commentary by Erickson and discussion with Ernest Rossi, Rossi's elaboration of Erickson's work, and exercises to guide therapists in developing their own skill in hypnotic induction. Chapter headings range from conversational induction, to mutual trance induction, to indirectly conditioned eye closure induction.

Fisher, G. L., & Harrison, T. C. (2005). *Substance abuse information for school counselors, social workers, therapists, and counselors* (3rd ed.). Boston: Pearson.

- Fisher and Harrison begin with a rationale for the role of the mental professional in prevention and treatment of substance abuse. Drugs are then categorized according to their main classifications of stimulants, depressants, and hallucinogens, with attention being paid to psychotropic medications as well. The authors define various models of addiction, with consideration given to assessment and diagnosis. There is a chapter dedicated to culturally and diverse ethnic groups, while the remainder of the book is dedicated to treatment and prevention for special populations, such as families, children, and those with co-occurring disorders.

Gingerich, W. J., & Eisengart, S. (2000). Solution-focused brief therapy: A review of the outcome research. *Family Process, 39*, 477–498.

- Gingerich and Eisengart give a summary of the solution-focused research completed as of 2000. Fifteen studies are reported and described in depth. They divide their article into three categories: well-controlled studies, moderately controlled studies, and poorly controlled studies. Tables are provided to make it easier for the reader to view the main components of each study.

Granfield, R., & Cloud, W. (1999). *Coming clean: Overcoming addiction without treatment.* New York: New York University Press.

- In *Coming Clean*, Granfield and Cloud present information based on interviews they conducted with individuals formerly dependent upon or addicted to drugs or alcohol. The book is divided into two parts. In Part 1, the authors present the strategies their interviewees utilized in overcoming addiction, reasons given for avoiding treatment, and resources that enabled natural recovery. In Part 2, the authors present the implications of natural recovery for professionals working with individuals affected by dependence and addiction. Additionally, the authors discuss the implications of natural recovery for the larger societal system in regards to prevention and policies.

Johnson, C. E., & Webster, D. (2002). *Recrafting a life.* New York: Taylor & Francis.

- This book is meant to be used as an aid to working with clients experiencing chronic illness and chronic pain. In Part 1, the authors share their philosophy of care about health and discuss how they may differ from their clients. The second part gives a more in-depth look at therapeutic approaches to use in session. Issues such as clinical hypnosis and caring for the caregiver are explored.

Lindforss, L., & Magnusson, D. (1997). Solution-focused brief therapy in prison. *Contemporary Family Therapy, 19*, 89–104.

- This article presents the findings of a two-year experiment in Sweden. Solution-focused network therapy was established and tested on prisoners being released back into the community. A case history is given to illustrate the specific treatment that was offered to prisoners. Results indicate that prisoners in the experimental group had lower recidivism rates (47%) than those in the control group (24%).

Lipchik, E. (2002). *Beyond technique.* New York: Guilford Press.

- Lipchik uses her book *Beyond Technique* to answer the questions of practitioners who want to learn more about solution-focused brief therapy. With a clinical focus, the author aids clinicians in understanding how to grasp and use the model. The use of emotions in solution-focused brief therapy is one misunderstood area that Lipchik clarifies. She also describes how to apply the model to couples, families, involuntary clients, crisis situations, and long-term cases.

Marlatt, G. A., & Gordon, J. (Eds.). (1985). *Relapse prevention*. New York: Guilford.

- In *Relapse Prevention*, Marlatt and Gordon provide a resource for clinicians and researchers interested in addiction. This book is divided into two parts. Part 1 provides a theoretical foundation and rationale for the relapse prevention model. It also includes assessment procedures, skill-training interventions, cognitive processes for relapse prevention, and lifestyle modification ideas. Part 2 provides a view of the application of the relapse prevention model when applied to problem drinkers, ex-smokers, and those interested in weight control. Specific methods and interventions are applied to these populations.

McCollum, E., & Trepper, T. S. (2001). *Family solutions for substance abuse*. Binghamton, NY: Haworth.

- McCollum and Trepper write about the application of solution-focused brief therapy with families dealing with substance abuse issues. They begin by talking about the family as a system. They provide basic skills for working with substance abusing families. Other topics include negotiating contracts for treatment, the ups and downs of change, and client termination. This is an excellent source for doing family work with the substance abusing population.

McCollum, E. E., Trepper, T. S., & Smock, S. (2004). Solution-focused brief group therapy for drug abuse: Rationale, content, and approaches. *Journal of Family Psychotherapy, 14*, 27–42.

- This article outlines a group format of solution-focused brief therapy that is focused on substance abusing and dependent clients. The emphasis is on providing a competency-based treatment approach in a group format for this specific population. Motivational interviewing is mentioned as a helpful approach to individual substance abuse treatment but not as a tool for group therapy. An outline of the solution-focused group format is given along with a case example of a solution-focused group therapy session.

Mee-Lee, D. (Ed.). (2001). *ASAM PPC-2R: ASAM patient placement criteria for the treatment of substance-related disorders* (2nd ed. rev.). Chevy Chase, MD: American Society of Addiction Medicine.

- This manual is used for patient placement criteria for those suffering from substance-related disorders. Criteria for adult patients are based on a four-level scale ranging from outpatient services to medically managed intensive inpatient services. Adolescent criteria are also provided. The appendix includes the Clinical Institute Withdrawal Assessment—Alcohol, Revised (CIWA-Ar) Scale.

Miller, G. (1997). *Becoming miracle workers: Language and meaning in brief therapy.* New York: Aldine de Gruyter.

- Miller begins his book by discussing brief therapy. Troubles as systems problems and troubles as language games are two chapters within this first section. Miller then goes on to write about the workings of brief therapy. He discusses the ecosystemic issues, such as change, problems, interventions, and solutions. The final section gives implications of brief therapy.

Miller, G. A. (1997). *The Substance Abuse Subtle Screening Inventory-III manual.* Spencer, IN: Spencer Evening World.

- The SASSI-3 is a screening device intended for identifying substance use disorders. The self-report measure takes approximately 20 minutes to complete and is easy to score. A reliability of 93% accuracy is reported for detecting substance use disorders. This instrument gives profiles of clients that can aid practitioners in delivery treatment. Adolescent and Spanish versions of the instrument are available.

Miller, G., & de Shazer, S. (1998). Have you heard the latest rumor about …? Solution-focused therapy as a rumor. *Family Process, 37,* 363–377.

- The authors use a unique style of discussing their model as a rumor in this article. Wittgenstein's views are covered as the authors explore topics such as the philosophy of language as well as aspects of postmodernist social thought. Therapy is also discussed in terms of ethical issues and political relations.

Miller, S. D., & Berg, I. K. (1995). *The miracle method: A radically new approach to problem drinking.* New York: Norton.

- This book offers hope and steps to follow from a solution-focused perspective and challenges the notion that formal treatment is the only way to overcome problem drinking. The authors suggest six keys for success for the problem drinker: (1) Make sure your miracle is important to you. (2) Keep it small. (3) Make it specific, concrete, and behavioral. (4) Be sure you state what you *will* do rather than what you *won't* do. (5) State how you will start your journey rather than how you will end it. (6) Be clear about who, where, and when, but not why (p. 66). The authors emphasize the value of learning from and building on what is already going well and the successes experienced by the problem drinker. The final chapter outlines suggestions and strategies for countering setbacks on the road to solutions.

Miller, S. D., Duncan, B. L., & Hubble, M. A. (1997). *Escape from Babel: Toward a unifying language for psychotherapy practice*. New York: Norton.

- In *Escape From Babel*, Miller, Duncan, and Hubble present a critique of dividing psychotherapy into several models and debating which model or approach is most effective. Rather than creating a new form of psychotherapy, the authors attempt to present factors of effectiveness that are common across methods or models of psychotherapy and supply a unifying language for all psychotherapists. The authors outline four factors that lead to effective psychotherapy: (1) the client and extratherapeutic factors, (2) a genuine therapeutic relationship between the client and the therapist, (3) the presence of hope for change or expectancy for the future, and (4) the specific models or techniques employed by the therapist. These common factors are illustrated and explained using case examples from the therapists.

Miller, S. D., Hubble, M. A., & Duncan, B. L. (Eds.). (1996). *Handbook of solution-focused brief therapy*. San Francisco: Jossey-Bass.

- This source provides a look at research, case examples, and practical clinical tools. The book is divided into the following three sections: foundations of solution-focused brief therapy, applications of solution-focused brief therapy, and research on solution-focused brief therapy. Topics of domestic violence, grief therapy, and inpatient psychiatry are just a few areas covered.

Miller, W. R., & Rollnick, S. (2002). *Motivational interviewing* (3rd ed.). New York: Guilford.

- The authors of *Motivational Interviewing* begin the book by providing an extensive background on the requirements for change, what leads people to make changes, and aids to understanding why individuals may feel ambivalent about changing. This section of the book is followed by a description of the basics of motivational interviewing (i.e., asking open-ended questions, listening reflectively, affirming, summarizing, eliciting self-motivated statements, etc.) and challenges one may encounter while utilizing motivational interviewing. Finally, the book concludes with additional contributors providing case examples of implementing the motivational interviewing model with various populations, including substance abusers, young people, HIV risk populations, and sex offenders.

National Institute on Drug Abuse. (2000). *Principles of drug addiction treatment: A research-based guide* (NIH Publication 00-4180). Washington, DC: U.S. Department of Health and Human Services.

- Available online at http://www.drugabuse.gov/PODAT/PODAT Index.html, this resource is a publication produced by NIDA on the principles of drug abuse treatment. The manual begins by addressing commonly asked questions about substance abuse treatment. The next section discusses drug abuse treatment in the United States by addressing various types of services. The last section talks about scientifically based approaches to treatment. Additional resources, including manuals and reports, are provided at the end.

Nelson, T. S., & Kelley, L. (2001). Solution-focused couples group. *Journal of Systemic Therapies, 20,* 47–66.

- The authors contribute to the solution-focused literature with this article by providing a guide for conducting couples' groups. A single case study was used to evaluate the effects of the couples' group. Measures of marital satisfaction and goal achievement were used to assess progress. On martial satisfaction, 7 of the 10 participants reported improvement. Goal achievement was self-reported by 8 of the 10 clients.

Nelson, T. S., & Thomas, F. N. (Eds.) (2007). *Handbook of solution-focused brief therapy: Clinical applications brief therapy.* Binghamton, NY: Haworth.

- This book includes solution-focused experts' advice on using the model with specific client situations. After an overview of the solution-focused brief therapy model is given, topics such as public schools, faith-based communities, relieving burnout in mental health practice, addressing depression, and supervision of training are covered. Attention is given to the role of exceptions, goals, and future possibilities.

Pichot, T. (2001). Co-creating solutions for substance abuse. *Journal of Systemic Therapies, 20,* 1–23.

- The author describes one agency's solution to substance abuse treatment by the use of solution-focused brief therapy. Pichot begins by giving an overview and history of substance abuse treatment. Then, an overview of the author's solution-focused approach is provided. The philosophy and application of solution-focused brief therapy are given. Topics such as women in treatment and supervision are also covered. Four outcome measures on clients who have experienced solution-focused treatment for substance abuse are reported in this article. Percentage of treatment plans completed by clients, tracking the decrease of negative client symptoms, rating clients' experiences, and client surveys are the four methods of evaluation presented.

Pichot, T. (2001). What's the big deal about solution focused therapy, anyway? *Professional Counselor, 2,* 39–41.

- In this article the author discusses the common confusion between problem-solving approaches and solution-focused brief therapy.

It answers the question of how solution-focused brief therapy is unique and therefore valuable to therapists.

Pichot, T., & Coulter, M. (2007). *Animal assisted brief therapy: A solution-focused approach*. Binghamton, NY: Haworth.

- The authors provide an overview of the basics of animal-assisted activities/therapy (AAA/T) and how this professional field shares common values and intersects with solution-focused brief therapy. The book offers specific considerations for implementing AAA/T, things therapists should know before engaging in a co-therapy relationship with a dog, and how to successfully use AAA/T and maintain professional and association standards. The authors also provide concrete guidelines for using AAA/T with special populations, employees, and within agencies. Case examples of sessions and treatment plans are provided as resources for those interested in incorporating AAA/T into their practice.

Pichot, T., & Dolan, Y. (2003). *Solution-focused brief therapy: Its effective use in agency settings*. New York: Haworth.

- The authors begin this book by providing a rationale for utilizing solution-focused brief therapy within an agency setting. The authors provide a summary of the fundamental techniques and principles of solution-focused brief therapy. An example of a solution-focused session format is provided for both individual and group sessions. The authors provide case examples and descriptions for applying solution-focused brief therapy when working with adolescents, collaborating with other agencies, observing as a team member, creating treatment plans, and providing supervision. This book also offers suggestions for how to creatively adapt the miracle question to meet the needs of different clients.

Prochaska, J. O., & DiClemente, C. C. (1984). *The transtheoretical approach: Crossing traditional boundaries of therapy*. Malabar, FL: Krieger.

- This book describes the authors' transtheoretical approach to change. Important topics such as stages of change, processes of change, and levels of change are covered. Then, their transtheoretical therapy approach is applied to various populations, such as addictive behavior problems and psychic distress, just to name a few. Various research projects are shared to discuss their theoretical approach.

Prochaska, J. O., & Norcross, J. C. (1999). *Systems of psychotherapy: A transtheoretical analysis* (4th ed.). Pacific Grove, CA: Brooks/Cole.

- The book provides an overview of several common theoretical approaches in psychotherapy. Each chapter addresses a different approach and the associated theory of psychopathology, therapeutic process, therapeutic relationship, general principles, considerations of effectiveness, common criticisms, and future directions of the approach. This book covers psychoanalytic, Adlerian, existential, person-centered, Gestalt, interpersonal, emotional flooding, behavior, cognitive, systemic, gender- and culture-sensitive, as well as integrative and eclectic therapies. This book concludes with a presentation of an overarching transtheoretical approach to therapy. The authors look at the similarities between the above-mentioned theories without overlooking fundamental differences.

Prochaska, J. O., Norcross, J. C., & DiClemente, C. C. (1994). *Changing for good.* New York: Morrow.

- In this book Prochaska, Norcross, and DiClemente present over 12 years and 50 studies of research on the process of change. The authors present a perspective about how change occurs, when people change, and methods for making change. Much of the book is dedicated to presenting the proposed six stages of change: (1) precontemplation, (2) contemplation, (3) preparation, (4) action, (5) maintenance, and (6) termination. The authors also include a chapter about recycling, or learning from relapse. The book concludes with specific examples of how these stages of change can be applied for smoking, alcohol, and distress.

Roth, A., & Fonagy, P. (1996). *What works for whom? A critical review of psychotherapy research.* New York: Guilford.

- Roth and Fonagy begin by describing the major schools of psychotherapy. Then, an outline of how psychotherapy researchers use research findings and clinical practice is given. Several chapters discuss specific issues, such as depression, giving detailed reports of research findings on effective treatments. The authors' main goals for this book include the following: what interventions benefit which patients, whether there is evidence to aid healthcare providers in determining the appropriate therapies for specific populations, and how much one can use efficacy research and clinical effectiveness to deliver psychotherapy.

Smock, S. A., McCollum, E., & Stevenson, M. (2006). *The development of the Solution Building Inventory.* Unpublished doctoral dissertation, Virginia Polytechnic Institute and State University.

- In this dissertation, the authors present the development of a new inventory: the Solution Building Inventory. An explanation of the differences between problem solving and solution building are given. The authors use the Problem Solving Inventory as a framework to develop their new instrument. It is hypothesized that solution building has three components. Results from the factor analyses found one factor in the new Solution Building Inventory. The authors state that the Solution Building Inventory can be used not only as an outcome measure but also as a therapeutic and supervisory tool.

Smock, S. A., Trepper, T. S., Wetchler, J., McCollum, E., Ray, R., & Pierce, K. (2008). Solution-focused group therapy for Level 1 substance abusers. *Journal of Marital and Family Therapy, 34,* 107–120.

- This article describes an outcome study on Level I substance abusers. Solution-focused brief therapy and a psychoeducational approach were given in a group format. Measures were given at pre- and post-treatment to measure client outcomes. The solution-focused group did significantly better on the Beck Depression Inventory and the OQ45.2 after therapy than before. The psychoeducational control group did not do significantly better on either measure. Authors address implications for practitioners and researchers.

Sournia, J. C. (1990). *A history of alcoholism* (N. Hindley & G. Stanton, Trans.). Cambridge, MA: Basil Blackwell.

- Sournia provides an overview of the history of alcohol and alcoholism with examples from around the world. The author addresses topics such as alcohol in various countries, alcohol as a medication, and alcohol as it intersects with race and religion. The author also provides a portion of the book that addresses alcoholism today. Clinical and biological considerations are presented, as well as methods of treatment and prevention of alcoholism. Cases are provided throughout the book to solidify presented information.

Wanberg, K. W. (1992). *A guidebook to the use of the Adolescent Self Assessment Profile—ASAP.* Arvada, CO: Center for Addiction Research and Evaluation.

- This booklet gives a report of the scales included in the 225-item assessment for adolescents. The domains of this measure are discussed in detail. Some of the domains include the consequences and benefits of drug use, family factors, psychological factors, school disruption, legal factors, and many others. This instrument stresses the importance of understanding multiple sources of information that influence substance usage in adolescents.

Wanberg, K. W. (2006). *A user's guide to the Adult Substance Use Survey— ASUS-R.* Arvada, CO: Center for Addiction Research and Evaluation.

- This manual gives clinicians a helpful guide to administrating the ASUS-R. This multidimensional assessment begins by examining the severity of the problem, type of useful treatment, and client motivation. The second level of the assessment aids clinicians in determining a treatment plan for the client. Other reports and self-report are both utilized to complete the assessment. Scoring and psychometric properties are discussed.

References

Alcoholics Anonymous World Services. (1976). *Alcoholics anonymous* (3rd ed.). New York: Author.

American heritage college dictionary (3rd ed.). (1993). New York: Houghton Mifflin.

Anderson, H., & Goolishian, H. A. (1992). The client is the expert: A not-knowing approach to therapy. In S. McNamee & K. J. Gergen (Eds.), *Therapy as social construction* (pp. 25–39). London: Sage.

Barnett, W. L., Branch, L. G., & Hunt, W. A. (1971). Relapse rates in addiction programs. *Journal of Clinical Psychology, 27*, 455–456.

Barr, A. (1999). *Drink: A social history of America.* New York: Carroll & Graf.

Beck, A. T., Steer, R. A., & Garbin, M. G. (1988). Psychometric properties of the Beck Depression Inventory: Twenty-five years of evaluation. *Clinical Psychology Review, 8*, 77–100.

Berg, I. K. (1994). *Family based services: A solution-focused approach.* New York: Norton.

Berg, I. K., & Dolan, Y. (2001). *Tales of solutions: A collection of hope-inspiring stories.* New York: Norton.

Berg, I. K., & Miller, S. D. (1992). *Working with the problem drinker: A solution-focused approach.* New York: Norton.

Berg, I. K., & Reuss, N. H. (1998). *Solutions step by step: A substance abuse treatment manual.* New York: Norton.

Berg, I. K., & Steiner, T. (2003). *Children's solution work.* New York: Norton.

Bertalanffy, L. von. (1968). *General system theory: Foundations, development, applications.* New York: George Braziller.

Bloom, M., & Fischer, J. (1982). *Evaluating practice: Guidelines for the accountable professional.* Englewood Cliffs, NJ: Prentice Hall.

Bobele, M., Gardner, G., & Biever, J. (1995). Supervision as social construction. *Journal of Systemic Therapies, 14*, 14–25.

Brecher, E. M. (1972). *Licit and illicit drugs: The consumers union report on narcotics, stimulants, depressants, inhalants, hallucinogens, and marijuana—including caffeine, nicotine, and alcohol.* Boston: Little, Brown and Company.

Brems, C., & Namyniuk, L. (2002). The relationship of childhood abuse history and substance use in an Alaska sample. *Substance Use & Misuse, 37*, 473–494.

Brennan, P. L., & Moos, R. H. (1996). Late-life problem drinking: Personal and environmental risk factors for 4-year functioning outcomes and treatment seeking. *Journal of Substance Abuse, 8*, 167–180.

Brennan, P. L., Moos, R. H., & Mertens, J. R. (1994). Personal and environmental risk factors as predictors of alcohol use, depression, and treatment seeking: A longitudinal analysis of late-life problem drinkers. *Journal of Substance Abuse, 6*, 191–208.

Budman, S. H., & Gurman, A. S. (1988). *Theory and practice of brief therapy*. New York: Guilford.

Byrne, R. (2006). *The secret*. New York: Atria.

Cantwell, P., & Holmes, S. (1994). Social construction: A paradigm shift for systemic therapy and training. *Australia and New Zealand Journal of Family Therapy, 15,* 17–26.

Cloud, W., & Granfield (2001). *Recovery from addiction*. New York: New York University Press.

Cook, C. C. H. (1988). The Minnesota Model in the management of drug and alcohol dependency: Miracle, method, or myth? Part II. Philosophy and the programme. *British Journal of Addiction, 83,* 625–634.

Cummings, N. A., & Cummings, J. L. (2000). *The essence of psychotherapy: Reinventing the art in the new era of data*. San Diego: Academic Press.

Davies, D. L. (1962). Normal drinking in recovered alcohol addicts. *Quarterly Journal of Studies of Alcohol, 23,* 94–104.

Davies, D. L., Scott, D. F., & Malherbe, M. E. L. (1969). Resumed normal drinking in recovered alcoholics, *International Journal of the Addictions, 4,* 187–194.

DeJong, P., & Berg, I. K. (1998). *Interviewing for solutions*. Pacific Grove, CA: Brooks/Cole.

DeJong, P., & Berg, I. K. (2008). *Interviewing for solutions* (3rd ed). Belmont, CA: Thomson Brooks/Cole.

De Leon, G. (2004). Therapeutic communities. In M. Galanter & H. D. Kleber (Eds.), *The American Psychiatric Publishing textbook of substance abuse treatment* (pp. 485–501). Washington, DC: American Psychiatric Publishing.

Department of Health and Human Services Substance Abuse and Mental Health Services Administration. (1999). *Brief interventions and brief therapies for substance abuse* (TIP 34, DHHS Publication SMA 99-3353). Rockville, MD: Center for Substance Abuse Treatment.

de Shazer, S. (1982). *Patterns of brief family therapy*. New York: Guilford.

de Shazer, S. (1985). *Keys to solution in brief therapy*. New York: Norton.

de Shazer, S. (1988). *Clues: Investigating solutions in brief therapy*. New York: Norton.

de Shazer, S. (1991). *Putting difference to work*. New York: Norton.

de Shazer, S. (1994). *Words were originally magic*. New York: Norton.

de Shazer, S., Dolan, Y., Korman, H., Trepper, T., McCollum, E., & Berg, I. K. (2007). *More than miracles: The state of the art of solution-focused brief therapy*. New York: Haworth.

de Shazer, S., & Isebaert, L. (2003). The Bruges Model: A solution-focused approach to problem drinking. *Journal of Family Psychotherapy, 14,* 43–52.

DiClemente, C. C., Bellino, L. E., & Neavins, T. M. (1999). Motivation for change and alcoholism treatment. *Alcohol Research & Health, 23,* 86–92.

Dolan, Y. M. (1991). *Resolving sexual abuse: Solution-focused therapy and Ericksonian hypnosis for adult survivors*. New York: Norton.

Dolan, Y. (1998). *One small step: Moving beyond trauma and therapy to a life of joy*. Watsonville, CA: Papier-Mache.

Duncan, D. F., Nicholson, T., Clifford, P., Hawkins, W., & Petosa, R. (1994). Harm reduction: An emerging new paradigm for drug education. *Journal of Drug Education, 24,* 281–290.

Eakes, G., Walsh, S., Markowski, M., Cain, H., & Swanson, M. (1997). Family-centered brief solution-focused therapy with chronic schizophrenia: A pilot study. *Journal of Family Therapy, 19,* 145–158.

Edelwich, J., & Brodsky, A. (1992). *Group counseling for the resistant client.* New York: Lexington.

Elkind, D. (1967). Egocentrism in adolescence. *Child Development, 38,* 1025–1034.

Engel, G. L. (1977). The need for a new medical model: A challenge for biomedicine. *Science, 196,* 129–136.

Erickson, M. H., & Rossi, E. (1979). *Hypnotherapy: An exploratory casebook.* New York: Irvington.

Erickson, M. H., Rossi, E., & Rossi, S. (1976). *Hypnotic realities.* New York: Irvington.

Flynn, P. M., Craddock, S. G., Hubbard, R. L., Anderson, J., & Etheridge, R. M. (1997). Methodological overview and research design for the drug abuse treatment outcome study (DATOS). *Psychology of Addictive Behaviors, 11,* 230–243.

Freeman, R. C., Collier, K., & Parillo, K. M. (2002). Early life sexual abuse as a risk factor for crack cocaine use in a sample of community recruited women at high risk for illicit drug use. *American Journal of Drug Alcohol Abuse, 28,* 109–131.

Galaif, E. R., & Sussman, S. (1995). For whom does Alcoholics Anonymous work? *International Journal of the Addictions, 30,* 161–184.

Granfield, R., & Cloud, W. (1999). *Coming clean: Overcoming addiction without treatment.* New York: New York University Press.

Gustafson, J. S., Anderson, R., Sheehan, K., McGencey, S., Reda, J., O'Donnell, C., et al. (1999). *State resources and services related to alcohol and other drug problems: Fiscal years 1996 and 1997.* Washington, DC: National Association of State Alcohol and Drug Abuse Directors.

Havassy, B. E., & Wasserman, D. A. (1992). *Traumatic events and post-traumatic stress disorder in treated cocaine abusers.* Proceedings of the 54th Annual Scientific Meeting: Problems of Drug Dependence, National Institute on Drug Abuse. Rockville, MD.

Higby, G. J. (2002). Drug quality and the origins of APhA. *Journal of the American Pharmaceutical Association, 42,* 831–835.

Janis, I. L. (1972). *Victims of groupthink: A psychological study of foreign-policy decisions and fiascoes.* Boston: Houghton Mifflin.

Johnson, C. E., & Webster, D. (2002). *Recrafting a life.* New York: Taylor & Francis.

Johnston L. D., O'Malley P. M., & Bachman J. G. (1997). *National survey results on drug use from: Monitoring the Future, 1975–1996.* Ann Arbor, MI: University of Michigan Institute for Social Research.

Khantzian, E. J., Golden-Schulman, S. J., & McAuliffe, W. E. (2004). Group therapy. In M. Galanter & H. D. Kleber (Eds.), *The American Psychiatric Publishing textbook of substance abuse treatment* (pp. 391–403). Washington, DC: American Psychiatric Publishing.

Laban, R. J. (1998, March/April). Treatment planning: Room for improvement. *The Counselor, 16,* 32–33.

Lindforss, L., & Magnusson, D. (1997). Solution-focused therapy in prison. *Contemporary Family Therapy, 19,* 89–104.

McHahon, M. O. (1990). *The general method of social work practice: A problem-solving approach* (2nd ed.). Englewood Cliffs, NJ: Prentice Hall.

McLellan, A. T., Luborsky, L., Cacciola, J., Griffith, J., Evans, F., Barr, H. L., et al. (1985). New data from the Addiction Severity Index: Reliability and validity in three centers. *Journal of Nervous and Mental Disease, 173,* 412–423.

McLellan, A. T., Luborsky, L., Woody, G. E., & O'Brien, C. P. (1980). An improved diagnostic evaluation instrument for substance abusing patients: The Addiction Severity Index. *Journal of Nervous and Mental Disease, 168,* 26–33.

Mee-Lee, D. (Ed.). (2001). *ASAM PPC-2R: ASAM patient placement criteria for the treatment of substance-related disorders* (2nd ed. rev.). Chevy Chase, MD: American Society of Addiction Medicine.

Mee-Lee, D. (2005). *Overview of the ASAM Patient Placement Criteria* (2nd ed. rev.) (ASAM PPC-2R). Washington, DC: SAMHSA's Co-occurring Center for Excellence (COCE). Retrieved November 15, 2007, from http://coce.samhsa.gov/cod_resources/PDF/ASAMPatientPlacementCriteriaOverview5-05.pdf

Metcalf, L. (1998). *Solution focused group therapy.* New York: Free Press.

Miller, G. A. (1985). *The Substance Abuse Subtle Screening Inventory manual.* Spencer, IN: Spencer Evening World.

Miller, G. A. (1997). *The Substance Abuse Subtle Screening Inventory-III manual.* Spencer, IN: Spencer Evening World.

Miller, G., & de Shazer, S. (1998). Have you heard the latest rumor about …? Solution-focused therapy as a rumor. *Family Process, 37,* 363–377.

Miller, S. D., & Berg, I. K. (1995). *The miracle method: A radically new approach to problem drinking.* New York: Norton.

Miller, S. D., Duncan, B. L., & Hubble, M. A. (1997). *Escape from Babel: Toward a unifying language for psychotherapy practice.* New York: Norton.

Miller, W. R., & Rollnick, S. (1991). *Motivational interviewing.* New York: Guilford.

Miller, W. R., & Rollnick, S. (2002). *Motivational interviewing* (3rd ed.). New York: Guilford.

National Drug Intelligence Center. (2006, October). *National Drug Threat Assessment 2007.* Retrieved October 2, 2007, from http://www.usdoj.gov/ndic/pubs21/21137/marijuana.htm

National Institute on Alcohol Abuse and Alcoholism. (2006). *The history of NIAAA*. Retrieved November 15, 2007, from http://www.niaaa.nih.gov/AboutNIAAA/OrganizationalInformation/History.htm

National Institute on Drug Abuse. (n.d.). *About NIDA*. Retrieved November 19, 2007, from http://www.drugabuse.gov/about/aboutnida.html

National Institute on Drug Abuse. (2000a). *Facts about drug abuse and hepatitis C*. Retrieved October 9, 2007, from http://www.nida.nih.gov/NIDA_Notes/NNVol15N1/tearoff.html

National Institute on Drug Abuse. (2000b). *Principles of drug addiction treatment: A research-based guide* (NIH Publication 00-4180). Washington, DC: U.S. Department of Health and Human Services.

National Institute on Drug Abuse. (2003). *Drug use among racial/ethnic minorities revised* (NIH Publication 03-3888). Rockville, MD: U.S. Department of Health and Human Services.

National Institute on Drug Abuse. (2005). *The link between HIV/AIDS and drug abuse*. Retrieved October 15, 2007, from http://www.drugabuse.gov/about/welcome/MessageHIV1105.html

National Institute on Drug Abuse. (2006a). *Trends in prescription drug abuse*. Retrieved October 2, 2007, from http://www.drugabuse.gov/ResearchReports/Prescription/prescription5.html#Trends

National Institute on Drug Abuse. (2006b). *NIDA infofacts*. Retrieved June 23, 2008, from http://www.drugabuse.gov/Infofacts/Drugabuse.html

Ouimette, P. C., Kimerling, R., Shaw, J., & Moos, R. H. (2000). Physical and sexual abuse among women and men with substance use disorders. *Alcoholism Treatment Quarterly, 18*, 7–17.

Pichot, T., & Dolan, Y. (2003). *Solution-focused brief therapy: Its effective use in agency settings*. New York: Haworth.

Prochaska, J. O., & DiClemente, C. C. (1984). *The transtheoretical approach: Crossing traditional boundaries of therapy*. Malabar, FL: Krieger.

Prochaska, J. O., & Norcross, J. C. (1999). *Systems of psychotherapy: A transtheoretical analysis* (4th ed.). Pacific Grove, CA: Brooks/Cole.

Prochaska, J. O., Norcross, J. C., & DiClemente, C. C. (1994). *Changing for good*. New York: Morrow.

Rotgers, F. (1996). Behavioral theory of substance abuse treatment: Bringing science to bear on practice. In F. Rotgers, D. S. Keller, and J. Morgenstern (Eds.), *Treating substance abuse: Theory and technique* (pp. 174–201). New York: Guilford Press.

SAMHSA. (n.d. a). *SAMHSA advisory committees*. Retrieved November 15, 2007, from https://www.nac.samhsa.gov/index.aspx

SAMHSA. (n.d. b). *SAMHSA's national registry of evidence-based programs and practices*. Retrieved June, 12, 2007, from http://www.nrepp.samhsa.gov/about-note.htm

SAMHSA. (1999). *Brief interventions and brief therapies for substance abuse* (TIP 34, NCADI Publication 04-3952). Rockville, MD: U.S. Department of Health and Human Services.

SAMHSA. (2005). *Substance abuse treatment for persons with co-occurring disorders* (TIP 42, NCADI Publication BKD545). Washington, DC: U.S. Department of Health and Human Services.

SAMHSA. (2006a). *SAMHSA's national survey on drug use and health*. Retrieved June 19, 2008, from http://www.oas.samhsa.gov/nsduhLatest.htm

SAMHSA. (2006b). *Substance abuse treatment: Group Therapy* (TIP 41, DHHS Publication SMA 05-3991). Rockville, MD: Center for Substance Abuse Treatment. Retrieved June 23, 2008, from http://www.ncbi.nlm.nih.gov/books/bv.fcgi?rid=hstat5.chapter.78366

SAMHSA. (2007). *Methamphetamine abuse in the United States*. Retrieved from October 2, 2007, from http://www.oas.samhsa.gov/treatan/treana13.htm

Simpson, T. L., & Miller, W. R. (2002). Concomitance between childhood sexual and physical abuse and substance use problems: A review. *Clinical Psychology Review, 22*, 27–77.

Sobell, L. C., Sobell, M. B., Toneatto, T., & Leo, G. I. (1993). What triggers the resolution of alcohol problems without treatment? *Alcoholism: Clinical and Experimental Research, 17*, 217–224.

Substance Abuse and Mental Health Services Administration (SAMHSA). (2002, November). *SAMHSA report to Congress on the prevention and treatment of co-occurring substance abuse disorders and mental disorders*. Retrieved August 6, 2007, from http://www.samhsa.gov/reports/congress2002/chap1ucod.htm

Timken, D. S., Wanberg, K. W., & Milkman, H. B. (2004). *Driving with care: Education and treatment of the impaired driving offender—Strategies for responsible living*. Thousand Oaks, CA: Sage.

Tonigan, S., Miller, W. R., & Schermer, C. (2002). Atheists, agnostics, and alcoholics anonymous. *Journal of Studies on Alcohol, 63*, 534–541.

Treatment Trends. (2003). *NIDA InfoFacts*. Retrieved June 12, 2007, from www.drugabuse.gov/infofacts/treatmenttrends.html

Wanberg, K. W. (1992). *A guidebook to the use of the Adolescent Self Assessment Profile—ASAP*. Arvada, CO: Center for Addiction Research and Evaluation (CARE).

Wanberg, K. W. (1997). *A user's guide to the Adult Substance Use Survey—ASUS*. Arvada, CO: Center for Addiction Research and Evaluation (CARE).

Wanberg, K. W. (1999). *ASAP II brief user's guide to the Adolescent Self Assessment Profile II*. Arvada, CO: Center for Addictions Research and Evaluation (CARE).

Wanberg, K. W., & Milkman, H. B. (1998). *Criminal conduct and substance abuse treatment*. Thousand Oaks, CA: Sage.

Werner-Wilson, R. J. J. (2000). *Developmental systemic family therapy with adolescents*. Binghamton, NY: Haworth.

White, M., & Epston, D. (1990). *Narrative means to therapeutic ends*. New York: W.W. Norton & Company.

Wolpe, J. (1969). *The practice of behavior therapy*. New York: Pergamon.

Wolpe, J. (1973). *The practice of behavior therapy* (2nd ed.). New York: Pergamon.

Women and Substance Abuse. (2006, October 13). *NIDA NewsScan*. Retrieved May 25, 2007, from http://www.drugabuse.gov/newsroom/06/NS-10.html

Yalom, I. D. (2005). *The theory and practice of group psychotherapy* (5th ed.). New York: Basic Books.

Zimmerman, G. L., Olsen, C. G., & Bosworth, M. F. (2000). A "stages of change" approach to helping patients change behavior. *American Family Physician, 61*, 1409–1416.

Index